Are You Laughing At Me?

John Wayne Sears

Chapters

Dedication

To my mother, Sybil, who inspired me to write letters home. And, way back, she loaned me her typewriter, which I soon wore out.

To my father, Stan, who bought me my own typewriter, then suffered through 200 pages of my first book (a western of all things, written when I was 19). After reading it, he said, more or less, "Gee, at times there it was almost like real writing."

To my brother Mike, who once laughed at something I'd written, thereby giving me the impression (which continues to this day) that I was funny.

To my wife, Patricia, who when the PC era dawned bought me my first keyboard. She bullied me into getting an article published in *Pacific Yachting*, thereby bolstering my confidence – hey, now I was a pro! She also provides, albeit unintentionally, subject material on a regular basis, critiques my work (and everything else I do), and freely passes my stuff around to colleagues, friends and family, acting like my agent.

To Lori and Teri, my special daughters, who up to this point at least, have never said, "Stop sending those stupid stories."

And to all my long-suffering friends who have been kind enough to encourage me by saying, "You should put this stuff in a book and get it published."

Well, finally, here it is. Now get out there and buy a copy!

Thank you. All of you. You've helped make a life-long dream come true.

John Wayne Sears
Harrison Mills, British Columbia.

Water, Water Everywhere...

On the day she left me, my wife had some final words of advice.

"You'll need emergency flares, a bailing device, the hand-held VHF radio, and a flashlight," Patricia said. "And don't forget your Personal Flotation Device," she added.

"Plus maybe the fire extinguisher," I said.

"Don't be smart," she said. "Being alone in the dinghy on the water is serious business."

"Yes sir," I said.

"And remember," she said. "The dinghy and the outboard are brand new, so don't break anything."

Patricia gave me a quick hug—she only hugs me when she thinks I might die—and got on the bus and went home to Vancouver, leaving me at Gibson's Marina, a days boat ride from home, without supervision.

As soon as she was gone, I opened a beer. I needed to strategize about my coming adventure, and beer always helped.

Our sailboat, *Temptation*, and I were on a week's vacation. Patricia had gotten us this far, but she wasn't on vacation and was required back at work, which meant I was free to sit on the lounge cushions in the cockpit and drink beer all day long in the sunshine. For an entire week. Or at least until the beer ran out.

And I never run out of beer.

What I was strategizing about was my offshore dinghy trip. Out into the open ocean I would go, braving wind, tide, and current. All by myself. Solo. Man against the sea. With the specter of capsizing, drowning, and death overshadowed by the potential for getting the virginal dinghy and outboard dirty, or even smudged. And if I broke anything, the Admiral – a.k.a. Patricia – would kill me in a painful way.

The thought of being killed in a painful way motivated me to open a second beer.

Tomorrow I would take both the inflatable Zodiac and the Yamaha and set off across the channel to the marine park at Plumper Cove on Keats Island, an offshore trip probably at least three kilometers long. Not much of a journey for some, but I was not the world's best boater. In fact, I was probably the world's *worst* boater.

What could possibly go wrong during the twenty-minute jaunt to Keats? Both the dinghy and the four-horsepower motor were brand new. Nothing could go wrong with them. The only thing that could go wrong was me, and I was determined to succeed.

The next day my hangover had cleared up by midmorning. The weather was perfect; blue sky, hot sun. A westerly of about twelve knots was blowing in, as it often did, from the west. I had spent much of the previous evening strategizing and I was now ready to put all that strategy into action.

The sea sparkled with sunlight. There were a few waves, but they were little ones as I fearlessly peered out across the ocean at Keats Island. Sure, I'd been in dinghies before, but rarely solo. Okay, *never* solo.

I loaded the dinghy with all of those things the Admiral said. I armed myself with my cell phone, a first aid kit, and—in case of a major emergency—a peanut butter sandwich

I got into the wobbly dinghy. I started the motor. It started smoothly on one easy pull. I cast off.

So far so good.

I glided out of the marina, past the gas dock, past the breakwater, and out into the channel.

Those little waves weren't quite so little now. The dinghy bounced over some of them, plowed through some of them, and chugged onward towards Keats, the wind at its back.

The mountains around Howe Sound were brilliant with sunshine, capped here and there with last winter's snow. North towards Gambier Island, the Langdale ferry plied the blue water. In the distance, a power yacht rumbled, and out past Gower Point a sailboat leaned into the wind.

"This is great," I said aloud.

The Yamaha coughed and died.

But it restarted easily on the first pull, before I had time to panic or even swear at it. Okay, fine. Everything was fine.

We made another couple of hundred meters. I was almost out in the middle now, Keats over there, Gibson's way back there.

The Yamaha quietly died.

Okay. No need to panic. I could now see the dock in Plumper Cove. I could easily row that far, if necessary.

But the Yamaha started on the first pull, again.

We purred through Plumper Cove and gently bumped against the gray dock planks. I tied us fore and aft to the dock cleats, grabbed my knapsack, and went ashore.

I sat at a picnic table and drank a celebratory can of beer. Through the trees I could see Gibson's across the wide body of ocean. I was successfully halfway through my adventure. I was alive, the dinghy was in pristine condition, and the day was bright with possibility.

Sure, the outboard had stalled, but maybe it was just new. Maybe it just needed to be broken in. Probably would never stall again.

I contemplated my peanut butter sandwich. Better hang on to it, just in case something bad happened on the way back.

Something bad did happen, but not on the way back.

It happened right there at the dock.

I was back in the dinghy. I switched the fuel on, plugged in the kill-switch thingy, and pulled the cord. The Yamaha just sat there. I pulled the cord. The Yamaha just sat there. I pulled and pulled. When I was out of breath—it took about three pulls—I sat back and wondered about two things.

One of the things I wondered about was if I was going to have a heart attack. The other thing I wondered about was throwing the Yamaha into the sea.

When my heart rate had stabilized, I pulled the cord again, savagely. The Yamaha remained in a coma. While I was savagely yanking on the cord, a small sailboat drifted in and docked beside me. Some people got off it and lined up on the dock, staring down at me. I was panting. They were smirking.

"Problem?" asked one of the guys.

"I think it's flooded," I said. The smell of raw gasoline wafted up in waves.

"Your face is purple," a woman said.

"Sunburn," I said.

Eventually they walked away.

I drank some bottled water. I let the motor sit there a few moments. I may have insulted it verbally.

After some more water, and possibly a few moments of additional verbal abuse, I could no longer just sit there patiently staring at the Yamaha. If the goddamned motor wasn't going to get me back home, I'd get myself back home.

I deployed the funny little paddles. I cast off the lines.

I began to row. Who needed a goddamned motor anyway?

The oars splashed in the water. Seagulls watched. Soon the dock was shrinking off the stern. I rowed. Hey, it wasn't so bad. Get the back and shoulders into it, no sweat. Well, actually the sweat started a few minutes later, and a few minutes after that my arms got tired.

About every seven oar strokes I wrenched around and discovered I was off course. The dinghy had a stubborn mind of its own. It kept seesawing at right angles to where I wanted to go. Eventually my neck got very stiff from cranking around, checking my direction. Now my neck *and* arms were stiff. The wind seemed stronger. Waves slapped against the rubber hull. Some of them sprayed me with cold salt water.

Over my shoulder, across the yawning channel, Gibson's failed to move closer.

The dinghy kept veering starboard, and when it wasn't veering starboard it was veering port. That's right and left in the real world. I spent very little time going straight.

A seal popped his big brown head out of the water and watched me for quite a while. It seemed to be smirking.

My mouth was dry, and I may have suffered blisters by the time I accomplished the halfway point. Anyway, I got blisters somewhere out there, and the halfway point is as good as any to get blisters. I debated trying the goddamned motor again. To do so, though, I'd have to stop rowing. If I stopped rowing and the motor failed to start, the wind and current would shove me way off course. I was already off course, but it would be worse, so I kept rowing.

A Suncruiser powerboat buzzed past, its wake making my little craft dip and fall. The sun was hot on my bald spot. I kept rowing. My mouth got dryer. If I ever got back to *Temptation*, I could very easily run out of beer immediately.

Another seal stuck his whiskery face out of the water to stare at the fool in the dinghy. Seals, I guessed, didn't get to see fools every day, thus the attraction to my progress in the funny rubber boat.

A sailboat hissed by on my starboard side on a leisurely broad reach. The man and woman in the cockpit stared at me. I pretended to be having fun. I smiled. Or maybe it was a grimace. They looked perplexed, then nodded and were gone.

Another powerboat rumbled by, paused, drifted closer. A woman with excellent cleavage leaned over the side and shouted something.

"What the hell are you doing out here?" I think she may have said.

I waved my oars at her in a friendly manner.

The powerboat came closer.

"Are you okay?" she asked.

Her husband was at the wheel on the flying bridge. I'm pretty sure he was smirking.

"Just getting some exercise," I replied.

"We could give you a tow," the lady persisted.

"God no," I shouted back. I couldn't stand the humiliation of being towed to the dock. Not to mention what the Admiral would say if she found out about it. "I mean, thanks, but I'm fine. Really."

I gave her a thumbs-up, clumsily dropping the oars as I did so. The wind immediately turned me in the opposite direction.

The lady waved farewell and off they went.

I splashed the oars in the water until I got turned around. Gibson's had finally moved closer. I knew then that I would survive.

I was maybe a quarter mile from the breakwater and safety when I decided to hell with it, I would try the motor again. If the wind and current blew me off course while I tried, no problem: I was almost home. Plus I was exhausted.

So I put down the flimsy oars and glared at the motor and pulled the cord.

It started perfectly. Like there'd never been a problem.

I may have called it a sonofabitch. Several times.

We purred into the marina and I tied us up snugly to *Temptation*, climbed aboard, and drank all my beer in about fifteen minutes. Fortunately, Gibson's has a cold beer and wine store not far from the marina.

Later, Pat called to check on the dinghy, the outboard, and me. In exactly that order.

"We had a great time," I said. "All the way over to Plumper Cove, all the way back. Beautiful."

"You sound tired," she said when I'd finished lying.

"And the oars really work great."

"The oars?" Pat said.

"Oops," I said.

"Are you all right?"

"Mostly. I think I may have drunk twelve beers, or was it fourteen? too fast. But it's helping with the pain in my shoulders, and my hands have almost stopped bleeding," I added positively.

"Oh boy," said the Admiral.

"I hate seals," I said. "Those bastards."

"Seals are bastards?"

"And no, I wouldn't let them tow me in."

"The seals?"

"The woman with the cleavage," I explained.

"I think maybe you got too much sun today," Pat said. "You'll have to tell me all about it when I get there on the weekend."

"You'll never believe it, and I'll never remember it."

"Maybe you should write it all down," suggested the Admiral, before hanging up.

So I did.

* * *

Tom's Cabin

From the covered front step of the cabin, where I'm sitting with my mug of morning coffee, I can see the shimmer of water through the trees. On my left, at an angle, sits the fire-engine-red pickup truck that got us here, and surrounding it is a wide swath of knee-high daisies. Their yellow centers and white petals add splotches of color to the tangled green of weeds and thistles that have overgrown the clearing. Fine rain slithers down in silver lines. The smells of wood smoke, which trickles skyward from the rusty chimney, wet brush, and moldy forest floor intermingle. There is no wind, and the silence—except for the sibilant falling rain— is unbroken and pure.

It is time to write, and time for you to join our trip.

We arrived at six-thirty Monday evening. When the truck rumbled around the final turn and he had his first look at the cabin, Tom was dismayed. A rear shutter lay flat on the ground, and a front shutter hung at a broken angle. It was raining, and we'd bumped and splashed along the narrow track, branches clawing at the muddy sides of the truck as the forest closed in. As always, we were hopeful that the cabin, deserted since October last year, had survived intact through the long months of winter, spring, and summer. But it hadn't. The hasp on the front door was broken off, and although the front door was closed and there was no interior damage, someone had been inside.

As dusk crept out from under the trees, we unloaded our gear, and soon the cabin was warm from its wood stove and Tom's dismay had changed pleasantly to relief that no damage had been done. After a hearty dinner of beans and wieners, and salad, we sought our beds early. Our usual nighttime campfire was rained out. Without the ritual of the fire, there was no reason to stay up.

Tuesday morning we slept late. The gloom of gray clouds and persistent rain made getting out of warm sleeping bags an insurmountable task. After brunch—a wild mix of juice, and thick boiled coffee, and chunks of cantaloupe and peach, and a ham sandwich, and a cob of corn each—we drove to the nearest hardware store, thirty minutes away, to replace the broken hasp. Range cattle blocked the logging road but moved lazily away when Tom touched the horn. We purchased a nine-by-nine blue plastic tarp as an investment against the rain. Clouds were low and solid across the sky, and if sunshine was in the future, it didn't seem like it would arrive soon.

So we strung the tarp in the light rain, and as soon as it was up, of course, the rain stopped and we enjoyed a brief hour of sunlight.

Taking advantage of the sporadic break in the clouds to gather firewood, I got wet to the knees trudging through rain-soaked grass and brush. Mosquitoes appeared, but they were logy and failed to feast on our blood, and soon disappeared.

The campfire took a long time to ignite, and smoke billowed long before flames appeared. The freshly deployed tarp shed a brief cloudburst, then Tom tinkered with his sagging dock and gathered water and started dinner while overhead clouds broke like river ice to reveal streaks of blue, and I scratched in my notebook and tended the fire. The nearby radio—atop a chopping block—sprayed country music and predicted more rain and chilly nighttime temperatures of four degrees. The fire, gaining momentum, snapped and popped and poured gray smoke skyward.

Once, a loon called; otherwise, the forest and lake continued their cloying silence.

My hands were black-smudged from stoking the fire and my fingers were starting to crack open from handling branches and logs. City hands, I guess. Not used to anything rougher than books and pens and telephones. My boots were wet and heavy and my jacket was damp, yet the fire heat made things comfortable. The logs turned first black, then gray, in the flames, and the raw smell of wood smoke permeated everything.

That Tuesday evening, Tom tromped over, the cabin door clunking shut behind him.

"How you doing?" he asked. He announced he had started dinner.

The radio informed us there had been a coaching change with the Canadian Football League's Argonauts, and we briefly discussed the situation while Tom tossed two wet logs on the fire, nearly dousing it. Then, as quickly as he appeared, he left, returning inside to his Coleman stove and steaming pots and pans.

Our conversations were like that. Moments of long silence, followed by a flurry of talk before we lapsed again into our private thoughts. But later, when night closed around the orange firelight, we would talk for hours, the press of darkness seeming to loosen our tongues.

Dinner was pork chops and vegetables served with red wine from Portugal, but during its serving Tom knocked the lid off the pepper and drifts of the black spice piled up over my food.

"Oops!" Tom said, grinning. "Sorry."

We both laughed and I refused to accept his offer to trade plates. Even after scraping wads of pepper off my cauliflower and broccoli and yellow zucchini, my mouth and stomach burned for hours afterwards.

Wet logs sputtered and hissed, coals flickered, and tongues of flame lapped at sticks while the surrounding trees solemnly watched.

For twenty-five years I'd been coming to this wilderness place, thirty-some miles out of 100 Mile House, and it still enthralled me. The poetry of wind and forest touched me at some elemental level that the city did not. It was a sort of shrine, a holy place, even when a gust of breeze sent hot smoke and ash into my eyes.

Through the trees, a late evening burst of sunshine spread gold across the lake and highlighted magically the trees on the far shore, while there by the fire, I was cloaked in dusk. Gray ash rose from the fire and floated on rising waves of heat, landing as softly on my clothing as snowflakes.

Later, when darkness had claimed the clearing, I asked Tom what single thing more than any other attracted him to this place.

"Solitude," he responded, staring thoughtfully into the fire. "It's a retreat from the demands of people."

With assistance from Tom's dry and carefully hoarded woodpile, we kept the wet logs burning until midnight and beyond, and finally at one in the morning we turned our backs on the diminishing fire and stumbled to our beds.

Wednesday morning was clear and sunny, but Tom had forgotten the tool which tightens the chain on his trusty chainsaw, so this day's work party would be restricted to using axes to cleave firewood from the forest, and to clear back some encroaching brush from the road.

My boots were still damp, and my clothing was ripe with the smell of wood smoke. My hands were rough and cracked, and the ball of my right thumb had a painful crack running across it.

The fire pit smoldered in the warm morning sun, and the lake glittered with bright light. Near the makeshift dock, dragonflies darted like mini helicopters above broad green lily pads.

After breakfast, while I stirred the coals to life and sat in the white plastic chair under the tarp and applied pen to paper, Tom stretched out on the cabin's yellow sofa and read the hardcover book he brought. When the flow of words dried up, I clomped into the cabin, stuffed my notebook in my packsack, and the workday, such as it was, began.

First order of business was the tilting outhouse. We managed, with much sweating and grunting, to untilt it. How long the thing stands vertical is subject to frost, rain and snow. Many of its boards are rotting and, although still reasonably sturdy, its life span is winding down.

"You're out of shape," Tom said as we lugged a two-hundred-pound log uphill. The monster log was part of the new foundation beneath the privy. My heart hammered in my chest and I gasped for air and wondered about having a heart attack. At least the ground was carpeted with moss and leaves so if I fell over dead, I would at least have a soft landing!

Tom made lunch—fruit, ham and mustard sandwiches on multigrain bread, and tea—while I scrounged wood for that night's fire from down near the lake. The sky was vivid blue, but a parade of white, puffy clouds ceaselessly marched across it.

The after-lunch work party consisted of dragging more wood than we would ever burn on this trip to the woodpile. Under my denim shirt, my T-shirt was soaked with sweat, and I was so tired I was almost dizzy.

Tom worked at twice my pace and seemed indefatigable. When the woodpile was stacked high, we set off up the road to hack at alder and brush that was infringing on the track.

Three o'clock found us wearily sitting in the white chairs, inhaling smoke from the remnants of last night's fire and taking deep drafts of water from plastic containers.

While I moved my chair out from under the shadowy tarp into full sunlight and wrote, Tom hiked out to his gate to nail up the numbers 7722 on his gate post. The property is 7722 Womack Road, but there are only two ruts in the mud making up this Cariboo road.

When Tom returned, he wordlessly entered the cabin for a thirty-minute nap.

My back hurt, my legs were stiff, my arms ached, and my hands trembled so much from all the pushing and pulling and lifting that I was afraid I wouldn't be able to read my wobbly writing when it came time to translate the words onto the keyboard. So, I closed my notepad—no use to write if I couldn't read the words.

A large cloud unfurled in front of the sun and the afternoon turned cool. There was a hint of autumn in the wind as it blew off the lake.

I limped to the fire and tossed on a log, and then another. Night was coming, the last night, and the fire would need to burn strongly if it was to ward off the night chill, and the sadness of leaving.

* * *

Hawaii

When she first won the trip, my wife, Pat, considered the Caribbean as a destination. But that was before she remembered what the fire coral did to her when she sat on it during her last visit there. Scratch, scratch, scratch for weeks. Plus, this time around it was hurricane season. The Caribbean was rejected.

Next, Pat considered the Cook Islands, but no one had ever heard of them. They were primitive. Not one hotel had microwaves, and only a few hotels had color TV. Down the drain went the Cook Islands.

At a lamb barbecue, Pat met a good-looking Greek. She stocked up on books on Greece. Folders and pamphlets about the Greek Islands and the Mediterranean littered all three levels of our condominium. Then someone at the Sears store, where Pat works, told Pat that Greek men were a bunch of lechers and adulterers. The Greek pamphlets, and Greece itself, immediately got the old heave-ho.

Finally, Pat decided on Hawaii as a destination. Hawaii didn't have fire coral or lecherous Greeks, but it had important things like microwave ovens, and color TVs were all over the place. Not to mention the occasional muscle-bound surfer.

Pat took me along because she needed someone to carry her luggage. And she took daughter Teri and Teri's partner, Doug, along, so she'd have an audience when she talked.

Off we went on a Qantas 747. The flight had an all-male crew. On the way to Hawaii Teri kept talking about nice buns, which was understandable, I guess, because Teri worked in a bakery and should know nice buns when she sees them.

The 747 took off in Vancouver and landed in Honolulu quite smoothly, considering how much of Pat's and Teri's luggage it carried.

Mid-Pacific Airlines flew us from Honolulu to Lihue airport on Kauai in a plane that had propellers. En route, two seagulls overtook the plane and beat us to Lihue. Now I know why they invented jet engines.

A rental Toyota awaited us. Playing on the radio on the drive from Lihue to Poipu were three songs I hadn't heard in decades: "House of the Rising Sun," by the Animals; "Let's Dance," by Chris Montez; and "Little GTO," by whoever sings 'Little GTO." With luck and careful planning, I was thinking, it would be even more decades before I heard those songs again. Little did I know…

Our Poipu Shores condo was right on the water where large waves shattered all over black rocks. Doug looked up in a book and proclaimed Poipu was one of the driest resort areas in the world. While Doug proclaimed, rain poured down in buckets.

First night on Kauai and we decided to go to Perry's Smorgasbord Restaurant for dinner. We forgot the map.

We drove this way and that way at high speed searching for Perry's. It was a dark and rainy night. Going north, we streaked past the Bullshed, Eggbert's, McDonald's, and the Ono Family Restaurant. Going south, we streaked by the Ono Family Restaurant, McDonald's, Eggbert's, and the Bullshed. Nowhere could we find Perry's.

Doug, who was driving, became very adept at U-turning in heavy traffic. The Toyota grew hot and tired and we grew hot and hungry and desperate.

Finally, Teri, who has large and strong hands, placed them around Doug's throat. Men usually don't like to stop and ask directions and often need persuasion to do so. Teri was very persuasive. Coughing and gasping, Doug decided to stop and ask directions.

We learned we'd driven right past Perry's nine or ten times. I've never driven so many miles to get to one single restaurant in my life. We all ate triple helpings in case it took us another four hundred miles to find our way back to the hotel.

The third day of our trip was Monday. On this day, and on each and every day until we left for home, I swallowed a quart of salt water, most of it through my nose. Although the surgeon general warns that swallowing salt water through the nose can be hazardous to your health, I do it anyway. I'm going to try to cut down to maybe a pint a day through the nose very soon. After awhile it begins to smart just a little.

On Monday—before my daily quota of warm Pacific Ocean—we packed ourselves into the still-warm-from-the-Perry's-hunt Toyota and sped to Wiamea Canyon.

The canyon was impressive and spectacular. What was even more impressive and spectacular was the fact that the wheezing Toyota made it all the way to the 4,500-foot summit without exploding.

Looking out from the top, Doug went into hallucinations. Probably they were caused by the dozen or so guava he and Pat pillaged at the side of the road and then ate by the fistful.

Doug looked out from the top and pointed, very excited by the beautiful white bird he saw floating on an air current. The beautiful white bird he saw floating way out there turned out to be a helicopter, and Doug hasn't even looked at a guava since.

At Polihale State Park we abused ourselves in the water. It marked the first time I had ever abused myself on a public beach while others did the same. Teri only abused herself a little bit. Pat abused herself after watching others do it. And I abused myself as long as I could. Doug abused himself more than anybody.

Some people call abusing yourself in the water "body surfing," but I know abuse when I see it.

The waves at Brennecke's Beach were huge. The large, breaking waves tried to kill Pat. The one wave in particular that tried to kill her was about as high as a wall. It picked Pat up, turned her over, and bounced her on her head in the sand. To this day, Pat swears that every time she shakes her head she can hear the tide ebbing and flooding.

During our one-week stay at Poipu Shores, we met an older couple named Cliff and Irene. Cliff was a Shriner.

Cliff and Irene loved to communicate with each other at 6 a.m. sharp each morning. Cliff would stand at one end of their condo, and Irene would stand as far away from him as possible. Both Cliff and Irene stood near an open door and an open window so they could share their hearty conversation with all their neighbors.

We were their very closest neighbors.

One morning their high-volume voices woke me out of a dream about string bikinis and smooth, tanned, female flesh. I was very upset when Cliff and Irene woke me. Girls who have smooth tanned flesh and wear string bikinis hardly ever chase me, even in dreams.

I yelled at Cliff and Irene to shut up.

The odd thing was, I enjoyed it. Further, yelling at Cliff and Irene felt so good I'm considering getting up at 6 a.m. every morning to yell at Shriners to shut up.

As early-morning exercise, it beats the hell out of jogging.

One dark, stormy night Teri entered the kitchen. She was alone, the rest of us in bed, sleeping. The lights were off. Wind billowed the drapes and rain lashed the windows. As Teri stepped carefully through the blackness, the floor was cool under her bare feet.

Suddenly, something alien gripped her toes!

A giant cockroach? A deadly spider?

Panic! Fright! Screaming terror in the dark. The horrible thing stayed firmly clamped to her toes. Teri desperately clawed for the switch and flicked on the lights.

She looked at her foot.

No cockroach, no spider.

Just a piece of curly grape stem lodged snugly between her toes.

In an hour or two, her heartbeat slowed, returned to normal.

Yes, she would live. But for a second or two there, it was touch and go.

On day seven, a Friday, Pat and I joined Captain Andy and sixteen other tourists on Captain Andy's trimaran. For Pat the most memorable part of the trimaran junket was eyeballing the diamond ring on one of the female tourists' fingers. The rock was huge.

The next most memorable event while on board the rolling vessel was the herd (gang, flock, pod, gaggle, bunch…) of dolphins that swam along with us, close enough to touch. Pat tried to talk to the dolphins using special dolphin language but received no reply.

Earlier, when Pat talked goat to the Wiamea Canyon goats, the goats seemed to understand, and replied politely. The goats and Pat carried on a lovely conversation for several minutes while Teri and Doug stood there, astounded.

It was the first time Teri and Doug had heard Pat speak goat. I've heard Pat talk goat *and* sheep, not to mention horse. So the conversation was no big deal to me. Although I did wonder a couple of times if they were talking about me, the way Pat and the goats kept snickering.

Anyway, the dolphins refused to speak to Pat. Maybe it was her West Van accent.

The final memorable thing about the trimaran experience was anchoring for lunch in a pretty cove. It turned out to be the location where *Fantasy Island* ("Boss...the plane! The plane!") was filmed. When Pat heard this, she beat all snorkelers ashore. Although she looked everywhere, there was no sign of Ricardo Montablan, which was too bad. Pat would love to talk to Senor Montablan even more than dolphins. Or goats.

The next day we drove to Prince Kuhio Beach. Prince Kuhio himself was nowhere in sight, but we fed Bird's Eye brand frozen peas to the assorted fish who lived there. The fish preferred the peas right out of the box, slightly thawed, without garnish or sauce of any kind. Plain eaters, these tropical fish.

Sunday morning another propeller-driven plane took us slowly but surely to the Kahului airport on Maui.

The candy-apple red Sentra that awaited us had a family of cockroaches included at no extra charge.

During the drive from the airport to Kahana Villa, our new home for a week, the radio blared out "Let's Dance." by Chris Montez, followed by "House of the Rising Sun," by the Animals, followed by "Little GTO," by whomever. All of us sang along. By now the words were burned into our brains.

On Monday, I rented two Boogie boards. Boogie boards are mini surfboards that you lie on to go shooting through the surf. Even on a Boogie board I managed to dip my nose into seawater to snort down a quart or two. It takes a certain amount of skill.

We discovered a nice little beach at the bottom of some cliffs. There were people down there, so we knew there must be a way down other than jumping. So Pat followed a dim trail down steep rocks with me following. Later, perspiring heavily and shaky from risking our lives climbing down sheer cliffs, we made it to the beach.

Two minutes later we discovered the proper trail, with steps neatly cut into the earth.

We fed the fish Cheez Whiz and more frozen peas. Appreciative, the fish swarmed around and nibbled the occasional finger.

For lunch, Doug ate a whole package of peanut butter cookies. Then, grabbing flippers, mask, and snorkel, he went down to the water's edge. Everybody spits into his or her mask before putting it on. The spit keeps the lens from fogging up. What Doug spat into his mask after eating all those cookies was far worse than any kind of fog he'd ever seen.

Taking his mask to the dry cleaners ruined a whole day's snorkeling.

The next morning, Teri and Doug showed a large amount of intestinal fortitude by getting up at two in the morning to embark on a mission to Haleakala. The volcano rises ten thousand feet. Watching the sun rise is spectacular, not to mention cold.

While Teri and Doug froze their buns off, Pat and I boarded the schooner *Windjammer* for a trip to Lanai for snorkeling, a beach barbecue, and a lesson in pineapples by an expert.

The heavy tub of a schooner pitched and rolled in large swells. Many tourists turned green. Pat and I pretended not to turn green. After all, we were veteran British Columbia sailors.

The beach was pretty, the snorkeling the best so far. Then came the beach barbecue and, at last, the lesson in pineapples by an expert.

We sat in the shade of a palm tree beside a sparkling blue lagoon, caressed by a fragrant ocean breeze. Ah, paradise! The expert they had on staff to give the pineapple demonstration, when asked, told us he was from Surrey.

Surrey!

Where cars are stolen every other minute. Where shootings occur regularly. Where all three hundred thousand residents deny living.

Kind of ruined the ambience of the moment. Ah, paradise! Ah, Surrey!

The vacation was drawing to a close. I could tell by the thickening wad of Visa receipts in my wallet. With only a few days left, Teri and Doug suggested flying over to the Big Island to look at fresh molten lava pouring into the sea. It sounded thrilling, so we flew to Hilo.

But the really BIG thrill came later, after the lava expedition.

At Hilo, Doug rented a Mustang convertible with four speakers. First thing we did was take down the top to enjoy the sun.

Instantly it started to rain.

While we scrambled to get the top back up, the Mustang's four stereo speakers blasted out our three all-time favorite hits by our three all-time favorite artists. (Artists?) Music by the Animals, Chris Montez, and some other group rattled through our ears.

As soon as the convertible top was up, the sun came out and the clouds blew away.

As we drove over a volcano and down the other side to where lava poured into the sea, the top went up and down and the rain came and went an equal number of times.

A footpath led over black rock at the sea's edge through jungle and back out to the sea. On the other side of the DO NOT GO BEYOND THIS POINT sign, dozens of tourists oohed and aahed at the red hot lava. One ranger wore a gas mask. The molten lava stank of sulphur and other acrid stuff. Millions of pictures were snapped.

Over the rough black rock and through snarled jungle tripped my blue sandals and me.

I hate my blue sandals.

You know the kind. With the thong around the big toe.

They're thin soled and floppy, and I have to walk funny to keep them from falling off.

Through the thin sandals I felt the heat of underground molten lava. It felt like walking on the kitchen stove. The one with the elements. Not the microwave.

I discovered something even more challenging then slurping salt water up my nose, and that was breathing lava stench. At first, lava stench hurts, then the hurt goes away. This is followed by a dizzy sensation so powerful you feel like you're going to die.

Other than that, it isn't too bad.

We enjoyed ourselves despite all the hard work with the convertible top. We visited the famous Painted Church but didn't see God. In Hawaii, he's probably on vacation like everybody else.

We visited a beach with black sand.

Across the lava flow, darkness gathered. Soon our plane, the last one of the day, would leave Hilo.

Not much time to get to the airport. About two minutes, in fact.

Teri drove. She passed some trucks, then some more trucks. Tick, tick, tick went the dashboard clock, eating away the two minutes.

It started to rain.

The Mustang hurtled through the countryside, passing cars and trucks and buses and screeching around schoolchildren. Teri combed her hair and applied makeup as she drove.

"Oh, God," exclaimed Doug as we neared the airport. "We have to top up the tank before we turn in the car!"

Teri cranked the wheel towards the last gas station before the airport. The Mustang leaped across four lanes of oncoming headlights into a 76 station.

A busy 76 station.

Out Doug jumped to pump gas. In the back seat Pat nervously glanced at her Timex. Less than a minute to go.

Back into the car jumped Doug. "No time, no time," he said. "Teri, get to the airport. Budget can top up their own tank!"

Teri slammed down the accelerator. The Mustang left smoldering streaks of rubber on the wet asphalt.

In a big hurry the radio played abbreviated versions of "House of the Rising Sun," "Let's Dance," and "Little GTO."

On two wheels the Mustang screamed onto Budget's lot.

We had fourteen seconds to catch our plane.

The desk clerk was just leaving for coffee.

Teri placed her well-manicured but strong fingers around his throat. Graciously but immediately the clerk postponed his coffee break.

Topping up the tank and finishing off the paperwork took up almost half of the fourteen seconds.

In seven and a half seconds the Maui- bound jet would take off.

In one second the clerk drove us the mile to the airport, whereupon Teri gave him his throat back.

Another whole second was wasted getting our gear out of the back of the van. We had picked up two male Canadian tourists who were also about to miss the last flight out.

I had the video camera bag. Pat and Teri had bags filled with flippers and beach mats. Fleet-footed Doug had the tickets. The two male Canadian tourists had each other.

"Run!" yelled Doug.

"Gate seven!" yelled Doug.

"Let's go!" yelled Doug.

Doug burst across the sidewalk into the terminal.

The brightly lit Hilo airport was a long, narrow building with a few retail shops. And, like all airports, people were hanging around, shopping or going on or off duty.

When we burst into the terminal in full flight, all of those people stopped whatever they were doing, and stared.

Now that we had everyone's attention, we couldn't help but sense that the next few moments would be the most exhilarating of the entire vacation.

Way down the bright length of the terminal was gate seven. We ran so hard towards it, the walls, windows, doors, and gawking people became a blur.

Doug led the pack. Teri loped right along behind him. Next came the two male Canadian tourists. Then Pat. Then my blue sandals and me.

Less than five seconds remained before the jet was due to take off.

We were halfway down the terminal before we hit top speed. We flew right by gate seven. Destination didn't seem to matter. Only speed.

As Doug sprinted past gate seven, he was worried about spending the long night on a hard airport bench. Teri worried about her knees, which sometimes locked up. She worried that if her knees locked up, she'd go rolling across the floor into the gift shop and wipe out the display of tourist novelties. Teri worried about how she'd pay for the damage, what with Visa already overspent.

Pat, who prefers to run at night when no one can see her, was horrified to find herself pounding down the center of a brightly lit terminal in bathing suit and flapping T-shirt.

All I could think about as I stumbled blindly past gate seven was my damned blue sandals and how I should have pitched them into the molten lava.

It was a good idea the builders had when they put a wall at the end of the terminal. Otherwise we might be still running out there somewhere in the jungle, searching for gate seven.

Arriving at the end wall, Doug screeched to a halt.

"Oops!" he yelled.

"Uh-oh!" he yelled.

"Gate seven is back thataway!" he yelled.

At the end wall I kicked off the damned blue sandals, turned, and then *really* began to motor.

But the others were already bearing down on gate seven and a nervous security guard who, unarmed and helpless, thought she was going to be badly flattened by the blitzing Canadian tourists.

In fact, it was probably a very good thing the female security guard *was* unarmed.

Then things might've gotten *very* exhilarating.

Maybe even *too* exhilarating.

So both our medical plan, and ourselves, were happy the lady had no gun.

We hurled our bags through the x-ray machine, grabbed them on the other side, and thundered out onto the wide tarmac.

One second left.

The jet was still there.

We had improved our aim. We missed gate seven, but we didn't miss our plane. We ran up the stairs and collapsed like dead people into nearby seats.

We'd made it!

Thank God.

Ten or fifteen minutes later the plane leisurely taxied down the runway and took off.

TEN OR FIFTEEN MINUTES LATER!

We could have walked.

Ambled.

Stopped for a cup of coffee, even.

But it wouldn't have been nearly as much fun.

Two days later the holiday was over, and all of us except Doug lived happily ever after.

To this day, Doug's dreams are tormented by...
...Gate seven, gate seven, gate seven...

Oh, by the way, I finally remembered who sang "Little GTO."
Somebody and the Daytona's.

* * *

Doing It!

Maybe it's all that fresh air they get. Or the sweet, seductive shapes involved, or the long, hard thrusts, or the thrilling, breathless climaxes. Whatever their reasons, sailors love doing it.

Under the right conditions they'll do it just about anywhere, with just about anybody, although they often have to get their partner's permission first. Couples do it together. Entire groups do it at the same time, which often takes precise choreography. And lonely sailors have been known to do it all by themselves in the dark.

Dedicated sailors will do it all day long and all night long, too. They are always exhausted when they finish and often have sore body parts.

Male sailors don't want to be known as premature finishers, but they usually start and finish faster than female sailors. This is something female sailors don't always understand. "If you enjoy doing it, why hurry to finish it?" female sailors will ask.

"It feels so good," answered John Timmerman, when asked the above question. "I can't wait to get to the end."

George Waibel, on the other hand, has a reputation as a slow finisher. He has never once looked at his watch while doing it, and those who have done it with him have hardly ever complained about how he finishes.

George doesn't do it as often as John does, which is probably why he prefers a slower pace. "Once I get started, I just hate to stop," says George. "If I have the right crew under me I can go for hours."

Regardless of whether it's a quick fast one or a long slow one, sailors can hardly wait to get together afterwards so they can ask each other, "Was is good for you, too?"

If it was really good for all parties concerned, sailors, wearing a wide smile, will talk for hours about doing it, sparing no detail.

Sailors who rarely do it, like me, can't help but get excited while listening to all the graphic detail. I'm sure I am not the only sailor who has spent a sweaty, restless night fantasizing about doing it.

Wait a minute—I don't want to give you the wrong impression here. I'm thinking about sailboat racing. What are *you* thinking about?

* * *

Viva Mexico

I didn't want to waste a lot of money going on an expensive Mexican vacation. Instead, I wanted to waste a lot of money on a big-screen TV.

My wife had other ideas.

Patricia argued, "Teri's lifelong dream has been to get married on a tropical beach. It's our duty as her parents to be there on a tropical Mexican beach for her when she marries Corbie."

"But the playoffs are coming and the big-screen TV is on sale," I said.

"You can visit your Mexican friend Enrique, whom you haven't seen for eleven years," she said, ignoring my whine.

Then she played her trump card.

"I hear there's a topless beach in the area."

"Viva Mexico," I said, and started packing.

The next day, the giant airbus dropped out of a hazy evening sky and thundered onto the Cancun runway. The rest of the wedding party had already been in Mexico for a week. Due to work commitments, Pat and I had been delayed. So our vacation would overlap the others; the first week we'd be with family, the second week the family would return home and we'd be with Enrique.

In the terminal, the humid, tropical air was like soup as we passed through the customs logjam and claimed our three overloaded bags. Outside, as darkness fell, a Mexican taxi driver approached us.

"Remember," Pat whispered, "these guys will try to rip you off, so bargain hard."

Confidently, I said to my wife, "Don't worry, I'm used to dealing with taxi drivers."

I greeted the cab driver with a snappy, *"Buenos nachos, senor."*

By using fluent Spanish, I was letting him know right from the get-go that I was a veteran at Mexican negotiation.

I could see respect dawn in his dark eyes. Or maybe it was something else.

"How *mucho* to Playa del Carmen?" I asked.

"Mucho dinero," he said.

"Great," I said. "Let's go."

"That's *bargaining*?" Pat said.

We crammed our luggage into the small trunk and Pat and I crowded into the Nissan's narrow back seat. Tires squealing, we rocketed through the darkness down a wide, four-lane highway, passing fleets of buses and taxis, and after forty tense minutes pulled up in front of the Mayan Paradise, our hotel.

The hotel was built around a courtyard filled with jungle, in the middle of which shimmered a swimming pool. Our room was nice, if you like dark. Dark walls, dark doors, dim light bulbs.

Then I removed my sunglasses.

It was still dark, but a lighter shade of dark.

The room had an air-conditioning unit located against one of the two narrow beds. Pat immediately chose the other bed, allowing me to sleep with the air conditioner. In order to bring down the temperature from a moldy, overheated forty degrees Celsius to a more livable thirty or so, the air conditioner had to run hard all night. It sounded like a jet taking off. Or landing. Or both.

In the morning we met up with the rest of the family, who'd already been in the area for a week, and joined them for a ferry ride to the island of Cozumel, thirty minutes across choppy water on an overcrowded, top-heavy ferry. Cozumel is noted for its white, sandy beaches, great diving, and world-class snorkeling.

Teri and Corbie were there—the bride and groom to be—and Lori and Peter from Whitehorse. (The wedding was still several days away.)

Peter and Lori had sunburns. Corbie and Teri didn't, but then this was the first time they'd left their hotel room in eight days. The honeymoon, evidently, was already well under way. First the honeymoon, then the wedding, I guess.

Our destination on Cozumel was a state park called Chankanaab, featuring a white sand beach, palm trees, palapa-roofed restaurants and bars, and beautiful green water.

The beautiful green water would try to kill me. I knew it, but I went in anyway.

Heavy rubber flippers on, rubber mask biting into my face, and rubber-tasting snorkel clenched in my teeth, I staggered across the blindingly white sand, almost tripping over a blonde topless sunbather (a female blonde topless sunbather, I should point out) and arrived, panting and sweat drenched, at the water's edge.

I looked at the ocean, and it looked back.

It seemed to seductively whisper, "Come on in and I'll drown you."

Or maybe I just imagined the whisper on account of how tightly I had cinched the facemask so water wouldn't creep in.

Taking my life in my hands, or flippers, I sucked in a huge breath of tropical air, maybe my last, and plunged into the clear green water.

Gulf of Mexico seawater is quite salty. I swallowed some.

Through my mouth.

Then through my nose.

While swallowing a few liters of salt water, I saw a few tropical fish. They looked back at me in a startled way. I think they thought I might be drowning. I sloshed around for a while, even going into water over my head, which caused me to panic and swallow another liter or two. The fish left the area. After maybe a minute and a half of snorkeling, I stumbled ashore and retraced my steps past the sunbather. I'm pretty sure she was still topless, but it was hard to see with the mask full of sandy seawater.

While the rest of the party frolicked in the surf, I spent most of the rest of the sun-blasted afternoon coughing salt water out of my lungs. Coughing salt water out of your lungs is hard labor, and when it was time to catch the return ferry, I was exhausted.

The honeymooners couldn't wait to get back to their room. The rest of us went out for dinner at a restaurant called Limone's. It reminded me of dining in a tree fort. It was open to the starry night sky, and a giant tree grew up through it, with branches everywhere. After a few cerveza's and a couple of rounds of gin and tonics, I managed to put behind me the ordeal of the green ocean trying to kill me.

Monday morning, Peter showed up with a T-shirt that said **LEAVE ME ALONE** in big, loud letters. He was haunted by a bad experience earlier in the trip with time-share salesmen, whom he labeled "rapists."

Fifth Avenue in Playa del Carmen is known as Restaurant Row. The buildings are a colorful assortment of shapes and sizes, and their rainbow hues include blues, greens, pinks, yellows, and all the shades in between. Occasionally among the chockablock businesses, crimson bougainvillea cascades brilliantly over walls and roofs.

Strolling along the car-free street, aggressive time-share salesmen, mobs of shopkeepers, and gangs of tour operators accost tourists, and at night waiters lurk outside restaurants, menus at the ready like weapons.

For Pat and me, ignoring the aggressive solicitation was no problem. Being from Vancouver, we were used to panhandlers, weirdoes, and street crazies, but for friendly, small-town types like Lori and Peter, who were polite to all strangers, the Fifth Avenue scene was sort of like being gangbanged several times a day.

The day's agenda included a trip to Xceret, a recent government-funded development featuring Mayan ruins, an underground river down which you can snorkel, turtle ponds, dolphin ponds, a manatee they were nursing back to health, and caves of bats and butterflies. Stone pathways shadowed by leafy trees connected these many attractions. All of this, plus restaurants, shops, and horseback riding were spread over several acres of jungled seashore.

The sun was out and fiercely hot as we lugged a heavy bag of rubber snorkeling gear through the entrance. We could've sat in the shade and spent the afternoon eating and drinking. But no. We were going to snorkel the underground river. Lungs still smarting from the flushing they'd received from seawater just twenty-four hours earlier, I couldn't help but wonder if I'd drown here, underground.

The good thing about the underground river was that it wasn't deep. The bad news, though, was that it was underground, with tons of rock and earth overhead, and mostly it was dark.

The other bit of good news was the river water wasn't nearly as salty as the ocean. I swallowed some just to be sure of that fact. There were fewer fish here to laugh at me, and my confidence soared. My snorkeling improved. We had so much fun, we snorkeled the river a second time. Unlike the ocean, the river didn't seem to want to kill me, and I survived comfortably.

After our aquatic adventure, we dined sumptuously and let the alcohol flow freely. Then it was time to watch a Mayan ball game in an arena—the first built for the sport in five hundred years. The players were costumed in animal skins and feathers and ornate headdresses, and the idea was to bump a resin ball with their hips through a hoop. In the old days, the losing team was often sacrificed to the gods. But in the modern era, the gods were deprived of human sacrifice and no blood was spilled.

Darkness gathered. The horde of tourists toured past costumed Mayan and Aztec dancers on their way to the next performance site. The primitive beat of drums reverberated through the grounds, casting a primeval ambience over the deepening night.

As the sky filled with stars, an amphitheater provided center stage for an array of Spanish dancers, singers, and musicians. After the show, there was a mad dash along darkened pathways to the fleet of waiting buses and taxis in the parking lot.

Around the corner and down the street from our room at the Mayan Paradise was a bakery specializing in cinnamon buns—sticky, gooey ones—but they were fresh and moist and totally decadent.

Lori said, "Bring some," when we were going to visit her in Puerto Morales, a twenty-minute bus ride up the highway.

So we did.

But I forgot to give them to her during the visit, and as we were about to leave she barred my exit, crossed her arms, and gave me one of those looks she surely inherited from her mother.

"Hand 'em over," she ordered.

Which I did, hurriedly digging into my knapsack, and only then we were allowed to leave.

The day before the wedding, Teri left a note on our Mayan Paradise door.

The note said, "Bring six cinnamon rolls when you come for the wedding."

That's how popular were the cinnamon buns.

I shopped early the morning of the wedding because the buns often sold out. I knew a non-delivery would cast a pall over the entire wedding celebration.

As far as wedding gifts go, the cinnamon buns were one of the most anticipated, if not the cheapest, we'd ever given.

Then it was Wednesday, and the wedding day had arrived. Enrique and his wife, Cristina, showed up from Merida, Yucatan, and Teri's friend Donna was there from Kelowna, along with her companion, Christina.

I hadn't seen Enrique in eleven years, since our banana-importing days in Texas. There was gray in his hair and mustache, and his girth had, well, gotten girthier. A friendly, funny hombre, with a zest for life, he remained otherwise unchanged.

Driving us to the scene of the wedding, a twenty-minute cruise north on the highway, Enrique had no hesitation at the security gate. The resort was guarded like a fort, the only way to keep out the riffraff, I guess. The uniformed and dour guard barely had time to remove the chain across the driveway before Enrique rammed through in his big, white Lariat Lobo crew-cab truck.

At the El Dorado Royale all-inclusive resort, the Gulf of Mexico rolled and crashed on the white sand beach, pillowy white clouds scudded across a vast blue sky, and the tropical breeze blowing off the ocean cooled the soaring temperature.

A white gazebo decorated with a red carpet, balloons, and flowers awaited the bride and groom. But there was a delay. The Mexican judge was late. We killed time in the handy nearby bar. The bride and groom grew increasingly nervous. Finally, the judge arrived.

Peter said, "That's a judge? He looks more like a waiter."

And he did look like a waiter. White shirt open at the neck, dark pants. The official documents he carried under his arm could have been menus. Maybe he was a judge during the day and a waiter at night. Or maybe waiters in Mexico were allowed to conduct wedding ceremonies.

As Enrique has often told me, "Anything is possible in Mexico."

The beautiful bride arrived in a golf cart. The ceremony went off without a hitch. Tears were spilled, and in their bare feet Corbie and Teri became husband and wife and began their official life together. There were roses and chilled champagne, and the wedding party took turns shooting hundreds of pictures of each other.

After a long day, and a long night of celebration, the bride and groom returned to their bridal suite. They locked the door and didn't come out for days—until it was time to fly home.

In the early morning hours, under a star- filled sky, the rest of the party returned to their various hotels in Playa del Carmen, Playacar, and Puerto Morales.

It had been a great day. Lori, the hairdresser, had scored big points making her sister, the bride, elegant and beautiful. Peter scored big points as official photographer. Donna and Christina had scored a heap of points by coming all the way from Kelowna. Enrique had scored big time for allowing himself to be dragged out on the dance floor for the first time in twelve years, and for not injuring anybody, including himself, while dancing with his wife. Corbie had scored by being voted macho hombre of the night for his performance with the band doing his own personal version of the Mexican hat dance, which, with luck, he will never do again in public. Ever. Teri had scored by being so cool and gracious and beautiful. Pat had scored a bunch for losing all that weight and for inter-fering hardly at all in the wedding plans. Everybody had scored big.

And just as the vacation had reached its heavenly zenith, things were about to plunge into hell.

The next day was a disaster.

Enrique had offered us the use of an apartment in Cancun, free of charge. We'd stay there for a few days and then join Enrique and Cristina in Merida. The free-of-charge part of the deal sounded especially good, as we'd been spending money like drunken sailors. But, as I'd learned many years before, an Enrique deal wasn't always a good one.

We said good-bye to the wedding party and started part two of our vacation. While the others were winding down their two-week vacation, which was just about over, ours was just starting.

Enrique drove Pat and me up the coast to the fabulous resort city of Cancun. Here swanky hotels rise like mini mountain ranges and downtown is like any city—all traffic and concrete. We drove past the swanky hotels, past the swanky shopping centers, past the views of sparkling green water.

Pretty soon we were passing not-so-swanky hotels, unswanky shopping centers, and for miles and miles there were no views of sparkling green water whatsoever.

And right after that, we were passing run-down hotels and the sidewalks were cracked and uneven, and the views were of vacant lots and weeds, and that's when I noticed that Enrique was sweating.

"I can't find the apartment," he said, making a hasty U-turn in thick traffic.

Now we could see boarded-up windows of gone-broke businesses, apartment buildings were crumbling to ruin, and the streets had deteriorated to potholed tracks. The gangs of youths in the alleys and hanging out in front of grimy cantinas looked at us hungrily, as though they were hoping we'd have car trouble and have to stop.

"It's around here somewhere," Enrique said.

Outside the air-conditioned truck, the apartment blocks looked like maximum-security prisons.

"Pat would prefer a nice hotel, thanks just the same," I said.

"I forgot my Coast Guard issue pepper spray," Pat mumbled. "And I don't feel safe without it."

"I can get you a deal," Enrique offered.

"On pepper spray?" I said, astounded.

"On a hotel room," Enrique added.

We exited the barrio and found a cheapo hotel, still miles from downtown Cancun.

Sure, the room was dirty, the furniture looked like it had survived at least two shoot-'em-out drug wars, and the shower stall was stained with three shades of yuck—mildew, mold, and possibly dried blood—but it was cheap.

As soon as we were checked in, Enrique and Cristina took off. Pat had to restrain me from running after them and heaving myself into the back of the pickup. That's how badly I didn't want to remain in this dump where we'd been, well, dumped.

"I want out," I fumed when I discovered the air conditioner was noisier than a cement mixer.

This discovery was right after I discovered the toilet barely flushed, and me with a sudden attack of stomach cramps.

Pat was calm. Which was understandable. She didn't have stomach cramps.

Pat said, "Let's go down to the lobby. Maybe the hotel is part of a chain and they can get us a better place downtown."

In the lobby a young, tall, and attractive Mexican woman who spoke perfect English was sitting behind a desk. She had very long legs and a very short skirt.

"I can't help you with your room," she admitted. "But I can sell you a fabulous overpriced time-share condo in a huge hotel complex, which you'll never use and never ever manage to pay off, no matter how long you live."

She smiled and crossed her legs. Long, tapered legs. Nicely tanned.

"I'll take them," I said. "It, I mean. It. The overpriced condo. That's what I'll take, uh-huh."

Always a sucker for a smooth sales pitch, especially when the pitcher wears stiletto heels, I would've signed there and then, except that fate intervened in the form of a stomach cramp attack. That, and Pat was giving me one of those steely looks in which wives seem to specialize.

I speedily exited the lobby, leaving Pat to sort out the details.

We never bought the time share.

But somewhere between the smile and the crossing of the legs, I'd agreed to take a tour of a fabulous, overpriced time-share condo.

In the morning, my stomach cramps were gone. And so were we. We took the time-share tour and said good-bye to the long-legged salesperson. Then we got the hell out of Dodge.

We went back to Playa del Carmen.

I needed beach time to recover from the horror of Cancun, so Pat found us a hotel on the beach, the Albatross Royale. It was clean and had a palapa roof.

Our room, number 207, reminded me of Tarzan's house. It was up a curving staircase that was made from what looked like driftwood. The bed's headboard was not attached to the bed frame but leaned against the wall and was hand carved, and, from the looks of it, by craftsmen using very dull knives.

There was no air conditioning, but the ceiling fan had overdrive, and when the turbocharger kicked in, the resulting wind drift could peel the sheets off the bed.

For several days we lounged on the beach, baked in the sun, and ogled topless female sunbathers.

Well, okay, *one* of us ogled.

When I wasn't busy ogling, I went in the water. But not over my head so as to risk drowning.

Pat watched the dive boats and went snorkeling and gradually became bored.

Lying prone on a beach lounge chair, Pat said, "We haven't met any-body yet...you know, made friends with anybody."

"Donna and Christina and Lori and Peter and Enrique and Cristina and Teri and Corbie," I said. "That's not enough people?"

I wasn't counting the time-share bimbo. For obvious reasons.

It was more than enough people for me. I could have gone the full two weeks of vacation speaking only to waiters and store clerks. Pat cannot go very long at all without being plugged into some kind—any kind—of social current.

A few minutes later, she dragged her lounge chair from the bright sun to the shade of a beach palapa. There was a woman already there, and Pat shoved her way in until she was elbow to elbow with the woman. Soon I heard the rhythm of their conversation, bro-ken now and then by happy laughter emanating from their patch of shade. Pat had found her social current and had plugged herself contentedly in.

I don't need people like Pat does, but I need to be plugged into my own current. Hockey.

The hockey season had ended during the past few days, and the Canucks had been in a fierce battle to finish in the playoffs. Not know-ing the outcome was starting to drive me slightly—only slightly—crazy. Our room had no TV or radio, and there was only one way to discover the Canucks' destiny. Find an American newspaper.

In hundred-degree heat, I charged from the beach, desperate for a hockey fix.

Up the street for ten blocks I hustled. The newspapers were all in Spanish. Away from the ocean breeze, the street radiated heat like an oven. I began to feel dizzy.

Down the street I sprinted, desperation setting in. Would I have to walk all the way to Cancun? Ten more blocks went by in a blur. Now I was really dizzy, and soaked with perspiration. I had to stop for bottled water. I resumed my search and finally succeeded when I found a *New York Times*. It weighed about fifteen pounds, and was three days old, and cost US$3.50, but it had hockey news.

The Canucks were in the playoffs.

Now, if only I had a big-screen TV…

Ah, well. No playoff hockey, but there was other stuff to watch.

Wobbly and bouncy female stuff.

Eventually—okay, the next day—Pat decided she'd made all the new friends she needed.

"Enough of this T and A," she said. "It's time to visit Enrique."

So I packed up my beach towel, said good-bye to the luminescent sea, not to mention the dozens of pairs of imported and tanned hooters, and boarded a bus for Merida.

The bus ride lasted four hours. We got to watch a filmed-in-Vancouver movie, dubbed in Spanish but with English subtitles. Or was it dubbed in English with Spanish subtitles?

Anyway, dusk and the Searses arrived in downtown Merida coincidentally. Our hotel was once a college, way back in the late 1800s. Well maintained, it had electricity, but like our earlier experience, *dim* electricity. Good thing I was too tired at night to want to read. Or maybe my eyes were already tired from, you know, the workout they'd had on the *playa*.

Enrique and Cristina were great hosts. They drove us all over the Yucatan in his Ford Explorer, A/C blasting high, cruising along at speeds so fast I declined to look at the speedometer.

We visited his *sandia* ranch, where a crop of seedless watermelon was growing heartily in rich, red soil.

We visited Campeche City, on the coast, which had an ancient Spanish fortress.

We visited the incredible, eight-hundred-year-old ruins of Uxmal. We toured Merida.

And everywhere we went there happened to be, quite by accident, one of Enrique's very favorite restaurants close at hand, just in time for lunch, or dinner. And—what a coincidence!—all the waiters and chefs just happened to be on a first name basis with my rotund *amigo*.

On the last night we were ensconced at a hotel near Uxmal, with an Enrique discount. From the balcony outside our door, Pat could see the modern swimming pool glimmering blue, and beyond it tangled green jungle, and, rising above the trees, the stone temple of Uxmal, built by the Mayan and then deserted by them almost a thousand years ago. While she contemplated the mix of modern and ancient, I was contemplating, once again, stomach cramps.

The next day we bused back to Cancun and taxied to the airport. When we were at thirty-five thousand feet, heading home, Pat turned to me and said, "Well, was it worth giving up the big-screen TV?"

I pondered for maybe three seconds.

"Lori and Peter were a lot of fun," I said.

She nodded.

"And Teri and Corbie made a wonderful bride and groom," I said.

"Yes."

"And it was great seeing Enrique again."

Pat nodded.

"And the food was exceptional."

"Yes."

"I have one little disappointment, though," I said.

"Oh?"

"Maybe we should've spent more time bargaining for a Cancun condo with that salesperson girl, who had those—"

"Long legs," Pat finished.

"Uh, yeah," I said. "Her."

It suddenly got very cold in the plane. Probably the air conditioning.

"I wonder if she'd still be there if we were to return next year?" I said. "And Enrique said for sure next time, he'll get us a rock-solid deal on a hotel room."

But later that year, just as hockey season began, a big-screen TV turned up in our living room. And what with playoffs to watch in the spring I forgot all about that salesperson girl. The one with the short skirt and the long tapered legs.

You don't think Pat planned it that way, do you?

* * *

Hurricane Tom

Packing up supplies for the annual trip to his Cariboo cabin, Tom Yipp is in his basement surveying his line-up of tools. Sort of like a surgeon checking his scalpels in the operating room just before the cutting starts.

Chainsaw, axe, machete…

This is Tom's stuff now, not the surgeon's.

Cut to my place, where, separate from Tom, I'm organizing my own tools for the four days of roughing it in the woods.

Lager beer, merlot, pilsner beer…

Back to Tom's. Tom fondles the heavy chainsaw. An evil grin parts his lips. He imagines the saw ripping through logs and trees. He tests the axe blade with his thumb. His grin broadens. He moves to the machete, hefting it. *Oh yes*, he's thinking. *Oh! Yes!*

While Tom imagines with delight cutting and slashing innocent trees and bushes with razor sharp implements, hammering nails, fixing and painting stuff—sometimes all on the same day—I am busy with my own thoughts. Different thoughts from Tom's. Way different.

I'm thinking of no running water, no electricity, and the ultimate deprivation—no TV. For FOUR days. Other gloomy thoughts concern an aching back from lifting heavy stuff, and blistered hands from lifting heavy stuff, and sore arms from lifting heavy stuff. I believe Tom takes secret delight in punishing me with hard labor. I'm also thinking I must be crazy to torture myself year after year on these hellish trips to Tom's place, seven hours' drive from the comfort of civilization.

Tom loves hard work because Tom is in great physical shape. Especially for an old, retired guy. He actually eats fruit and vegetables. And he eats them morning, noon, and night. He exercises. His mind is full of pure thoughts. Okay, *most* of the time his mind is full of pure thoughts unless he's had a few beer. And that's another thing about Tom. A few beers to Tom is two, and if he's really on a binge—three.

So Tom is healthy.

I'm not so healthy.

All day at work, I sit at a desk. I drink strong coffee. Sometimes I even eat doughnuts. For me, exercising is picking up the phone. Then, at night, exhausted from picking up the phone, I ride the couch. Sometimes, if I'm in the mood for a cardiovascular workout, I operate the TV remote control for up to twenty minutes at a time.

Tom has tools. I have books. Tom does his own around-the-house repairs. I hire it out. Tom takes the stairs. I use elevators. Anyway, you get the picture.

This year, it's a Chevy Silverado 4X4 Tom rents for the trip. That's the only thing Tom and I have in common. Old cars. Too old and frail for the dirt roads of the Cariboo. Tom is in charge of provisioning, supplying tools, and cooking. I'm in charge of bringing my own toothbrush and doing the dishes.

I help Tom load the truck. Mostly what we load, other than booze for me and tools for Tom, is food. And most of the food is fresh fruits and vegetables. Not a box of doughnuts in sight. It's gonna be a long four days.

Hours later, on the drive in from Highway 97, the truck shudders over the washboard gravel road, tires thump over cattleguards, and fat Cariboo bugs explode against the windshield. Out the bug-splattered window I notice mailboxes and road signs riddled with bullet holes. It appears as though deer and moose might be out of season, but mailboxes and road signs have been killed by the dozen.

The Silverado lurches off the forestry road and enters the road to Tom's place. Tom shifts down into four-wheel drive. The mud puddles are deep enough to drown in, and alder and pine branches claw at the side mirrors. In the deep forest, dusk is gathering and shadows stripe the narrow track of road.

"I've got the meals all organized," Tom says over the country music pouring out of the radio speakers. "We're going to dine on gourmet specialties. There's fresh-caught sockeye salmon, lamb chops, and chicken breasts. And for lunch, there's fresh-baked bread and all kinds of luncheon meat. And of course we've got lots of fresh fruits and vegetables."

"Of course," I say.

"Wait a minute," Tom says, frowning. "I think I forgot the salmon and the chicken. Left them at home. Sorry."

"Don't worry," I say. I'm in a forgiving mood. There's lots of booze, and there's still the luncheon meat and the lamb chops. "No problem."

"Uh…," says Tom, a moment later. "Darn, I think I forgot the luncheon meat, too."

"Oh boy," I say. "How many lamb chops are there?" I fail to keep the panic out of my voice. The nearest store is thirty miles away.

"Lots," says Tom. "And I brought extra grapes, so we'll be fine."

As we pull up at his cabin near the lake, I realize it's been a long day and I'm starving.

I'm envisioning a fabulous gourmet meal when I ask, "What's for dinner?"

"Wieners," Tom replies.

Once the truck is unloaded, the lanterns lit, the cabin's stove hot and chasing out the dampness, and the outside campfire pouring smoke, Tom plunges into the forest, machete in hand.

In a few moments he returns and thrusts a six-foot sapling at me. I wonder if he's expecting me to go pole vaulting, or maybe we're about to have a jousting match it's so big.

"For roasting your wiener," Tom explains.

The wieners are still mostly frozen.

Tom skewers a frozen wiener on the end of his stick and shoves it into the flames. Seconds later the wiener is no longer frozen. It's charred black and sizzling and dripping globules of fat. It crunches when he bites into it.

"This is the life," he says, grinning his enjoyment.

I impale my wiener with some difficulty. It's not easy impaling a frozen wiener on a six-foot stick, the pointy end of which is thicker than the wiener.

I nod in agreement. It's the life, all right.

That night, Tom sleeps and snores. Mostly what I do is stay wide awake listening to Tom snore.

In the morning, Tom leaps out of bed just as I'm about to doze off.

"Today," he says, full of enthusiasm, "we're going to cut and haul firewood, slash some brush back from the roadway, fix the dock, and paint the cabin. Then in the afternoon..."

Then he's gone into the kitchen, turning on the radio, making coffee, assembling breakfast, and hauling water from the lake before I can even find my socks.

Tom always makes the coffee with his back to me, as though it's a secret formula. It's instant coffee, so the formula can't be all that secret. It's probably the portions part that is the secret. Anyway, I've never been witness to how much coffee he shovels into the mugs before adding boiling water. But I can feel my heart lurch with each swallow, and the black-as-coal concoction sets my blood zinging wildly through my veins for the entire day.

After gorging ourselves on a hearty breakfast of seventeen blueberries each and a banana, it's time for work.

Lugging the chainsaw, Tom sprints into the bush. The saw snarls and bites into the wood, spewing great drifts of sawdust. I try not to get too close, just in case Tom turns my way and accidentally lops off one of my arms. I'll need both for what is to come. In about three minutes he saws up a cord of wood. The chunks of wood are strewn all over the forest floor about a mile from the cabin.

Tom's job is to spend three minutes using the chainsaw. My job is spending the rest of the day transporting the cord of wood, by hand, to the cabin. It's a tough job.

There are spider webs out there in the trees, and the ground is lumpy and root infested and low branches knock my hat off, mocking my career as a lumberjack. Little bits of bark and sawdust somehow get inside my shirt and itch like crazy. My lungs heave, my heart hammers, my arms grow weary, and my legs tremble with fatigue. And that's just transporting the first piece of wood, and there are hundreds more that require movement.

It's a long, long morning.

But for lunch, there is a nectarine and a slice of melon. Fortified with this, I'm able to complete my chores. Barely.

Then there's another sleepless night for me, while Tom's snoring rattles the glass in the windows.

Friday morning while I'm searching for my toothbrush, groggy from lack of sleep and cranky from doughnut withdrawal—it's been two days, five hours, and sixteen minutes, but who's counting?—Tom washes the windows, hauls more water, stirs the fire, cuts another cord or two of wood, fixes the sagging dock, and finishes painting. All this without even breathing hard. Tom the hurricane.

Then, after a lunch of twenty-three red seedless grapes each and an apple, there's more brush to clear, things to fix, logs to lift and drag. As I gasp and stagger trying to keep up, Tom takes pity on me and declares a time-out.

We sit by the campfire and read and enjoy some wine. While I read a trashy thriller, Tom studies a pamphlet about the nutritional value of antioxidants in leafy green vegetables.

"Anything in there about the nutritional benefits of french fries or doughnuts?" I ask.

Tom gives me a savage look over the tops of his reading glasses, which broke earlier and have been mended with about three yards of masking tape. The look shuts me up and I go back to guzzling wine. You don't mess with Tom and leafy green vegetables, is the lesson learned.

Gray clouds with charcoal bellies drift in from the northeast and unload their cargo of rain. It makes a rustling sound in the fir trees, drips in silver strands from the porch roof, and brings the surface of the lake to a boil. And, best of all, all work parties are canceled and the slave labour camp is temporarily closed for the day.

I actually sleep a few hours during the night despite Tom's wall-shaking snores. Probably due to the four bottles of wine I drank during the respite from work.

And the next day, the last, I spend mostly walking to and from the outdoor biffy, a result, no doubt, of the consumption of grapes, melons, apples, bananas, and nectarines. Fresh fruit in, not-so-fresh fruit out.

Nighttime, and I'm sinking into a coma in the lawn chair. Hard work, fresh air, and wine—thus a coma. The campfire roars, pulsing heat and smoke, and sparks fly and Tom keeps busy heaving ever-larger chunks of wood on the blazing fire. The fire gets so big and so hot we have to move our chairs back to the edge of the clearing to avoid barbecuing ourselves. Overhead, the sky is like black velvet, pierced by the light of a billion cold and distant stars. Around us the forest is black and the trees circle us like a fortress. Tom serves hot chocolate laced with Bailey's, and when that's gone, there's snifters of Cognac, and when that's gone it's time to seek our beds.

On this, the final night of the ordeal, I sleep soundly, ignoring Tom's thunderous snoring, for I am dreaming of a return to civilization. Electric heat and hot showers and doughnuts. Lots and lots of doughnuts.

* * *

Blowing Smoke

People go to Mexico for many reasons: the sun, the beaches, the food, the fun. Enrique and I went for the chayote of it.

It seemed like a good idea at the time, the idea being to cut a deal with some of Enrique's amigos to pack and ship the pale green chayote squash to the distribution company in McAllan, Texas, for which we worked.

We jumped into Enrique's brand new shiny red Dodge Ram pickup and drove twelve hours south of the Rio Grande on narrow, bumpy highways through the state of Tamaulipas to green and lush Vera Cruz.

Chayote has several growing areas, but the one we wanted was the most difficult to reach by far. Enrique and I had a policy of never doing things the easy way if it was possible to find a more difficult way, which explains why we are no longer together in the fresh produce business.

The highway out of Actopan, Vera Cruz, going towards the mountains rapidly dwindles from pavement to gravel, from gravel to dirt. Both the gravel and dirt sections had some pretty heavy-duty potholes. The mountains squeezed into a narrow valley. There was a village of dirt, kids, chickens, burros, pigs, tiny houses, and growers of chayote.

We met up with Mauro, who is actually Enrique's godson, yet Mauro is older than Enrique. Even Enrique is at a loss to explain how this relationship came to be, and usually he can explain just about anything.

Mauro led us to the chayote fields, and that's where all the trouble started.

Enrique had to reverse uphill on a narrow lane to get turned around. The lane between fields of chayote vines growing up and along wire trestles was choked with tall grass and weeds.

Finished with the chayote inspection, we waved good-bye to Mauro and left the weed-choked lane and drove from the dirt road to the gravel road in late afternoon. We were on our way back to the city of Vera Cruz.

On a street corner in a town close to the paved highway, a pretty girl waved, and Enrique, ever the gallant hombre, pulled over in a cloud of dust to offer her a ride. But what Enrique didn't know was, a man accompanied her. While she stood at the roadside with her thumb out, the man stood out of sight in some bushes. When the dust settled there were four of us sharing the pickup's bench seat. Hiding his disappointment at the girl's small deceit, Enrique drove on.

At first I thought the funny outdoorsy odor came from the two hitchhikers. But a mile later I identified the smell. Smoke. *Well*, I thought, *maybe they attended a barbecue and are a little smoky.*

The smell of smoke grew stronger.

I tried to sniff the young lady who was crammed in beside me, cheek to cheek, so to speak. Was she on fire, or merely smoldering? I didn't want her to think I was a weirdo gringo or anything, so I tried to sniff discretely. I inhaled perfume, shampoo, a little bit of sweat, but mostly what I smelled was smoke. Definitely smoke.

When the highway forked to Jalapa, Enrique dropped off the passengers. When they departed, however, the smoke didn't. It got stronger. Enrique had been flirting with the girl and seemed oblivious to the problem, which shows his power of concentration when flirting. Enrique has the biggest nose in all of Vera Cruz. Looking at it, you'd think he could smell everything, even at great distances.

Only when smoke started pouring out of the air vents in the cab did Enrique take notice.

"That stuff, it looks like smoke," he said.

We were flying down Highway 180, speedometer at 120 km/hour.

"Yes," I agreed. "I think we're on...FIRE!"

"How could we be?" asked Enrique.

"I don't know," I said, looking over my shoulder out the rear window. "There's so much smoke I can barely see the car behind us."

I may have screamed the last part.

"Shit!" Enrique said, pronouncing it *Chit*, as he always did.

He pulled over and we got out. A thick tangle of grass and weeds was snarled around the muffler and other underbelly truck parts. In the dark of the undercarriage, branches and sticks glowed red. I tried to yank some weeds away from the muffler but it was hot work, plus the undergrowth was firmly attached. The reason I volunteered for the dirty work was because Enrique weighed 280 pounds and, sure, he could get down on his hands and knees, but there was a chance he might not be able to get back up. For my efforts I was rewarded with singed fingers. I gave up.

"We could walk away, let it burn, and claim the insurance," I suggested helpfully.

But it was a brand new truck and Enrique refused to abandon it.

We decided to get back in the cab and drive to the nearest town, Cardel, where Enrique hoped to find a garage. His idea was to get the truck up on a hoist. Once on a hoist, access to the brush fire would be greatly improved. There's not a lot of garage owners, at least in Canada, who would allow a burning vehicle onto their premises, never mind on their hoist, but this was Mexico and maybe Mexican garage owners weren't as discriminating as their Canadian associates. Enrique tends to be an optimist in all situations anyway, so I just kept quiet and tried not to inhale too deeply.

"I'll drive slower so as not to fan the flames," Enrique said.

Slower was 110 km/hour.

Along the highway to Cardel, people gave us funny looks. Probably the first time they'd seen a traveling forest fire.

Cardel is a small town strung along Highway 180. There were shops and fruit stands but there was no garage with a hoist. There was no fire department, either.

However, there was a sort of lean-to arrangement where a young man had a tire repair business. The young guy gave us a very hostile look as we drove up.

"No way I'm crawling under there," he said.

He said it in Spanish, but there are times when translation isn't needed, and this was one of those times.

"The gas tank could blow any second," he added.

"*Chit*," Enrique said. "The truck won't blow *any* second. You got two whole minutes, maybe even three, before it blows."

Hands on hips, the three of us studied the problem. A few nervous passersby stopped and peered at the smoking truck. Nobody seemed curious enough to get very close.

Eventually, Enrique persuaded the young man to crawl under the Dodge with a machete. One of the persuasive arguments Enrique used was a fist full of money.

After the young man disappeared into the smoke, Enrique and I made sure we stood several yards away as we supervised, not wanting to crowd a man while he worked.

Gradually the smoke eased, then stopped.

A blackened young man belly-crawled out from under the truck and staggered to his feet. Enrique paid him.

"The next time your truck catches fire," said the young man, "take it somewhere else!" He didn't seem at all grateful for the work. He also called out several more Spanish words, which to this day I have never been able to locate in my Spanish/English dictionary.

And that's the true story of the day Enrique's truck caught fire.

Okay, okay. I'll rephrase that.

And that's the *almost* true story of the day Enrique's truck caught fire.

* * *

Texas Love Letter

Down in the Rio Grande Valley in south Texas, the trees still have all their leaves late into October, daytime temperatures get close to ninety degrees, and the only way I know it's fall is Carl's Grocery store is selling pumpkins.

I'm sitting in apartment ninety-four working on my beer belly (Old Milwaukee—smells like the Whitehorse Inn at closing time, tastes like Drano) and a letter, both at the same time. Today's topics will include tits, handguns, avoiding creditors, and Patricia.

Let's start with Patricia. We'll save the *really* interesting stuff for later.

After an absence of a mere eight months, upon returning to Vancouver I discovered a few things had changed. Radically. But one of the things that hadn't changed was the cat.

Just got in the door, home in Vancouver from the airport after eight months working in Texas, when the cat walked in, looked at me like she'd never seen me before, walked right back out. Felines have short memories, I guess. But being ignored was something I was going to get used to.

I knew eight months was a long time to leave my wife alone, but I was hoping for the best. There were forty-seven messages on the answering machine that first night. Male voices, every one.

Hmmm.

At eleven o'clock, Patricia jumped into a hot, steamy shower, naked. Oh boy! I thought.

But when Patricia jumped out of the hot steamy shower, she didn't remain naked very long. On went a flashy blouse and skirt. Off went the steamy and hot.

"Special lesson at the yacht club," she said, after explaining how much money she'd saved buying the new blouse and skirt. (Every time she spends money she knows exactly how much she's saved by spending it.)

Patricia continued, "The special lesson is how to get your spinnaker up after dark. I'll be home before dawn and don't forget to feed the cat."

The door went slam.

Oh boy! I thought.

Okay, no problem. Another night alone, just like all those nights in the Rio Grande Valley. I took a cold shower. Cold showers are much colder in British Columbia than in Texas, by the way.

At midnight, the guy next door banged on the front door. I opened it.

"Oops," the neighbor said. "Didn't realize you were home. How soon before you go back to the States?"

"Take a cold shower," I said. "I'll be gone in a week or so."

The neighbor went back to his apartment. In a few minutes I heard water running through the pipes next door.

When Patricia came home at dawn, I told her about the neighbor.

"Yes," she said. "He comes over a lot, mostly at night. He's *very* friendly."

Is that a bunch of strange shirts in my half of the closet? I asked myself the next morning. Or did I just forget I owned them?

Down at the marina, Patricia introduced me to several more men. Each was handsome, intelligent, young, and in good shape. Whatever happened to dim, middle-aged guys with beer bellies? I wondered. Maybe they all moved to Texas. The state is full of them.

One of those good-looking guys owns a—oh no—oh yes—power boat! And Patricia even spoke with him at length. God! Talking to a power boater! What next?

Next, he asked her to go bungee jumping. Bungee jumping? While everybody else stands around talking about what they did on the weekend, I mentally wrestled with bungee jumping, evidently the new "in" sport in British Columbia.

Pat couldn't accept the bungee-jumping invitation from the good-looking power boater.

"Nah, I can't, Jer," she said. "Gotta take my husband, old whatshis-name, sailing."

So a-sailing we went. To Gibson's.

Where I remet Mom and Dad, who didn't recognize me at first. Had to show them my driver's license to prove I was part of the family. It was beginning to look like eight months was a lot longer than I'd thought.

Later that night, back on the boat at Gibson's Marina, a guy wandering along the dock recognized Patricia and came aboard.

"Bob," Patricia grinned. "I sure enjoyed those marine etchings you showed me last time I was here. Got any new ones?"

"No," Bob replied. "But I varnished my bulkhead recently. Shines real nice in the dark. You wanna see it?"

Away they went to Bob's sailboat to gaze at his shining bulkhead.

I fell into bed alone. No cold shower was available, either.

Much sailing and many boyfriends later, we returned home and Patricia returned to work.

One night the phone rang. It was my old buddy Tommy Yipp. At last a male voice on the phone for me!

"Hey, Tom," I said. "Great to hear your voice! How are you doing?"

"Is Pat home?" Tom asked, straight to the point.

"Well, no," I said. "She's working late again. Taking men's inventory—I mean menswear department inventory. Or something."

"Tell her our first hockey game is the twenty-fifth," Tom said, and hung up the phone.

My *former* buddy Tom Yipp.

Looked like not only was eight months a long time, it was *too* long!

A few days later, Pat said, "You look tired. Why don't you try one of my vitamin pills?" She took a bottle from a row of about twenty-three bottles and shook out a big white pill.

"Take one of these," she said, winking. "And you might get lucky tonight."

She stripped off her clothes and jumped into a hot, steamy shower.

I swallowed the pill. It tasted like three pounds of chalk dust. I went to the fridge and drank nine bottles of Granville Island Lager to wash down the chalk dust. Horrible stuff. The chalk dust, not the lagers.

By the time Patricia emerged from the shower I didn't feel so good. In fact, I felt like going to sleep and going to the bathroom at the same time. Feeling like that doesn't bode well for the romance department. Not even in Texas, where nine beers a night is a way of life.

"While you're deciding whether to go to sleep or go to the bathroom, I'll go down to the club, see what's happening," said Patricia.

On went the fishnet stockings, lipstick, and two liters of Paul Mitchell hair spray. She headed for the door. I headed for the Tylenol.

Soon after that I headed back to lonesome old Texas. Just the air conditioning, my pickup truck, and me.

One night the phone rang. Patricia.

"We came in seventh," she gloated. "Out of forty boats."

"We?" I said, knowing what was to come.

"Me and Larry," she said. "He's a wonderful sailor for an old guy."

Oh ho! No more bright, young, fresh-faced boys for Patricia. Now she was lowered to liver-spotted, grumpy old lechers. No sympathy from me.

"Yeah," she complained into the phone. "Larry must be just about as old as you."

"Thanks for calling," I said. "See you in another eight months."

"Wait," she said, before I could hang up. "I lost another five pounds this week."

I said goodbye. I was very depressed. I went to the fridge and opened the door. There was stuff growing in it from before I went to Vancouver. The growth made it hard to spot the seven or eight sixteen-ounce cans of Old Milwaukee lurking inside. Uh oh. Just about out. Time to drive, not walk, to the local Circle K for another six-pack. Later, maybe there'd be a wrestlin' show on TV.

Crown Fruits Inc. teeters on the brink.

Crown is the company I work for down here, importing Mexican bananas and other items. We owe everybody money, including me. Creditors circle like vultures. Each morning begins with a tense strategy session during which we decide who to pay, who not to pay. The criteria for who gets paid usually is who can inflict the most damage in a violent confrontation.

That party gets paid, usually. Others have to wait. And wait.

Enrique handles the Mexican side of things. I handle the rest. At Crown we believe in sharing the harassment. The majority of our business is conducted in Spanish, which is one reason why Enrique is involved. Another reason Enrique is so valuable to me is his size. He's big enough to hide behind should anything dangerous happen.

In Mexico there are three main parties who want money, all growers: pineapple, limes, chayote. There is a fourth Mexican source who is hostile, but we'll talk about him later.

The objective each day is to dodge the creditors, keep the goods rolling, and hope that one day soon accounts receivables catches up to accounts payables. If we fail, the only thing we'll catch is bankruptcy.

Most of Crown's phone calls are in Spanish; therefore, most of them are for Enrique. It's hard to tell the creditors from the customers, so Enrique doesn't answer the phone, just in case. Carmen answers and takes messages. She has learned to be very creative.

Carmen, screening callers, answers the phone, "Enrique has been attacked by severe stomach pains and went. to the doctor. Would you like to leave a message?"

But really Enrique and his massive stomach are fine and dandy. He lurks in his darkened office, phoning out, selling. Or trying to sell. Chayote isn't everybody's favorite vegetable.

He calls Chicago, New York, Los Angeles, Miami. I can hear his strong voice vibrate through the wall. "You want chayote, we got it. How fast do you pay?"

At noon Carmen gets, well, sick to her stomach of Enrique's sick stomach and suddenly changes her routine. Now it's Enrique's back that has gone out, and Enrique has gone out with it. To the chiropractor. "Wanna leave a message?" asks Carmen into the phone. "He'll call you back soon as he gets out of bed."

We even have to drag Cristina, Enrique's wife, into the charade, as many calls go directly to his house. She tells the callers Enrique's back is so sore he's taken some pills and gone to sleep in bed. He'll phone back soon as he's able.

Every now and then there's a minor slip-up, so many lies, stories, and illnesses going around. Enrique and I are in my office. It's like being in a bunker under siege. Carmen sticks her head in the doorway.

"Manny called," she says. "He also called once before and I couldn't remember what I'd told him earlier. So this time I told him you were halfway between your doctor's office and the chiropractor's office driving in your car. Told him I'd try to reach you by car phone."

Enrique dials, unperturbed. "Make car noises," he says.

"Vroom, vroom," I say. "Beep, beep." I wail like a distant siren. The distant siren part is tough. Make it too loud; the guy on the other end will think Enrique's being pulled over for a speeding ticket.

It's probably bad enough as it is. Manny must be wondering what the hell the racket is all about in Pharr, USA.

Regardless, Enrique has a long conversation with Manny. The crazy sounds I'm making don't bother him a bit. When you're used to Mexican telephone lines nothing will bother you.

Luis the lime guy, calls. Twice. First call, he's told Enrique is sick with a cold. Second call, he's told Enrique is sick with a sore back.

"You better talk to Luis before he thinks you died," I tell Enrique.

So, Enrique picks up the phone and reaches Luis at his home in Mexico City. Snuffling from a make-believe cold, and from time to time moaning with make-believe back pain, Enrique talks for a long time before hanging up.

He grins.

"Two more loads of limes on their way," he says.

"But how are we going to pay for them?" I ask.

He shrugs the famous Mexican shrug. "One thing at a time," he says.

Right. One thing at a time.

We already owe Luis $5,000. And two more loads rolling. That's another ten grand. Yikes!

Times like these I wish I had a chayote box brim full of Pat's vitamins to help get me through the day. And a lime box full of Granville Island Lagers to wash them down.

The chayote guys drive twelve hours straight, Cordoba, Vera Cruz, to Pharr. We're only two or three loads behind in payments. What's the hurry?

Herberto has a glass eye. He keeps rubbing his crotch. Doesn't he know he can go blind, playing with himself like that? He's already halfway there. Maybe he should fondle come chayote instead.

Fernando, Mario's assistant, has Indian features and flashes a stainless steel tooth when he smiles.

They're good guys but they want money, which makes them bad guys.

"Hey, Enrique," says Herberto. "How come you didn't return our calls?"

"Let's not talk here," says Enrique, pushing them out the door. "Let's go to the Tex-Mex."

Parking lot full of cars. Square, one-story building with no windows. Place your hand on the outside of the walls, you can *feel* the music. Bouncer big as a fridge at the door. The dark room is smoky and full of men watching topless girls. They dance on the stage or at your table, or both. The topless girls, I mean, not the men. Everywhere you look there's tits, all sizes and shapes. A regular art gallery of flesh.

Herberto and his single eye have to work hard to keep track of all the action. Fernando's metal tooth glints in the spotlights. I pay for the lite beers on my Visa card. Crown is broke and there's no expense money left. That's why it's rounds of beers I buy, not Scotch. The chayote guys get pretty zonked pretty fast. The twelve-hour drive on Mexican highways, the sea of breasts, and the steady stream of Miller Lites. Who wouldn't be zonked?

At the right moment, 2:30 a.m., Enrique pitches his plan. We'll give them a check for ten thousand and they'll cash the check at their bank in Cordoba. Meanwhile, Crown will put a stop on the check, but it will take fourteen to twenty-one days for the check to clear Crown's Lone Star Bank account. So, the chayote guys will have a couple of weeks' worth of free money, enough to buy some more loads. Who knows, in two or three weeks, Crown might even have enough funds to cover the check. Unlikely, but it's a possibility.

Numbed by nipples and exhaustion, brains a-quiver from the loud rock music, the chayote guys agree to the deal. They stagger out to their Suburban, get in, and drive south, Crown check in hand. Or wallet.

Now a different story. The handgun story.

Enrique has just hung up the phone. We're alone in the office. Night has fallen.

Enrique's brown eyes are very serious.

"You got a gun?" he asks.

"You're kidding," I say.

"Not kidding."

"Guys from False Creek don't carry guns," I say.

"Better to have a gun if you need it than not to have a gun if you need it," he says.

It's hard to argue the point, especially when it's spoken in a rapid Spanish accent.

"So you think Geraldo will shoot me?" I say. The office is a pleasant, air-conditioned sixty-eight degrees, but I'm sweating profusely.

"Well," Enrique says, "this guy is real mad. And you can never be sure what a Mexican will do when he's mad."

Earlier Geraldo stormed out of the office, cursing and making dire threats. Now his partner, Pete, just called to tell us the obvious. Geraldo is pissed off. John better be careful.

Enrique says, "He wants a meeting tomorrow night. Or else."

I have more experience with meetings than with gunfights, so I agree to the meeting. Nothing happens to me on the way home. Nothing happens to me during the night. But I think about Geraldo a lot.

He's a crazy guy. He wears thick Coke-bottle glasses, behind the lenses of which he has wild, magnified eyes. Bushy beard. Loves to talk. He's had lots to talk about. He sold us some mangos, which we shipped to Vancouver, but the settlement was $8,000 short. That's what you get when you ship second-rate fruit. I had tried to explain to him that Crown would pay him the agreed price, providing the mangoes arrived in Vancouver in acceptable condition. Something got lost in the translation. To compound the problem, the fruit did not arrive in good shape, thus the problem.

Just before Pete and Geraldo arrive for the five o'clock meeting the next day, I send everybody home. No sense having innocent bystanders gunned down when the real target is a double-crossing Canadian cheat. I'm half of that. The Canadian part is true, but not the cheat part.

When their rattletrap car turns into the parking lot, Enrique gives me one of those cold, flat stares. Exactly the same stare he had watching the roosters tear each other's guts out in Vera Cruz six weeks earlier during a cockfight.

"If these guys want to talk, we'll talk," Enrique says. "But if they want to fight, we'll give them a fight."

He takes a 9 mm Ruger pistol out of his briefcase and shoves it in his belt, then pulls out his shirttail to cover it up.

Seated comfortably in an office chair, Enrique says in a relaxed way, "If their shirttails are out, they're carrying. If they're tucked in, they're unarmed."

"Yes," I say, like Canadians know about stuff like that.

Outside, the car doors slam shut.

All I've got in the way of armament is the office stapler. Probably just as well to have nothing at all. It's pretty hard to stop a full-grown, angry adult male by firing off a round of staples.

Geraldo enters first. Shirttail out. Uh oh.

Pete follows, shirttail neatly tucked in.

But during the two hours of heated negotiation that follow, the only shots fired are verbal ones. Eventually a very disgruntled Geraldo agrees to split the loss, accept some banana boxes instead. He's not joyful: banana boxes aren't exactly the same as cash money. They leave. And that's the main thing; they're gone.

Enrique and I grin and shake hands. We got through another day. Alive.

So, please understand. If you phone and ask for Enrique and are told he's home, sick as a dog in bed, unable to come to the phone. Believe it, even if you hear a strong Spanish accent in the background saying, "You want chayote? We got it. How fast do you pay?"

And if you call and ask for me, well, I'm out to lunch, even if it's only nine o'clock in the morning. But please leave your name and number. I'll get back to you.

Probably.

* * *

A Wimp Goes Winter Cruising

Patricia said, "Let's go sailing."

"It's three below," I said.

"We have a new spray dodger to cut down the wind and the kerosene furnace has just been reconditioned," she said.

Okay, I was in. Thoughts of a toasty warm furnace clinched it.

I'd spent the past year working in south Texas, where the temperature never drops below 90°F unless you turn on the air conditioning. To my thinned-down blood, Vancouver seemed about two degrees warmer than Baffin Island.

During my lengthy absence, Patricia had laid claim to *Temptation*, our twenty-eight-foot San Juan sloop. While she was busy teaching herself to sail solo in all kinds of weather, I was in Texas, busy forgetting everything I knew about boating in general and sailing in particular. But mainly what I forgot was how cold it gets on the water on a sailboat in winter.

We left Heather Marina in False Creek early on a Saturday morning. English Bay was flat calm, without even a breath of wind to tempt the sails. Except for a few anchored freighters, the water was deserted. There were no boats fishing at Cowen Point or Cape Roger Curtis.

First, my hands went numb. Then my feet. I could see my breath. (In Texas the only time I saw my breath was after eating Tex-Mex chili!)

At Gibson's Marina, our first night's destination, frost and duck guano made the docks especially slippery, but I wasn't worried about sliding into the water and drowning. If I slid off the dock, I'd land on the ice that covered most of the water in the marina.

In the middle of the night my chattering teeth woke me. It was too cold to get back to sleep, and now that I was awake I needed to use the head.

My scream woke Patricia.

"What's the matter now?" she grumpily asked.

"Er," I said. "The seat is a little chilly." Which was a gross understatement. I was frostbitten clean to the bone.

"Don't be such a wimp," she ordered. She hates being disturbed at 0200 hours, especially when what disturbs her is me, screaming.

At 0300 hours my butt finally thawed. At 0400 hours my feet got warm. At 0500 hours I pulled my ski toque down around my ears. Pretty soon my teeth stopped chattering, and sleep finally came.

Not for long. Patricia kicked me awake at 0600 hours. "Isn't this fun?" she asked, grinning.

After using the deck mop to smash the ice that had frozen around the boat, we headed for Snug Cove. There was a pub there, I'd heard, and it was probably warm inside.

Up went the sails and *Temptation* tilted into a fresh easterly. Winching in a sheet as we tacked, I whacked my hand against the new dodger and didn't even curse since my hand was numb from cold anyway.

Howe Sound was gorgeous. Sunshine glittered on smooth water. Snow sparkled on mountains. In a weak moment I thought winter cruising might not be so bad after all.

Snug Cove was even colder than Gibson's because the government dock didn't have power. Also, the ferry's wake bounced us around like a cork. To help me make it through the night, we hiked up to the comfortable Bowen Pub, where I took on some Scotch as antifreeze.

In the blackest hours of the night the wind blew up. Aggressive swells marched into the cove, shoving docks into motion and pushing boats to the limit of their lines. Then the island ferry docked just before dawn, adding its lumpy wake to an already rolling sea. Right after the ferry arrived, the dredging equipment—on hand to expand the marina—roared to life.

Temptation pitched and heaved. Docks groaned, rigging clattered, lines creaked. In the bucking cabin we stumbled like drunks into our yellow cruiser suits. When we clambered out on deck I saw whitecaps in the channel. *Lots* of whitecaps.

"We're not going out in that, are we?" I asked.

"Perfect day for sailing," Patricia said.

Again, I glanced out towards the channel. Spray blew from the tops of the whitecaps. While I wished I were back in hot, flat, boring Texas, Patricia reefed the main.

The only thing I remembered about reefing the main was, it usually meant you were in a hurricane, or worse. Before I could protest further, she cast us off.

"Don't worry, Tex, I'll have you home in no time," she said with a smile.

Home: solid ground, hot air vents, fireplaces, and thermostats turned high. Home is where the heat is, as they say.

Still, we made it, whitecaps and everything.

The next time I go winter cruising, it will be in the summer.

* * *

My Wife, the Skipper

Right from the start I knew I wasn't cut out to be a skipper. The instructor of our basic sailing course agreed with me. He took me aside and said, "I'm passing you only because your wife did so well, and you'll always be sailing with her, right?"

Right.

Okay, so my career as a sailor didn't take off with a bang, but the only previous nautical experience I'd had was with a canoe. Plus, I was left handed and figured that had something to do with my problems.

If my career as a sailor didn't take off with a bang, it certainly ended with one. Shortly after Pat received her basic sailing certificate, and therefore I did, too, we ended up owning our first sailboat. The very first time I tried docking the thing was the very last time I tried docking the thing.

Pat's voice boomed over the crunching fiberglass. "*Beside* the dock, not *on* it!"

After that horrible incident, all I was good for was ballast. Being used for ballast was pretty humiliating, but at least I was contributing. Also, it was hard to screw up being ballast, even if you were left handed.

When Pat announced she was joining Power Squadron, I thought it was a group of militant feminists. I was wrong, as usual, but the result was the same. After learning all about safety and navigation, Pat was more qualified than ever to boss me around. She became skilled as the yeller, and I became skilled as the yell-ee.

Some wives I know take classes in things like Japanese cooking, knitting, or flower arranging. Pat took a course in diesel mechanics.

After completing the course, she brought home a rubber tube and some odd-looking attachments. I wondered if the apparatus was for her, me, or the boat. Or, perhaps, our sex life was about to take a new twist. I try to keep an open mind, so I'm still not quite sure if I was disappointed or relieved when Pat explained the kinky stuff she had brought home was for changing the diesel's oil, and was not for personal use.

Pat is always lugging home vast quantities of vitamins, so I didn't pay much attention when she started talking about how important it was to change the zincs. I agreed wholeheartedly. If changing the zincs would make me healthier, I told her, I'd swallow a couple every morning along with my vitamin E tablets. She gave me a strange look and has never again brought up the subject, so I guess I'm doing fine, health wise.

At Christmas a friend of mine gave his wife some jewelry and some sexy lingerie. Pat got a power drill and a set of Blue Johns for winter cruising. I can't speak for my friend and the lingerie, but I never before realized how attractive long underwear can be when modeled in the appropriate atmosphere, like below freezing.

The other day I went down to *Temptation*, otherwise known as *her* boat, and caught Pat with another man. There he was, in a very compromising position: in a bosun's chair at the top of the mast, held in place by a line she had wrapped around a winch and was casually tailing off.

Pat claimed the guy was replacing the Windex, which sounded pretty suspicious. I mean, give me some credit for knowing a thing or two about boats. I know Windex is for cleaning windows, and I also know there's hardly ever any windows at the top of masts.

But before I could protest, Pat said, "I'll take you out sailing later, if you'd like. Providing you don't do anything dumb, or get in my way."

For a moment she thought about what she'd just said, and then she smiled.

"What the heck, I'll take you out anyway," she added, finally.

Ah, my wife, the skipper.

Maybe for her birthday I'll give her a jumbo-sized bottle of zinc pills, a couple of liters of diesel fuel, and a jug of Windex. After all, it pays to stay on the skipper's good side.

Believe me.

* * *

Trouble in Paradise

Summer is coming. Vacations, holidays, long weekends. Now is the perfect time to kick back, reminisce about past boating adventures, remember the good times, and recall the disasters.

Speaking of disasters…

We're in the Caribbean, Pat and I, guests on my brother-in-law's trawler, *Manana*. (Yes, we're ashamed to admit we holidayed on a powerboat, but, hey, we all have our little sins.) We meet two other couples which are also touring the British Virgin Islands on a powerboat. This pair of couples have three strikes against them: 1) they are from Ontario. 2) they are new to boating, and 3) their luck has just run out.

Please meet them.

Gary is a handsome wheeler-dealer salesman. Pat sunburns her eyeballs gawking at his muscular body wedged into a tight pair of swimming trunks.

Nancy is Gary's girlfriend. She is a flight attendant. Nancy looks terrific in her bikini. Luckily, I have sunglasses so my eyeballs don't suffer the torture of sunburn while gawking.

Duncan is a rich man's son who knows everything about boating on Ontario's placid lakes. He thinks the ocean is, well, just a big lake. He will soon learn the difference. If intelligence can be measured in terms of light bulbs, Duncan is a forty watter.

Sherrie is Duncan's blonde girlfriend. She also looks smashing in a bikini, and if intelligence can indeed be measured in terms of light bulbs, Sherrie has a great set of headlights, if you catch my drift.

One afternoon they join us hunting for conch shells, taking under-water pictures and other snorkeling activities. We're in *Manana*'s dingy with Mike and Judi, our hosts. And the Ontario foursome is in their dingy. We decide to dingy race back to the boats, which are anchored half a mile away. We take the lead. No wonder. Their motor sputters. Keeps going. Sputters. Suddenly it pops off the transom. Splash, right in the drink it plops.

Duncan and Gary grapple with the dripping motor. Clamp it back on. Just because the entire motor took a saltwater bath doesn't mean it won't start. Duncan, the boating expert, grabs the frayed starter cord in a strong fist. Yanks hard. Oops! The cord snaps. Tension free, his arm slashes back. The broken cord is like a short whip. Duncan accidentally slashes girlfriend Sherrie across the face. In heated fashion, Sherrie explains to Duncan her lack of appreciation for the stinging pain he has inflicted.

We win the dingy race.

Our reward? We get to tow the other dingy back to their boat, *The Sandees*.

Duncan assures us he knows how to fix the dinghy motor, while Sherrie races for her makeup kit.

Time passes. Gary approaches *Manana* in the dingy, rowing. Seems Duncan *wasn't* able to mend the Evinrude. Does anybody know anything about Evinrudes?

Pat and brother Mike love to play with screwdrivers and wrenches and stuff. They volunteer mechanical services.

Gary borrows *our* dinghy, the one with the working motor. Roars off. Pat and Mike get in the nonroaring dingy. I join them. Three's a crowd. I'm given one of those don't-bother-the-experts looks.

Then I'm assigned to the bow, where I am used as ballast while they fiddle with the motor. I do a great job as ballast and the Evinrude gets fixed. Sort of. At least it runs. Sort of.

That night not only do the heads on the *Sandees* back up, but the sail mysteriously unattaches from Gary's rented sailboard, which is tied to his boat, and silently drifts away.

In the morning, before we leave, Gary tells us he plans to anchor that night in Spanish Town.

"The anchorage there isn't very protected," Mike warns him.

Gary shrugs off the warning and proceeds to search for his missing sailboard sail.

It's a free country, and if Gary and his troupe want to rock and roll all night long, it's their right to do so. Their heads are still backed up. The odor is so strong the four Ontarians can barely breathe.

Later, we anchor in a nice, secure spot in Marina Cay. Spend a peaceful, restful night. Very early the next morning Pat spies the *Sandees* headed our way.

"Gee, they're up and on the move early...say, where's their dingy?" she says.

The *Sandees* grabs a vacant mooring buoy. The crew collapses to the deck. Gary dives into the water, swims over, and hauls himself wearily onto *Manana*'s swim grid. We gather in the stern, staring, waiting for his tale. It goes like this...

During the night anchored off Spanish Town, Gary woke up several times. Large swells tossed the boat and wind lashed the rigging, making sleep almost impossible.

In the darkest part of the night, Gary continues, he peered out a window. Yikes! The bow of an anchored sailboat was only inches away. Their anchor was dragging. He jumped up, awakened the others, and feverishly started the big diesels.

Steering to avoid clobbering other boats Gary tried, and tried, and tried again to anchor. Took forever to get a hook.

Finally the anchor flukes caught.

Gary gave the engines a quick reverse to set the anchor, but no one was on dingy watch. Undetected, the thick, black painter (rope) sucked around a prop.

Okay, no problem. They're firmly anchored. The panic is over.

Calmly, Gary will get a knife, dive down, and cut loose the painter.

But Gary's string of bad luck has yet to run out.

He could only find a very small kitchen knife. The painter was thick and tough. Underwater for long periods of times, Gary nearly burst his lungs trying to saw through it. The prop was finally cut free and Gary and his lungs survived. But things got worse.

The sea rolled, the wind gusted, and once again the anchor dragged loose. Gary went up on the bridge. He banged the throttle back and forth—reverse, forward, reverse again—at two in the morning, trying to reset the anchor. Until, at last, a firm hook.

Not wanting to repeat the painter-prop entanglement, Gary yelled at Sherrie to pull in the dingy so he could reverse and set the anchor deeply. As he reversed, Sherrie pulled in the painter. Oops! No dingy on the other end. She paused to consider the implication, then she flew up to the bridge and reported the missing dingy to a very harassed and perspiring Gary.

She asked him, "Are we going to die, Gary?"

Gary didn't answer. Before he could set the anchor, it had come loose. He and Duncan were keeping busy trying not to sink any nearby sailboats. Sherrie and Nancy, using their flight attendant training, broke out the life preservers, and, figuring they were going to be dead soon anyway, they started drinking heavily.

In the bow, Duncan crouched over the anchor line in the pitch-black dark. The boat rocked and pitched. This wasn't like Lake Muskoka, Duncan thought.

The anchor caught; Duncan squatted down, tugging on the line, making sure it was caught. The line stretched taut. Duncan crouched even lower, not wanting to get chucked overboard by the bouncing deck. Suddenly the anchor rode released. Duncan was dealt a stiff *whack!* dead center on the very end of his, er, male member. Duncan screamed in agony, soprano style, and swooned. The girls, putting aside their martinis, rushed to his rescue, helping him stumble below. Again their flight attendant training came in handy. Sherrie whipped out the party ice and dipped Duncan's blackening bruise into it.

Somehow the anchor caught and stayed and they made it through the rest of the night without further misadventure.

Sherrie's quick work with the ice saved a possible serious bit of damage. Duncan and his member were okay, but even now, years later, he refuses to use ice in his drink.

Leaning on the swim grid, Gary concluded his story. Now he wanted us to help rescue his wayward dinghy, which had washed up on a rocky beach, the poor Evinrude once more over the side, dangling by its wire.

It's the least we could do. But this time it was terminal. The Evinrude was dead.

A couple of days later, after their anchor dragged again, this time in Cane Bay amid a crowd of boats, the Ontario foursome cut their vacation short and returned home.

Ah, yes. Summer is coming. Boating holidays, boating weekends, boating disasters. I can hardly wait for the next adventure to begin.

* * *

Agony and Ecstasy

I was sick of golf, and golf was sick of me. I'd hooked and sliced so many balls into the rough that Greenpeace was starting to protest I was a danger to the environment. I'd excavated enough divots to fill a dump truck. When I stepped onto the tee box, local birds would start early migration just to be on the safe side.

Humiliated, frustrated, and mortified with one sport, I was ready to try something different.

Patricia said, "Let's go sailing!"

"Yessir," I replied.

Sailing couldn't be worse than golfing. Couldn't possibly. Could it?

Mother's Day weekend arrived, and we decided to sail to Gibson's. A nice and easy half-day sail. Kind of like a tune-up for the season. See if the three of us—the sailboat, Pat and I—could get along for longer than fifteen minutes without the threat of mutiny, violence, or, worse, boredom.

Maybe the Admiral wasn't really Captain Bligh. Maybe sailing wasn't the miserable experience I remembered. Maybe it would be better than golf.

We left the dock with the usual rules and regulations in place. The Admiral's main job was dispensing orders in my direction. And my main job was to obey those dispensations. I wasn't allowed to do any of the important stuff —like steering, navigating, or using the VHF radio. Mostly what I was allowed to do—make that *forced* to do—was the grunt work. Hoisting sails, winching, fetching coffee for the skipper, stuff like that.

I smacked my head on the boom. Banged up my right ankle on a shackle. Wrenched my back. Ripped my fingers to shreds hauling on lines. Whacked my knee, somehow, against the mast.

Then we cast off.

I survived waves, wind, and the Admiral, and made it alive to Gibson's.

I survived Gibson's.

I survived waves, wind, and the Admiral, and made it alive all the way home.

I was okay, but the head died. With beer on board, having a functioning head was critical to the morale of the crew.

The Admiral said, "I'll look after the head, you get the boat cleaned up. Next weekend we're sailing to Newcastle Island with the yacht club."

Relieved, I said, "Yessir."

I was glad the Admiral was looking after the head. Installing a new one meant wrenches and tools and stuff, and, as everybody knows, wrenches can kill you.

Newcastle Island is thirty-eight nautical miles across the yawning, watery expanse of Georgia Strait. There was tide out there, and currents and swells. And the ocean was very deep and very cold. And *Temptation* was very small. And my skull was still bruised, my fingers bloodied, my knee stiff, my back throbbing in pain from the Gibson's trip.

Following orders, I attacked the sailboat with boat wax. I scrubbed and waxed vigorously. Until my shoulders hurt, and my left elbow swelled up (I'm left handed, one of my many problems); even my neck was sore.

The night before disembarking for Newcastle Island, the Admiral installed the new head. She worked long into the night, using wrenches and other dangerous tools, until the head was firmly in place.

Saturday morning arrived, and the four of us—*Temptation*, the Admiral, the new head, and I—set sail across Georgia Strait. One big happy family.

The wind was fierce, the swells were high, the rain clouds were low, and so was the temperature. But the good news was, due to hypothermia I couldn't feel the pain in my shoulders, or my throbbing back, or anything at all.

Maybe it was the pitching and rolling. Or maybe it was the beans I ate the night before. Whatever the reason, sixteen nautical miles into the voyage, nature called. And the brand new shiny head beckoned.

Down into the cabin I went. Upon the throne I contentedly sat.

And while I sat, the swells got bigger and the boat bounced and rolled and shuddered and pitched with increasing enthusiasm.

The screws, so carefully inserted into the floor by the Admiral and her Craftsman screwdriver in the wee hours of the night, suddenly ripped loose. The head was like a wild animal off its leash. It bucked and heaved and galloped all over the boat. I crashed into the bulkhead, smashed against the wall, slammed into the roof. But through all this I was glued to the saddle like a broncobuster.

Eventually, the swells diminished and I was able to, er, dismount.

Staggering back into the cockpit, exhausted, I sagged onto the lazeret, glad to be alive.

"Are you all right?" the Admiral said. "You were down there a long time."

"Yes," I said. "But I'm thinking maybe golf isn't so bad after all."

* * *

Gulf War

Just before our vacation started, the Admiral called a meeting.

She pulled out a thick wad of charts, slapped 'em on the dining room table, and said, "Listen up, crew. Here's the plan."

I looked around. The only crew in the room was me.

"We're gonna invade—I mean, we're gonna spend a week in the Gulf Islands."

"Oh, good," said the crew. "Full-service marinas with pubs, hot showers, and plug-in power."

"That's *not* the plan," Patricia said, glaring.

"Oh," mumbled the crew.

"Government docks with no facilities, lonely anchorages, and no restaurants, let alone pubs. *That's* the plan."

"Oh."

"It'll be wonderful to enjoy the best the Gulf Islands have to offer. Just the sailboat, Mother Nature, and us. Plus, I just bought two thousand pounds of food and we only have a week to eat it."

On Saturday, the first day of our vacation, there was no wind, no swells, and no excitement. We motored across Georgia Strait under overcast skies, arriving at Whaler's Bay, Galiano Island, in the early evening.

As the government dock came into view, I said, "It looks kind of grungy."

The dock looked like it had been hammered together from driftwood by drunken carpenters, and the boats moored to it were rusting buckets of bolts.

"There's a spot open for us," announced the Admiral, and she turned abruptly and parked.

As soon as the engine was off and the diesel fumes had abated, I could smell rotting fish. But this was a working government dock and Pat was happy and I had a fresh supply of cold beer, so I was happy, too.

The next morning, Sunday, over coffee brewed in *Temptation*'s galley, the Admiral consulted a stack of tide tables, charts ,and horoscopes. Whenever she spent long moments scanning stuff like that, I knew we were about to embark on a suicide mission.

The Gulf War, Sears style, was moments away.

The Admiral pointed to a chart. "This is Whaler's Bay, and right here is Active Pass."

"Active Pass!" I blurted. "It's narrow and has dangerous currents, and the big passenger ferries plow through there every thirty minutes."

The Admiral quickly explained everything, as all great nautical commanders do. "I checked the tide chart. Flood tide flows north to south, and west to east, but it's not flood tide, so forget what I just told you. It's ebb tide, which changes everything. But I also checked the astrological chart and it's a great time to risk our lives. Batten down the hatches, we're outta here!"

We left the safety of the government dock, turned south, went past Sturdies Bay, and then the gaping maw of Active Pass opened before us.

Into the maelstrom we chugged. Current swarmed through the pass like great white sharks, silent and deadly. The rocky shores of Mayne Island on the port side and Galiano to starboard closed like the grips of a vise. We kept chugging. Active Pass is viciously doglegged. We made it past the first turn and approached the second.

Suddenly, a great shadow fell over us.

I looked back.

A mammoth ferry loomed over our stern. It was so wide,; its steel sides scraped the rocks on each side of the pass. Tourists gathered on its high decks to watch our little sailboat get flattened.

Ferries travel at twenty knots. *Temptation*, flat out, can do maybe six.

Within seconds the ferry closed on us. The entire pass trembled with its power, weight, and speed. I considered wetting my pants.

But they don't call the Admiral the Admiral for nothing.

Calmly, she reached for the radio mike, and calmly clicked it on.

"Mr. Big Shot Ferry Boat Captain, this is *Temptation*," she calmly said.

"*Temptation*," answered the radio. "This is Mr. Big Shot Ferry Boat Captain, go ahead."

"I'm a member in good standing of the Coast Guard Auxiliary, Unit Six," she calmly continued. "And the Coast Guard Auxiliary is connected to the real Canadian Coast Guard, which is on very good terms with the U.S. Coast Guard."

"Uh, could you talk a little faster," I interrupted.

The Admiral was unperturbed. "And the U.S. Coast Guard has really big boats with really, really big guns, and if you run over us, Mr. Big Shot Ferry Boat Captain, and my American buddies find out about it, they just might launch missiles and stuff at the British Columbia ferry fleet. And with all the ferries burning or sunk, you'd be out of your high-paying union job. So there."

"Yikes!" came the radio response. "I need at least two more years to top up my extravagant union pension!"

And the ferry took a sharp turn, gouging out a big chunk of Mayne Island, sending cabins, cottages, and homes splashing into the sea. But the ferry avoided us and we were safe. I reconsidered about wetting my pants and decided not to.

Eventually, Active Pass spit us out the other side, where we emerged onto mirror-flat water unruffled by wind, breeze, or zephyr. The Gulf Islands were all around us. We took a left—oops, I mean port—turn down Navy Channel, which is the narrow channel that separates Mayne and North Pender. As we passed Hope Bay, Pat spied a vacant slip at the government dock and gunned it in there, cutting off two fishermen and a sailboat.

"It's mine, it's mine," she screamed. "I saw it first!"

In all the mountain of food stored on board there was one item missing. Diet Pepsi. Pat had looked it up on the Internet and discovered that Diet Pepsi caused all of the inner organs, and some of the outer (depending on sex), to rust. So she immediately and forever swore off the stuff, not wanting rusted-out organs in her later years. So instead of drinking Pepsi, she was guzzling bottled water. Lots and lots of water.

The Gulf Islands were beautiful, their wonderful silence broken only by the whisper of tree branches, the gentle slap of waves on the beach, or the distant cry of seagulls. Until we arrived, that is. Now there were two new Gulf Island sounds everywhere we went. The glug-glug-glug of Pat upending another water bottle, shortly thereafter followed by the pump-pump-pump sound as she flushed the head. But at least she wasn't developing organ rust spots!

Hope Bay government dock had no water, no power, and no showers. The nearest store was forty-seven kilometers away. We were fresh out of absolutely nothing, but Pat hadn't been in a store for almost forty-eight hours, and she was getting desperate. So we set off, walking, in search of provisions. Along the roadside we saw wild deer, wild eagles, and wild blackberries, which we picked and ate. The berries, I mean. Not the eagles and deer. Having realized when we got to the store that we in fact needed nothing, we returned to the dock.

Monday, we celebrated Labor Day by departing Hope Bay and laboring east across Plumper Sound to Winter Cove. Winter Cove is a spectacular little cove nestled in the protection of Saturna Island. Here we were badly outnumbered by large U.S. boats, both power and sail. Cottages and waterfront homes peeked through arbutus and hemlock. We dropped the hook and for two days and nights swung languidly at anchor.

Pat unslung the crab trap and plopped it overboard, using a ripe fish head for bait. I could practically hear the rustle of crabs as they stormed the trap, trying to gain entry.

Tuesday morning, *Temptation*'s cockpit became a hell storm of screaming crabs, slashing machete, and exploding bits of crab shell as Pat harvested her catch.

"Some of 'em look kind of small," I commented, ducking lopped-off crab parts as the evil machete swooped down, slicing and dicing.

"I measured every one of them," Pat snarled. "They're all legal." In her tightly clenched fist was the killing machete, dripping with the blood and guts of innocent crabs.

"Yessir," I said, and scuttled crablike to a safe distance.

For lunch we feasted on—yes—fresh crab. It was succulent and delicious, but my conscience curtailed my appetite. Murdered crabs are, after all, murdered crabs.

In the evening, while a swollen orange sun sank below the horizon, setting fire to the flotilla of clouds as it went, Pat cleaned and sharpened her machete in anticipation of tomorrow's crabathon.

But crabs are smarter than most people think, and the remaining herd avoided the trap, shopping elsewhere for fish heads. The next morning when Pat wrenched the dripping trap from the sea floor it was empty, and she was bitterly disappointed.

To get her out of her blue funk (sometimes when in the throes of a blue funk she grabs the machete and…well, you can imagine), I took her and *Temptation* across Plumper Sound to the long harbor of Port Browning, where I plied her with butter pecan ice cream until she released her hard grip on the machete handle and I was able to store it safely away.

We plugged into the marina's electricity, the weather forecast calling for gale force winds, rain, and other bad stuff. Although Port Browning marina has been for sale for several years—it must be a real money loser—and the service is consequently lousy, there's power, and showers, and, wow, a pub! Not to mention a restaurant. And a shopping mall—North Pender style—half a mile away. Port Browning, in other words, had it all.

One of the first things we did, as storm clouds closed in, was hotfoot it to the showers. The shower stall was a narrow cylinder, and I shared it with a very large spider, which didn't really appreciate the steaming hot water. I flicked the creature out with my big toe, and soaped and rinsed. Because the stall was so narrow, every now and then I couldn't help but rub a body part or two against the walls. Unclean walls. I imagined catching some incurable disease, and lathered soap until I was raw. Then the spider reappeared, at eye level, crawling up the soiled shower curtain. Its fangs dripped venom as it closed in. Trying to bat it away, I dropped the soap. The second bat sent the killer spinning beyond kill-ing distance, but now I had to pick up the soap. Not an easy task in the confined space of the shower. As I bent over, my butt wedged against the rear—so to speak—wall, my head jammed against the other wall, and I was trapped. For one scary, claustrophobic moment, I figured I was stuck, bent over like a you-know-who, waiting for a you-know-what, until morning when the caretaker arrived and would have to pry me loose. But I managed to wriggle free and got out of there with every-thing intact except my dignity.

Dodging rain drops, I fired up the barbecue that night. The unit was attached to the pushpit at the side of the cockpit. There was a great whack of meat to grill—five or six pork chops, a dozen beef ribs—as well as corn on the cob, so I filled 'er up to the brim with chunks of easy-to-light charcoal. When I applied match to charcoal, a great explo-sion occurred, sort of like a volcano. Roaring, blazing, snapping flames leaped high into the air.

The Admiral, who was below, called out, "Are you okay out there?"

I couldn't see her, immersed as I was in a thick column of black smoke.

"I think my hair just caught fire," I replied.

"Don't burn my beef ribs," she warned. "I hate when you burn my beef ribs."

I plunged my head into the cold sea, promptly dousing the fire in my hair.

"I'll be okay," I reported. "Maybe a week in the hospital, max."

A few minutes later, she squinted through the smoke and said, "Put some sauce on my ribs. Looks like they're drying out."

I couldn't get closer than throwing distance to the conflagration, so I picked up the bottle of honey garlic barbecue sauce and heaved it in the general direction of the inferno.

"Your beef ribs look fine, sir," I said.

She examined the height of the flames, which would measure about three feet high if you could get close enough to measure with an asbes-tos measuring tape.

"You used too much charcoal," she said. "Again."

"I like a *hot* fire," I countered.

"And what happened to your eyebrows?"

I ran burned fingertips over what was left of my eyebrows. They felt crispy. But she was gone below before I could respond.

I noticed a boater on the dock nearby, frantically waving his arms.

"Here, take my fire extinguisher," he offered.

"No thanks," I said. "My wife hates when I get fire retardant on her ribs."

The boater walked away through the cloud of hot smoke and ash, shaking his head.

Eventually, the smoke lessened and the flames died back and I was able to get close enough to the molten barbecue to shovel sizzling, blackened chunks of meat onto a plate and take dinner below.

No big deal. Just another barbecue a la John.

Thursday morning, when dawn should have been happening, the sun decided to take the day off. It was gray, gray, gray. Gray sky, gray sea, gray prospects. The gale force winds arrived in full force, and wind gusted into the long, narrow bay, flapping flags, causing halyards to sing, and rippling the dark skin of the ocean. And rain fell, puddling on the wooden dock boards and pooling on the cockpit sole. Shards of water burst against the windows and poured down the glass. Raindrops hammered on the hatch cover and *Temptation* stirred restlessly against its lines and fenders.

We were snug in the small cabin while the storm boiled around us, the electric heaters keeping dampness at bay, overheating the interior, making me bored, tired, and lazy all at once. Sort of like some sales meetings I'd been forced to attend in the past.

It was a long day of murky light, newspapers, books, dominos, and napping. The day was made longer with the prospect that tomorrow would be much the same.

But tomorrow, Friday, proved the weather forecaster dead wrong.

The sun broke through multilayered, rumpled clouds, illuminating patches of water, and further south the San Juan Islands beckoned. But there was no more time. The Admiral's pager beeped, and when she phoned, a message from the Coast Guard waited. Night shifts were available at Kitsilano base and the long-range weather was not promising, so the decision was easy. We were going home.

Leaving Port Browning, we turned north. We planned to go to Degnen Bay on Gabriola Island, anchor overnight, then cross Saturday morning to False Creek. We'd get home in plenty of time for Pat to start her Saturday-night night shift.

There was wind but it was right in our face. We crisscrossed Plumper Sound and Navy Channel, fruitlessly tacking against wind and strong current. Finally, the motor was kicked into action and we powered a couple of miles into Trincomali Passage, which separates Saltspring and Galiano islands. The wind changed direction a little bit, and the current eased, and we killed the motor and sailed while clouds split apart and blue sky brightened the morning. A rain squall moved in briefly, but the skies cleared again. Skirts of rain swept across Saltspring's green flank. To the northwest a huge purple stain of cloud blossomed and expanded, threatening the afternoon with gloom.

As we drew abreast of Porlier Pass, the gap between Valdes and Galiano that provides access to the northern Gulf Islands, we could see Georgia Strait was bathed in sunshine and its blue waters were calm. Vancouver was twenty nautical miles away.

"Let's go," I said.

And maybe for the first time ever, the Admiral complied.

It was slack tide, and we motored easily through Porlier, which, like Active Pass, can be rife with current.

Most of the distance was covered under power, but the sun was out and the afternoon was pleasant. As we approached the Point Grey bell buoy hours later, a bank of cloud settled in, blocking the sun, and the day chilled, the wind strengthened, and swells tied the sea in knots.

The sun set, and it was like the last ember of a dying fire. Darkness gathered, and now, as the wind increased, we had too much sail up and the wind drove us hard. *Temptation* surfed down the long backs of the swells, then slewed and climbed again, then fell again.

Ahead, the lights of the big city twinkled, but home was still two hours away and we were in trouble.

The waves were steep and aggressive, the wind relentless. Out of the descending dark came tugboats pulling barges. Tugboats to starboard, to port, and coming straight on from the harbor. Almost like we were under attack. Tugs don't move fast when they've got chip barges in tow, but they don't give way, either.

Chip barges are huge when you're in a small twenty-eight-foot boat. Hell, even tugboats are huge, built from iron and steel, and they could run over a sailboat in the dark and not even feel the slight bump.

The Admiral had the tiller. I was on lookout.

"Look out," I kept screaming. "Here comes a tug and barge!"

Which the Admiral would barely dodge.

Then I'd holler, "Look out! Another tug and barge!"

And the Admiral dodged that one, too. Very calmly. Maybe all that Coast Guard training was paying off.

And I'd had a series of heart attacks, or were they strokes? And after we'd successfully passed through the minefield of tugs, and got the sails down, and were approaching Burrard Bridge, and beneath it, the quiet, friendly waters of False Creek, a bright moon rose over the city and frosted the ragged clouds with reflected light.

The Gulf War was over, and the troops were home.

* * *

Ode to Sailing

Another nautical vacation, but with a difference.

A week before the start of our holidays, the Admiral says, "This time you're in charge. You get to pick the places you want to go. And don't screw up, or it'll ruin everything."

Oh, boy. Or, sticking with the nautical theme, oh, buoy!

She downloads thirty-seven pages of charts from the Internet and prints them off and thrusts them at me and says, "Start picking right now. We're not leaving till we have a plan."

"I want to go to Telegraph Harbor," I say. I *love* Telegraph Harbor.

"No," she says firmly. The Admiral always says everything firmly. "We've been there already. Pick someplace else."

"But…"

She rips the charts out of my hands. "I knew you'd screw it up. We'll go to Cabbage Island," says the Admiral. Firmly.

"Yes, sir," I say.

I've never heard of Cabbage Island. It doesn't sound very exotic, but it doesn't matter. Wherever goeth the Admiral, so goeth her crew.

As our vacation draws closer, I check the weather forecasts. The weather experts are forecasting intermittent rain, rain showers, and periods of rain. The newspapers, the radio, and TV all forecast the same thing.

"Maybe we should just stay home and watch the playoffs," I suggest to the Admiral.

She gives me one of those Admiral looks.

"Or, maybe not," I quickly add.

So we pack up most of the Admiral's clothes closet—wardrobes for summer, winter, and spring, just in case the weather changes—buy all the groceries our credit card can manage, load up on crab bait for the Admiral's commercial-sized crab trap, and, with a convoy of wheelbarrows piled high, we off-load all this stuff on *Temptation*. *Temptation* is *our* sailboat, but mostly it belongs to the Admiral.

One wheelbarrow is packed to the brim with cans of beer. When you go sailing with the Admiral, you need a lot of beer.

We set off early in the morning under a mostly overcast sky, but with sunny breaks.

We clear English Bay and the wind strengthens. The sails go up and the engine is switched off, and we sail.

Cabbage Island lies just off the eastern tip of Saturna, thirty nautical miles down the Strait of Georgia. Right next to—get this—Tumbo Island, a marine park. Cabbage and Tumbo. Sounds like some kind of... of Ukrainian dinner menu!

But we can't get there from here. The wind is from the southwest and that's where Cabbage Island is. So we bear away a few degrees and sail towards Porlier Pass as a high, thin cloud slides across the sky. Hidden now behind a gray veil, the sun loses its heat and the temperature plummets. We reach for toques and jackets like it's the middle of winter.

From Vancouver, there are only three gateways into the Gulf Islands. To the north, there's Gabriola Passage. To the south, there's Active Pass, which the British Columbia ferries use on their journey to Swartz Bay. And in the middle is Porlier, with Valdes Island north and Galiano on the south side. Each of these passes is subject to strong currents, unless taken during slack tide. Even at slack, eddies swirl and ripple and the sullen green water plucks at the keel and rubs against the tiller, like a friendly warning it could get nasty if it really wanted to.

Some sailors, while they cruise, listen to music or just enjoy the symphony of wind and water, but not the Admiral and her crew. No sir. Channel 16 is turned up to full volume, just in case there's an emergency to which she can respond.

Motoring through Porlier, the radio crackles to life. We hear of a sailboat in distress just south of Clam Bay, about eight nautical miles away. The sailboat is up on a rock (it's low tide, and there is some mysterious magnetic force that draws sailboats to rocks at this time.) Not only is the sailboat on a rock, but also it's *Canicula*, a boat we know very well, owned by a couple from Gibson's.

The Admiral guns our diesel engine up to five and a half knots (that's full blast). She yells at me to check the chart, which I have to put aside my beer to do, and she asks, "How long will it take to get there?"

"Maybe an hour and a half," I say.

She grins and reaches for the radio.

"*Canicula*, this is *Temptation*. Help is on the way," the Admiral says.

"We could be dead by the time you get here," answers *Canicula*. "There's a fish boat close by and we're going to ask it to tow us off this rock."

"You old fart," yells the Admiral so loud it's likely *Canicula* can hear her without the radio. "You better wait for me to save you, or I'll never speak to you again!"

For years now, the Admiral has been waiting to save somebody with her sailboat. She's saved all kinds of people and all kinds of boats as a member of the Coast Guard, but never once has she saved a life with her own boat. She tried to save a wild bald eagle once, but the eagle had other ideas, and that was the closest she's ever come to saving anything while aboard *Temptation*.

"What kind of friends would rather be rescued by some fish boat they don't even know, instead of me?" fumes the Admiral, slamming down the VHF mike.

We're rocketing along now at darn near six knots. It's almost fast enough to throw out a visible wake.

"We'll go over there anyway, just in case the fish boat screws up," she says.

So we chug along, going an hour out of our way. Eventually, after turning past a small island, we can see that *Canicula* is off the rock, and there's a fish boat leaving the scene. For a moment there, I'm thinking the Admiral might try to ram and sink *Canicula* for letting the fish boat do the rescue, but we merely cruise on past, Pat throwing them a serious glare.

Motoring down Tricomali Channel, we take a left turn into Montegue Harbor Marine Park. It's narrow and sheltered, with many mooring buoys available. The marine park is mostly deserted this time of year—May—and we have our choice of buoys.

"We'll take that one near the beach," decides the Admiral. "Get the boat hook out, get up on the bow, and hook the buoy ring when I get close."

Again, I put aside my beer (not the same one) and leap into action.

Up on the bow, the buoy seems to be closing in fast.

I give the Admiral a slow-down-dammit arm motion.

She sends me a finger signal back.

She still has the engine in rescue mode. We're closing on the buoy like a shark on an overweight swimmer.

Bending through the lifelines and stainless steel pulpit, I turn myself into a pretzel trying to harpoon the buoy, and get it, the boat hook nicely snaring the ring. Very smooth. Very professional. Especially considering our rapid rate of speed. Professional, okay, but not too bright.

The sailboat weighs more than three tons. (Maybe four tons, counting the weight of my beer.) It has no brakes. I weigh a lot less than three tons. My arms likely have less muscle than just about any other adult male arms in all of North America. Okay, maybe the world.

I've got the ring, but the boat keeps moving. The buoy slides past. The boat keeps going.

If I drop the boat hook in the water, the Admiral will kill me. If I *don't* drop the boat hook in the water, the effort of trying to stop six thousand pounds of moving sailboat will kill me. Under my winter toque and coat, I'm sweating like it's Florida.

At the last possible nanosecond, just before my arms are ripped completely and absolutely out of their sockets, I manage to release the ring. Which is good news/bad news.

My arms are still attached to my shoulders (good news), but now (bad news) I have to explain to the Admiral about my failure to capture the ring on the first try. It probably would've been less painful in the long run to lose my arms.

Now it's late afternoon. The Admiral and I have just shared a two-hour conversation about how to hook a mooring buoy. (*She* was driving way too fast. *He* is an incompetent hooker of buoys.) The argument ends in a tie, which means the Admiral automatically wins.

The water is dark, the nearby trees are dark, and the sky is dark and getting darker.

With the aid of about nine hundred bungee cords, we rig a blue plastic tarp over the cockpit just as raindrops begin to fall. First just a few, then more, then it's raining with a vengeance.

I sit in the cockpit, listen to the rain crackle on the tarp, open another beer, and tell myself to move the tarp a little before lighting up the barbecue. A missed buoy ring is one thing; catching the boat on fire is yet another.

I avoid losing my eyebrows during the lighting of the charcoal, but barely, and don't even come close to setting the boat on fire. My pork chops have that black look of cinder, and Pat's steak is slightly crunchy, but we're not complaining.

We're on holidays.

* * *

The furnace pants throughout the night, keeping the cabin cozy warm.

Golden rays of sunshine spear through the windows and wake me at seven o'clock. The sky is scrubbed free of clouds and is a perfect blue. The sea is mirror calm; the boat tugs gently on its mooring line. I'm first up on this morning—mainly because my bunk is narrow and hard, and Pat's is wide and luxurious. (The crew doesn't get to sleep with the captain. Or the Admiral, either.)

After dismantling and folding the tarp and all those bungee cords, I sit languorously in the cockpit and work on my suntan. I can hear crows fussing at each other in the forest, and high overhead four bald eagles glide in expanding circles above the land. Higher still, a seaplane drones, going east to west. Over by the dock, a dinghy's outboard leaves a thin trail of blue smoke behind it as it motors over glassy water. Occasionally, swallows swoop over the water. There's a campsite nearby, and up under the big evergreens it's shaded and cool and peaceful.

For two days we sit and enjoy the sun.

We take a walk along a trail on Grey Peninsula and look out through arbutus trees, with their smooth, red bark, at the moored boats and watch the color of the sea change from green to blue as the sun climbs in the sky. Along the path the thin soil is fertile, and Indian paintbrush, Oregon grape, salal, wild sweet pea, and ferns crowd each other for growing space.

In the afternoon, the wind picks up and thrashes the branches of oak and cedar and fir, ruffles the water, and steals away the sun's warmth.

But the long evenings are calm and pleasant, and around seven each night, charcoal smoke lifts lazily from the barbecue and the air is redolent with the aroma of sizzling meat, not all of it charred black.

One afternoon, Pat digs some clams from a deserted beach, where the crushed shells of hundreds of thousands of their ancestors that cover the beach gleam white in the sun. We dine on the clams that night, giving the barbecue a rest.

Then, on Saturday, I have a near-death experience.

The Admiral gets out of bed uncharacteristically jolly. She even percolates the coffee while whistling a happy tune. Well, no she doesn't. I'm exaggerating. But she makes the coffee and isn't too surly about doing it.

"Aux Six is coming over," she informs me as I'm cleaning up a pile of empty beer cans.

"Ox who?" I say, a fierce hangover stabbing knitting needles in the backs of my eyeballs.

"The boys from Coast Guard Auxiliary Unit Six, that's who," she declares, grinning.

"You invited them on our vacation?"

"The Coast Guard Auxiliary *never* takes a vacation," she says, firmly. "They're meeting with the Ganges unit and with the Galiano unit to inform boaters at Montegue Harbor Marina of safe boating procedures."

"How nice," I say. I'm busy trying to decide what to have for breakfast, coffee or beer.

"We might have a little surprise for you," she says, no longer grinning. Now she's smirking.

I decide on coffee for breakfast, with a beer chaser.

"Great, great" is what I think I say. It's hard to concentrate with knitting needles skewering the backs of your eyeballs.

"Let's go over to the marina and say hello," she suggests after I've finished breakfast.

She shrugs into her bright yellow and red Coast Guard jacket and pulls on her Coast Guard Auxiliary hat, the one that makes her look like she's about to invade Cambodia. A jungle kind of hat.

The knitting-needle-hangover thing is almost fixed, and I agree to go to the marina with her to say hello to the crew of Ox Six.

The Hurricane Zodiac they rode over on from the North Arm of the Fraser River, crossing sixteen miles of Strait of Georgia in about fifteen minutes, is tied to the dock. It's red, with two gigantic outboard engines on the aft end.

Three Ox guys are standing casually on the dock. They're wearing ball caps with fancy Coast Guard logos, jackets with Coast Guard shoulder patches, and nearby, on the side of their Hurricane Zodiac, in foot-high lettering. is "Coast Guard Auxiliary" spelled out boldly. They're wearing radios and pagers and cell phones along with Spyderco rescue knives, which are so sharp you can shave with 'em. The knives, not the cell phones.

"We're with the Coast Guard Auxiliary," they point out.

"Nice dinghy," I tell them, nodding at their overpowered, seven-plus meters of rocket ship resting benignly at dockside.

They're wearing sunglasses. Greg, the tall one in the blue uniform with the broad shoulders and square chin, shifts his gaze. Reflected in his sunglasses is the Admiral standing behind me. Smirking.

"Okay, boys," she says. "Grab him!"

His two cohorts grab me by the arms and throw me onto the floor of the Hurricane. They quickly follow me aboard, and before I can leap back to the dock, they stuff me into a Coast Guard cruiser suit. Then they shove me onto one of the rear seats, the kind you sit in like a saddle, and they strap me in.

The Admiral is watching from the dock, arms folded.

"Stop screaming and struggling," she orders. "They're just gonna take you out for a little spin, show you how fast the boat is."

"No no no no no no," I protest.

"It's something you've always wanted to do," she says.

I stick with the "no no no no no" routine.

"It's a special vacation bonus I arranged for you," she adds. "So you better enjoy it."

There's only room for three of us in the red rocket ship. The guy who stays behind on the dock, and whose seat I've taken, turns to the Admiral, and says, "And if he doesn't make it back, Pat gets the insurance money."

And Pat's smirk gets smirkier.

Greg steps on board, taking the forward seat, the one that belongs to the coxswain. He turns a key and the twin engines rumble to life. It reminds me of those dragsters you see at drag strips, just before they explode down the track.

Pat and Larry, the guy who's been left behind, toss free the lines, and very slowly the Hurricane drifts away.

The gap between the dock and me widens. Then widens some more.

"Say goodbye to the cat for me," I holler beseechingly at Pat across the yawning patch of cold sea that separates me from safety.

The Admiral waves good-bye, and I think this could be the very last time I see her. Hey, maybe this isn't all bad, I think next. Then I realize I could die. I mean, this rescue craft is really just an air mattress on steroids attached to about two thousand horsepower.

Greg maneuvers us carefully around a fleet of anchored sailboats and motor yachts. Sunlight sparkles on the water. People are sitting relaxed on their boats, enjoying the day. They watch us go by, none of them realizing that I'm like a condemned man going to the gallows. Will we explode in a fiery ball? Will I fall overboard at fifty-five miles per hour and drown? Will my heart simply give out as we approach the sound barrier?

One female person with long blonde hair, sunglasses, and tanned cleavage is lounging on the bridge of a sleek yacht. She seems to give me a close look as we pass slowly by.

I sit up a little straighter; adjust my sunglasses, giving her a little nod. Maybe she thinks I'm a rescue guy. I've heard girls go for macho rescue guys. Especially girls with cleavage.

Before I can give the sleek girl on the blonde yacht—I mean blonde girl on the sleek yacht—a second Tom Cruise how-ya-doin' nod, Greg turns to me.

"Ready?" he says.

"Huh?" I reply.

We're now at the mouth of the harbor, staring across the open water of the channel towards Parker Island. This could be the spot where we get blown to smithereens.

"Nope," I say. "Definitely not ready."

"Better hang on," Greg says.

The guy I'm sitting beside gives me a nod of confidence. "You'll be fine," he says.

"Fine?" I retort. "Compared to what?"

Suddenly, the engines scream.

No, wait a minute. It's not the engines.

It's me. Screaming my lungs out.

The engines merely whine as they hurtle us forward. Instantly we're going so fast, the wind so hard in my face, that I can barely breathe. I wonder if I can hold my breath for the twenty or so minutes we'll be out here, jetting across the water like a cruise missile. No, probably not for twenty minutes. Running out of oxygen at one hundred miles an hour is not much fun. It's way less fun than, say, running out of oxygen at a sedate thirty miles an hour. I quickly learn to duck my head a little so I can breathe. Now I can take a moment, look around; enjoy the sights, the thrill of—

Oops, almost lost my sunglasses.

The red rocket ship surges forward, coming out of the water like it's going to fly into the wild blue yonder. The nose lifts and we're fast and smooth over the surface, sheets of white water spraying off the sides and a white, foaming wake churning behind us.

Fast and smooth until—oh God! Yup, that's me screaming again.

Until we hit the wake of a big powerboat, then we're, *yikes*—so this is what it's like to go off an Olympic ski jump!

And—*whump!*— so this is what landing is like after going off an Olympic ski jump!

Yeah, I'm fine, okay, no problem, except maybe for my spine, which is probably only slightly broken.

I turn my head to the left and the wind tries to peel my face off. The shoreline is a blur, the water is a blur, and everything is a blur. Any faster and we'll be in the next time zone.

Roaring down the channel towards Active Pass, the shore on either side of us—rocks, trees, cottages, docks, boats—looks like it's been chucked into a high-speed blender. In sixty seconds we've covered more ground than *Temptation* could in, well, a week. At least that's what it feels like as I'm swept at light speed down the road to hell. Make that the waterway to hell.

One small mistake could send us bouncing, careening, and skittering out of control. I picture engine parts and body parts showering into the sea.

The rocket ship is outfitted with about a million dollars' worth of electronics, at least. Including radar, GPS, chart plotter, and a dozen or so VHF radios.

Radios!

If I could just reach over and grab a radio, I could call, say, the Coast Guard to put an end to this insanity.

Then I realize, wait a minute, this *is* the Coast Guard!

I'm doomed.

Greg wrenches the wheel and Ox Six does about nineteen very tight doughnuts, the boat listing hard over, green water sloshing close to me. We're sitting at right angles to the water. The engines whine, and water boils, and Greg is smiling.

"It can turn within its own length," he boasts.

"I think I may be having some kind of marine heart attack," I croak.

"What?" he says.

But we're under way again, leaping forward, and this time it's the engines screaming, not me. It's hard to scream and have a heart attack simultaneously.

We're headed back to Montegue. We slow down, and now I know I'm going to survive. We pass the blonde and her tanned cleavage, and I try to look like I'm capable of saving dozens of stricken boaters at a time, should the need arise. But she ignores the red rocket ship. Wait till you're out there alone at sea, I'm thinking. That gloriously tanned cleavage barely keeping you afloat—then—*then* you'll appreciate rescue guys like me. Then you'll be sorry you ignored me. Er, us. Okay, them.

The Admiral is waiting at the dock for our return.

"How was it?" she hollers, as we get close.

"Damn near killed me," I mutter.

"What was that?"

"Fine, dear. It was fine," I say, louder this time.

A few hours later, I stop shaking.

* * *

Sunday, it rains.

All day.

We huddle in warm clothing under the blue tarp. We read books for hours, until we're almost blind. Then we read some more. Drinking beer in the cold and rain just isn't the same. Plus, there's no TV for playoff games.

In the morning, which is overcast and threatening rain, we leave Montegue and sail on the jib across to Ganges Harbor on Saltspring Island.

Ganges Harbor is long—really long—and narrow, and it's mined with crab traps. We deke around the crab traps and pull into Saltspring Marina.

Ever wonder what happened to all those hippies from way back in the hippie era?

I'm here to tell you what happened to them. All of them moved to Saltspring, that's what happened. They're there by the thousands. And there are thousands of art galleries. After the night in Ganges, we're down to one more night before going home.

Why am I not surprised when we head south for Cabbage Island? There's no wind, so the motor is on. The sky is only partially marred by cloud, and as the day unfolds, the clouds disappear and the weather is like summer. *Temptation* motors past the rocky cliffs of North Pender Island, where expensive glass-sheathed homes with commanding views sit precariously among the rocks. Near Bedwell Harbor, porpoises play tag with a sailboat. We leave North Pender off our stern and chug along the deserted shore of Saturna. Not much well water available on Saturna, so fewer homes there.

Then we turn the corner past the southern tip of Saturna, and we can see Tumbo Island. On the flat, sun-drenched rocks of East Point lie many seals. They might look kind of cute, but they sure smell horrible! The western shore of Tumbo is a stone palisade, and the breeze carries the smell of shaded forest. Once a privately owned island, Tumbo is now a marine park. There are no homes, cabins, or cottages, but there are a few wilderness campsites tucked beneath the evergreens.

On a stony beach on Tumbo's southern shore, two bald eagles are feasting on the pink remains of a dead seal. One eagle watches from a nearby log while the other rips into its meal with a bloodied, hooked beak.

Cabbage Island is far prettier than its name. It's small, only a few acres, but with a sandy beach, and it's forested. The entrance is between outstretched reefs, their rocky teeth barely visible above the glossy surface of the sea. There are ten mooring buoys, only one of which is taken. It's a kinder, gentler Admiral at the helm, and we attach ourselves to the buoy on the first try. With a long view up the strait, Tumbo protects us on the west, and Cabbage on the east. Thirty miles away, clouds the color of dark bruises hover over Vancouver, but down here, the sky is clear and the sun is actually hot.

Parked for maybe thirty seconds, Pat plunges below and emerges with her huge blue crab trap. It's almost as big as the dinghy she heaves it into.

"There must be crabs here," she tells me. "There's a good sandy bottom and crabs like that."

"Yes," I agree. "There's nothing like a good sandy bottom."

The Admiral jumps into the dingy and grabs the oars and starts rowing, the excitement of catching crabs energizing her. Muscles ripple in her strong, brown arms. But she's not going anywhere, despite all that power. Then she realizes the dinghy is still tied to the starboard cleat and she yells at me like it's my fault, which it isn't, but she yells anyway. And I untie her and the dinghy vaults over the water. About a hundred feet away, she grunts the huge trap overboard, and it splashes and quickly submerges.

She returns to *Temptation* and fidgets, looking at her watch every fifteen seconds, and keeps glancing expectantly towards the float that marks the crab trap.

An hour later, she says, "I think it's time."

And she leaves me alone with my beer and rows out to the crab trap and hauls it up, then deploys it again, and heads back to the boat.

Halfway back, I hear her yell.

"What's wrong?" I holler.

"There's a crab loose in the dingy and it's scuttling towards me, claws open," she hollers back.

She starts to row faster.

At *Temptation*, she leaps out of the dingy a moment before the crab bites her in the...well, use your imagination.

I whip out the measuring tape and measure the width of the crabs. Legal. Barely legal. And, once the two crabs are safely in a plastic bucket and cannot attack, I marvel at these armored creatures, the result of a million years of evolution. Their legs and claws scratch futilely at the sides of the too-slippery bucket. There is no escape for them. No hope.

In a matter of moments, Pat is grinning triumphantly as she reaches for the killing knife. The cockpit's sole is suddenly awash in crab guts, and the sweet, succulent crabmeat is bagged and on ice.

Opening another beer, I brood about the crabs. They survived countless threats—other crabs, starfish, seagulls, all manner of aquatic carnivores—and they made it this far through a tough, cruel life, and now they've met their crab god, their shells and guts chucked like garbage overboard, their sweet white meat jealously hoarded, their life force smashed to eternal nothingness. Just so we can momentarily savor a crab dinner.

Dare I mention my regrets of their passing to Pat, who is wearing a butcher's smile and clutching with a firm grip twenty inches of rusty steel blade? There's a special hunter's glint in her green eyes, and I can picture her ancestor ten thousand years ago, hunching over a fresh kill deep in the forest, guarding the carcass with a snarl and a show of sharp white teeth.

Yup, that's the girl I married, all right.

And no, now might not be the best time to express my regrets over the slaughter of a few crabs.

Dinner that night consists of garlic and broccoli and garlic and cauliflower and garlic and crab and garlic, with melted butter and a dash of soy sauce.

There are only two boats here, and it is so quiet, so peacefully quiet. A gull lands on a nearby vacant buoy, flexes its wings for balance, and stays and watches, just in case food like a miracle falls from the sky or drifts by on the outward-bound tide. The sun, above the dark island shapes of Mayne and Galiano, is lowering quickly, and the heat has fled, and with the evening stealthily come the cooling temperatures across glass-smooth water. A gull cries. The boat creaks. Clouds streak the silent sky. Thirty miles north, clouds pile up against the North Shore Mountains. And, out of sight, the throbbing, stinking, racketing noisy city of Vancouver calms itself for night, and through the dusk gathering in its harbors and along its rivers and waterways, lights will glow like embers in some great furnace, and tomorrow upon our return we'll be swallowed whole into its convulsing innards.

But for these last hours of vacation, it is peaceful here. We're drenched in soft light, and the satin-smooth skin of the water darkens slowly to ebony. *Temptation* bobs gently, a heron plies its gawky trade in the shallow waters near the beach, and the land, which separates us from the horizon, is turning purple under a shelf of lavender cloud.

The sunset is a collage of fiery red, cherry, and salmon with copper highlights illuminating a third of the western sky. The sun descends beyond the earth's curvature and pulls the beauty of the sunset with it as it goes. Darkness rushes out from all angles and conquers the evening and turns it into night.

To the north, the distant lights of Grouse Mountain emerge, and overhead a half moon brightens the night sky.

In the small cave like shape of *Temptation*'s cabin, the lights glow yellow, and we listen to gentle music and lie looking at the ceiling and wish the vacation could last forever. But I'm out of beer, and nothing lasts forever.

The Admiral calls to me from her luxurious, wide V berth and says, "What was the best part for you?"

I'm tossing and turning on my narrow and hard bunk, trying to get comfortable.

I stop and think about it.

"The beer," I say. "Definitely the beer."

There's a moment of silence.

Then she hollers, "Well, go on! Ask me about my favorite part."

"Okay," I reply. "What was your favorite part of the vacation, sir?"

"Well, it wasn't the near rescue of *Canicula*."

Near rescue? We weren't even close, I'm thinking.

"And it wasn't seeing how pale you got on Aux Six."

Great.

"And it wasn't catching and killing those crabs."

"No?"

"No. My favorite part was yelling at you about screwing up the boat hook/mooring buoy thing."

"It wasn't my fault," I protest.

"Maybe not," she concedes. "But you always screw up, and I always enjoy chewing you out about it."

"Why, thank you," I say, a little embarrassed with the Admiral's sweet talk.

"I hope you never change," she says sweetly.

"I'm sure you'll always be able to find fault with the things I do, sir," I say.

"I'm sure I will," she agrees cheerfully, and reaches out and turns off the light.

Thus another blissful vacation grinds to a halt.

* * *

Worse for Wear

When Patricia and I first married, she seemed normal. It was only after she discovered sailing that she began to go weird.

Recently, she discovered *racing*, and now she is weird no longer.

Now she's certifiably *insane*.

After her first English Bay race, she limped home and couldn't sit down.

"Fell on my tailbone," she explained, wincing. "I was up on the foredeck and we caught a wave and down I went, right on a cleat. My whole spine feels bruised. I've never been in such agony."

Then she grinned a little.

"We came in fourth," she added.

The next week she came home shivering after a race in Indian Arm.

"I didn't realize how hard it rains up there," she said through stiff, blue lips. "I'm so cold I think I've got pneumonia, but we finished seventh."

Those afternoon races were only mildly damaging to Patricia. She didn't get seriously beaten up until the Southern Straits race.

She staggered in the door after the twenty-four-hour race looking a little glassy eyed.

"Are you okay?" I asked.

"I think I have a concussion," she said. "The winds were thirty knots, with huge swells. I was thrown down the companionway and struck my head, knocking myself out."

Seawater dripped from her clothing, forming a puddle at her feet.

"But I wasn't the only one hurt this time," she went on. "The skipper is on his way to the hospital with a broken collarbone. And one of the crew couldn't stop being seasick for the entire race."

Patricia paused to give me a bleary smile.

"It was great!" she said.

The Entrance Island overnight race was her next challenge. Strong winds and heavy rain were forecast.

In anticipation of her return, I purchased a first-aid kit, a bottle of aspirin, and an electric blanket and placed them near the front door.

Patricia sloshed right past the first-aid kit, the aspirin bottle, and the electric blanket when she got home. There were dark circles under her bloodshot eyes.

"I'm dizzy from lack of sleep," she slurred. "Plus, I think my pneumonia is acting up again."

And she weaved into the bedroom and crashed into bed.

After all these races crewing on other boats, Patricia entered us in a Jack and Jill race across the strait to Silva Bay on board *Temptation,* our San Juan 28.

Patricia was the skipper. I was everything else.

"If I yell at you and call you names while we're racing, don't take it personally," she advised. "The yelling and swearing are all part of racing."

"I thought it's supposed to be a *fun* race," I said.

But the glint in her eye told me there was no such thing as a fun race.

After three and a half hours of yelling and swearing and sailing, we finished the race, placing fifteenth.

"Last year when you were out of town, Larry and I finished a lot better than fifteenth," Patricia told me. Several times.

The following morning I could barely move, let alone get out of the V berth. The aches and pains were from scrambling all over the boat trying to do three things at once, and from winching. Grinding, they call it. But the only thing that got ground was me, as in ground beef for hamburger.

There have been no races lately, but last week Patricia took the boat solo to the Gulf Islands. I couldn't go. I had to work. Also, I was still recovering from the Jack and Jill fun race.

Patricia phoned from Maple Bay to give me the bad news.

"I was motoring along at five knots when the keel hit a rock," she said.

She quickly added, "It's not my fault, the rock had no business being there."

"Of course," I said.

"I'm sorry," she said. "But there's been some damage."

"To you, or the boat?"

"Both. The boat will have to come out of the water and the keel might have to be refitted. I just hope it's not too expensive."

"What about you?" I asked. "Are you okay?"

"Oh, sure. The jolt threw me around a little, that's all. No big deal. My little finger is likely broken, but the bleeding has stopped and I'm fine now."

"I guess that means you're having a great time," I said.

"A *wonderful* time," she said. "But I can't wait to get home to do some more racing."

She sounded happy as a clam.

* * *

Bottoms Up

In Stamp's Landing Pub there was always a lot of talk about bottoms.

When a girl wearing tight jeans went by, I heard a guy say to his buddy, "Nice buns!"

I'm pretty sure he wasn't talking about bakery products.

Likewise, a moment later when a guy wearing tight jeans walked by, I heard a gal say, "Cute butt!"

All the girls at the table turned to look.

That's how normal people talk about normal bottoms.

However, there is a group who frequent Stamp's who often spend whole evenings discussing bottoms and nothing else. This group of bottom specialists is called Stamp's Landing Yacht Club.

Just the other night I overheard John Timmerman's booming voice announce, "I'm going to scrub her bottom!"

I half expected him to grab Jean and haul her off to the shower. But John and Jean just sat there looking at each other.

"Scrubbing's good," Jean said, with a sparkle in her eye. "But first you have to scrape it until it's smooth!"

"There's nothing like a smooth bottom," George said.

"And nobody knows more about smooth bottoms than George," Keith said, with a wink.

"I ran my bottom onto a rock," Buko said, grimacing.

"I'll bet it stung," I said.

Buko gave me a funny look. Sailors are always giving me funny looks of one kind or another.

"I just got rid of some mussels on my bottom," Charlie said.

Muscles? I thought. I had never heard of guys trying to get rid of muscles. George, for example, spends countless hours in the gym trying to grow them.

I glanced over at Charlie to see if losing his bottom muscles made him sit funny. He didn't seem to be sitting any funnier than usual, but he was smiling a lot.

The bottom talk continued.

"My bottom has osmosis," said a glum sailor.

"Try Preparation H," I suggested. "It works for me."

My wife gave me a withering look. My wife is always giving me withering looks of one kind or another.

"I bought a battery powered grinder to use on my bottom," Ellie said.

"Is it a big one, or is it medium sized?" asked my wife.

"Her bottom?" I said, trying to keep up.

"Her grinder," said my wife.

Ellie held out her hands to indicate the grinder's size. "You can borrow it any time," she offered, looking at me.

"Your bottom?" I said.

"My grinder, you idiot!" Ellie said.

"You better lay off the pale ale," warned my wife.

"Just as soon as I finish the three in front of me," I replied.

Barry seemed quite upset about some kind of weird growth all over *his* bottom.

"Does that mean you'll get it, too?" I asked Marsha.

"Excuse me?" Marsha said.

"Maybe we shouldn't sit too close together," I told her. "So far my bottom doesn't have any weird growth all over it and I want to keep it that way."

Later that night, when we were walking home along the sea wall, my wife said, "Were you making an ass of yourself again in the pub tonight?"

And the bottom line answer to her question was, yes.

As usual.

* * *

How Cookies Conquered the Coast Guard

Our kitchen stove, a General Electric model, is a burned-out, exhausted wreck. The oven is so weary it groans every time it's switched on. When Patricia (a.k.a. the Admiral) enters the kitchen, the stove cringes. When Patricia reaches into the fridge for cookie mix, the stove would run and hide if it had legs, which it hasn't.

Ah, the fragrance of baking cookies.

The only sustenance we ever have in our home is cookies. The only food in the fridge is raw cookie dough. (And, occasionally, a beer or two.)

The Coast Guard lives on cookies, thousands of them, each and every cookie lovingly baked by Pat and the reluctant General Electric.

A quick look at our monthly expenses shows cookie payments just slightly less than the mortgage payment.

Pat has cookies in inventory at home, in her office desk, in her MR2, and always on *Temptation,* her—I mean our—sailboat.

Some people falsely believe that through hard work, dedication, and loyalty, they will be advanced up the ranks. The Admiral has found a short cut. Cookies. Better than sex. Okay, *almost* better than sex. Better than anything else for launching a Coast Guard career.

She takes them to meetings. She packs them aboard the *Guardian*, the high- powered Zodiac the auxiliary uses to madly dash up and down the Fraser at the slightest opportunity of rescue. She bribes the boys at the Coast Guard base here in False Creek. Everywhere the Admiral goes, she is welcomed with open arms. Make that open mouths.

Undoubtedly there are cookie crumbs on every Coast Guard vessel on the West Coast.

But the Admiral can't attribute all her kamikaze Coast Guard success just to chocolate chip, oatmeal, or peanut butter cookies. Her buddies have all recognized a kindred spirit.

One night, the crew drove the *Guardian* at full speed up onto a log boom.

Onto a log boom!

And these guys are highly trained watchdogs of the sea, with about a zillion dollars worth of radar and stuff on board. I guess somebody should work on that. Invent some kind of gadget that sets off a log boom alarm. Such a device could save lives, or at least cut down on embarrassment.

The Admiral wasn't on duty at the time of the log boom trip, and nobody got hurt, except for a few bruises to the pride. Nor was the Zodiac damaged. But the bagful of cookies sustained heavy damage and was deep-sixed with all the respect and ceremony of a burial at sea.

Not satisfied with a simple Zodiac, this band of wild-eyed would-be lifesavers went out and purchased a bigger boat. Something to impress wives, girlfriends, and the boys back in the pub. *Smoke* is/was a twenty-six-foot multihull with a cabin, a ton of electronic gear, including windshield wipers, and two ferocious engines.

They put Sean in charge of boat renovations. Sean didn't know anything about boats, but he owned a Craftsman table saw, so he automatically qualified as the master fixer-upper. They put Larry in charge of the rewiring. Larry's qualifications as an electrician were that he had at one time taken a flashlight apart and came darn close to putting it back together.

About six months after purchase, Larry and Sean had *Smoke* ready for sea trials. *Smoke* will never be the same, nor will Sean and Larry. But at least its big engines worked, and from its rigging proudly snapped the Coast Guard Auxiliary pennant.

Then they took poor *Smoke* out onto the river, pushed it up to full power, and seconds later struck a log! Damn those logs and log booms anyway! The engines were bent and twisted, and there was even more damage to parts of its anatomy I can't remember the names of.

Now they're thinking of selling *Smoke*, which is good news for *Smoke*, but Sean will have to retire his Craftsman saw, and Larry will sadly go back to taking apart flashlights. Ah, well. There are always the cookies, which came through the incident unscathed.

The Admiral wasn't on board during the incident. She misses all the fun.

Patricia's Coast Guard career has affected almost everything in her life, including sailing. There was once a time when she thrilled at sailing before the wind, hitting speeds of five or six knots. Well, she still does get a thrill sailing, but sailing isn't what it used to be.

One of the first things you'll notice boarding *Temptation* is the gun. Just like in a pickup truck in the Cariboo with a rifle in the gun rack. Of course, the Admiral's gun is actually a water cannon, but a gun is a gun. Next thing you'll spot is the Coast Guard Auxiliary pennant flying boldly from the starboard shroud. By the time she drags out the high-power binoculars, snaps on the—get this—*two* VHF radios, and plugs in her cell phone, you know this lady is no longer an ordinary sailor person. She is transformed into the Admiral.

As *Temptation* chugs out into English Bay, the Admiral scans the horizon, seeking boats in distress. Usually there aren't any. So to fill in the time until the radio urgently crackles with a mayday call, the Admiral fishes. Fishing is almost as expensive as cookie making. Onto the line go spinners, flashers, weights, hooks, and a string of glittering stuff intended to attract the attention of starving salmon. I guess if all this junk actually hit a salmon smack in the head, then somehow managed to hook it while its groggy, it just might work. Mostly it doesn't, at least when the Admiral is on the other end of the line.

Some kind of weird mutant underwater thing must eat fishing gear. Where else would it all go? All I know is, before each sailing trip

Patricia has to load up a wheelbarrow full of lures to replenish what went missing on the previous jaunt.

Once, the Admiral did get to rescue some people while sail boating. I think they ran out of gas and she towed the hapless boaters back to the dock.

Rest assured, the kamikaze Coast Guard auxiliary is out there roaring up and down the south arm of the Fraser day, night, and afternoons, too, dodging logs, scaring fishermen, and ready—boy, are they ready—to rescue somebody. Anybody.

Just so long as they are not on a cookie break, that's all.

* * *

Divorce, Yukon Style

My vacation was coming up, and I was dreaming of a tropical destination, like Bora Bora or Tahiti or maybe even Playa del Carmen again.

Until my wife, Patricia (who, when we're sailing, or even when we're not sailing, is known as the Admiral), said, "I spent all our money renovating the bathrooms, so forget about an expensive vacation."

Then she gave me the good news.

She said, "Because I've started a new and very important job at Hurricane/Zodiac, the manufacturers of the best darned inflatable boats in the world, I won't get holidays this year. So you'll have to vacation alone."

Alone didn't sound so good. Unsupervised, I could get into all kinds of trouble.

"I'll go to the Okanagan and play golf with my friends at BC Tree Fruits, where I used to work," I said to Patricia at dinner the next night.

"No," declared Patricia, "you won't."

"But…"

"You'll just drink and carouse every night with your buddies and spend money like crazy."

"But…"

"Here's what you'll do. You'll go to the Yukon and visit our daughter Lori and her partner, Peter. I already booked your flight, using those air-mile points you'd accumulated so it won't cost a cent."

"The Yukon…," I said. "Isn't that the place that's famous for sled dogs and blizzards?"

"Don't be ridiculous! It's summer. You can take your clubs. They have golf courses in Whitehorse. Plus, you can sponge off of Lori and Peter while you're there," she added.

No sense arguing with the Admiral. I'd never won one yet. My record was 2,016 arguments, 2,016 straight losses.

"But," I explained, "there won't be a Starbucks within a thousand miles of anywhere."

"Stop sniveling," said the Admiral before I could even get off a small second snivel. "Lori and Peter have been together for twenty years and you've only been up there once," she added. "Plus they're a happy, contented couple, and they're too mature to want to carouse and stay up late."

The next day I e-mailed Whitehorse and received an immediate reply.

Peter's response was, "You're welcome to join us on a five-day canoe trip on the Yukon River to Dawson City. See Teri for details."

I visited Teri, Lori's younger sister. Teri was everything I was not: adventurous, brave, and female. Teri had been to the Yukon several times. She had rafted the Yukon River, camped in the wilds of Klondike country, and if she'd had more time she likely would've trapped for fur-bearing animals while up there.

"First thing you'll need is lots of toilet paper," Teri advised.

"Toilet paper?" I asked.

"Well, yeah," she said. "There're no facilities of any kind along the river."

"Where will I plug in my electric razor?" I asked.

Ignoring me exactly like her mother, Teri said, "Second, you've got to be careful about bears."

"Bears?" I think my voice may have cracked.

"Moose can be dangerous, too," she said. "And wolverines can rip your organs out in seconds."

"Wolver—what?"

"I have bear repellant I can lend you," she offered.

I borrowed a tent, air mattress, and a half ton of other assorted camping gear from Teri. I refused the bear repellant on the grounds I might appear wimpish. When I got home from Teri's place, I packed it all up, adding several liters of bug-off juice, a dozen rolls of two-ply toilet paper—the real good, soft stuff—and, just in case of a sudden blizzard, a pair of warm mittens. I'd heard that blizzards could occur without warning in the great white north, even though it would be the middle of July when I arrived.

The next day Peter sent me what was probably a lifesaving e-mail.

The message said, "Forest fires are raging and the river is flooding its banks. River trip is canceled. Bring your clubs."

I threw everything out of my suitcase (except the mittens) and repacked.

I was thinking: This is great. Now bears won't eat me. All I have to worry about is humiliating myself on the golf course, something I am comfortable with.

I flew Zip Airlines to Whitehorse. The plane was painted vivid pink but it got me there, plus my golf clubs arrived without loss or damage, so I forgave them the pink paint job.

Whitehorse had a temperature of twenty-five degrees Celsius. I hoped no one would notice the mittens I tried to discretely stuff into my pockets.

Peter picked me up in a big SUV.

"Hi, how are you? After twenty years together Lori and I have split up," he announced.

"Fine, thanks, you?" I asked.

"Fine, thanks. Yeah, we just can't live together anymore."

"It's warm here," I said.

"Hottest summer in two decades," he said. "Sorry we didn't tell you about the breakup earlier."

"No problem. Where's the golf course?"

"Tomorrow we golf, tonight we dine."

We drove downtown to Georgio's, a fabulous Italian-style restaurant where Lori was waiting.

"So, did Peter tell you the big news?" she asked, after a welcome hug.

"Yes, we're golfing tomorrow," I replied.

"No, you idiot. About us splitting up?"

"Oh, that. Yeah, too bad. Say, you look different."

"Yes, my hair is blonde this week," she said. "And you're okay with that?"

"I think the blonde look suits you," I said.

"No, dummy. About us breaking up."

"Oh, that. Does your mother know about it yet?"

"Are you kidding? The Admiral will kill both of us. It's your job to tell her."

I paused. "Maybe later, after some golf," I decided.

We were shown to a corner table, where we ordered dinner.

"So here's the deal," Lori told me, sounding exactly like her mother when she was ordering me around. "Because we're not really living together anymore, Peter and I are going to share you. Tomorrow, you belong to Peter. Sunday, you're mine. And so on."

"Sort of like a custody battle and I'm the child," I said.

"Another round of drinks," Peter ordered.

"We're being very amicable about the whole thing, don't you think?" Lori said.

"Very mature," I agreed. "Make mine a double."

The next day, Saturday, Lori attended the Yukon's very first legal gay wedding while Peter and I played a manly round of golf at the nine-hole Meadow Lakes course. The fairways were narrow and the boreal forest closed in tightly. Basically what we did was, we hit all the balls we owned into the trees, long grass, and water hazards. Good thing it was merely a nine-hole course.

After hitting a drive off the tee maybe twelve feet past the ladies' tee, Peter turned to me.

"Now that I'm single again, what I'm looking for is a woman with big hooters and a pleasing smile," he said. "Who owns a pub," he added.

"I'd settle for a small-breasted woman who enjoys vacuuming and ironing," I said. "But don't tell the Admiral."

"No," he agreed. "She frightens me."

"Me, too," I said, and blasted a huge divot beyond the flight of my ball.

Peter and Lori had a log cabin home on the shores of a lake. The view from their private sandy beach was of distant mountains, a wide and perfect sky, vast spruce and aspen forests, and the air was so pure my lungs kept asking, what is this stuff? Around the hot tub and the deck Lori had planted colorful annuals.

While Lori danced and partied all night long with three hundred wedding guests, Peter and I did our best to deplete his inventory of single-malt Scotch.

Sunday belonged to Lori. On our way to an afternoon barbecue, Lori drove through a red light in downtown Whitehorse.

"In Vancouver," I said, "most of the time we stop at red lights."

"Yes, but I was talking," Lori explained. "It's hard to talk and pay attention to traffic stuff at the same time."

Yukoners are great gardeners. The yard in which the barbecue took place was bright with blossoms, and the late afternoon sun was hot. One thing Yukoners do even better than gardening is being friendly and welcoming and, evidently, making great margaritas. I had ten or fifteen of the best margaritas I've had anywhere while at the party.

Monday morning arrived and all three of us went golfing at Mountain View, located along the high banks of the Yukon River. Temporarily, at least, there was no squabbling over who owned me. Today was a sharing day. At Mountain View the fairways were lush, the greens perfect, and the views outstanding.

Lori played golf like most people played croquet, knocking the ball forward a few feet at a time, mostly along the ground. That was the good news. The bad news was, sometimes she'd hit the ball farther than Peter and I. Each time she swung her club she made a sort of squawking sound, sort of like a Canada goose might make if it was being strangled.

When the golfing was over, Lori strong-armed me into her Corolla. The Corolla had rust around the wheel wells and there was a nasty side-to-side crack in the windshield so that the little car didn't look like it could handle speeds of, say, three hundred mph. But I was soon to find out looks can be deceiving.

Speakers blasting music, we screamed along the streets of Whitehorse. Okay, it wasn't the car that was screaming. It was me.

Lori drives like a maniac.

When I'd settled down from screaming, Lori said, exiting onto the highway, "I'm going to take you to meet the new man in my life."

"New man?" I said.

"I'm in love," she said, grinning.

"But you and Peter have only been split up like maybe fifteen minutes," I said.

"This happened *after* the split," she said.

We went flying over a little hill. I was pretty sure all four wheels left the pavement. I had questions, but they could wait. I knew all about Lori and her difficulties talking while driving.

Around us the forest was uninterrupted by civilization. I hadn't seen another car in either direction for probably fifteen minutes. (And I wouldn't see another until the next day.)

"His name is Hans and he lives way out of town," Lori said.

"We're already way out of town."

"What did you say?" Lori asked, turning to look at me.

We were approaching a tight curve.

"Don't talk, just drive," I said.

About two hundred miles later, the Corolla shot off the paved highway onto a dirt road. The forest closed in. There were no power lines on the roadside. Or telephone poles. Ahead, a mountain range loomed, the rocky peaks well above tree line. I began to wonder exactly how far out of town "out of town" actually was.

"Hans doesn't need power lines; he's got a generator," Lori explained as though reading my thoughts. "And he has a satellite phone, although it's not hooked up yet."

"I see," I said, even though I didn't.

"Of course, we're way past cell phone range now," she said.

"So if we have car trouble…?" I faltered as the Corolla bounced over potholes.

"Someone would come along in a day or two," Lori said, seriously.

The sun went down behind a mountain and it was dusk.

After about an hour we came to the Wheaton River. Glacier fed, the water seethed and tumbled over rocks. Trailing a cloud of dust, the Corolla pulled off the road and into a driveway and jerked to a stop. Ahead were two guys sitting outside at a wood table drinking beer in cans. On the right was a log cabin bristling with antlers as decoration. Behind the house a huge mountain rose steeply. On the opposite bank of the fast-flowing river bulked another huge mountain.

Hans had long hair, a big mustache, and twinkling blue eyes. If he'd been an actor he would've been perfect as Wyatt Earp. His buddy Joe had linebacker shoulders and a handshake powerful enough to crush rocks.

"Welcome," Hans greeted me. "There's been a grizzly wandering around the area, but I think we're safe enough. And sometimes wolves hang around. We got guns inside so don't worry."

"Guns?" I said.

"Yeah, shotguns, rifles, handguns. You need 'em out here."

"Oh," I said.

"Hey, you want to throw an axe?" Hans asked.

"Throw a what?"

"There's a target all set up over by that pine tree. And here're the axes."

"Gee," I said. "I'm a little out of practice."

Hans and Joe exchanged looks that probably said, ah, a wimpy *city* guy. I think I failed my very first Yukon test.

"I work on a deep-sea fishing boat and sometimes off the coast of Alaska the waves get sixty feet high," Hans said. "And Joe here is a wilderness guide. What kind of work do you do, John?"

"Uh, I sell produce," I said. "You know, at a desk, with a telephone. Sometimes I operate a pencil."

"Produce," Hans said.

"Hmm," Joe said.

"He specializes in fruit," Lori said, helping out.

"Ah, a fruit salesman," Hans said, nodding grimly.

Joe nodded, too.

"Well, we're all men out here," Hans said. "How about some vodka to celebrate your visit?"

"I don't know much about guns or axes," I admitted. "But I know a little about drinking."

Hans brought out a bottle of Russian vodka and we drank several glasses straight.

The world began to grow a little tilted.

"I think I'm ready to throw an axe now," I said, a little while later. "Or maybe go moose hunting."

That's when Lori took me home.

The next day was Peter's turn. In the afternoon we drove one hundred of the most scenic miles in all of North America, from Whitehorse through Carcross and into Alaska. The lakes were bright green, the mountains awesome, and, crossing the Continental Divide into Alaska, the terrain was rock crusted and the trees no bigger than shrubs. Arriving in Skagway, we checked into Sergeant Preston's Lodge.

In the 1890s, Skagway was the port that facilitated the gold rush to the Klondike. Today it's a town of eight hundred people making a fortune from another gold rush. Each day four or five cruise ships from Vancouver disgorge their passengers onto the streets and boardwalks of Skagway. The buildings, cafes, bars, and shops bulge with tourists. The melody of busy cash registers fills the air.

Skagway lies at the end of North America's longest and deepest fjord, which is named Lynn Canal. Mountains strewn with glaciers dominate the skyline and ocean winds blow hard through the town. The coastal trees—fir and cedar—are big and tall, and the air is humid and scented with ocean and forest.

Peter had booked tickets on the White Pass and Yukon Route railway. The rail line had been built in 1899 to move people and freight to the gold fields, but now it moved camera-toting tourists up the narrow and steep canyons. Our ride would take us twenty miles, from sea level to almost three thousand feet in elevation, terminating at the White Pass summit. The tracks would climb along canyon walls, into tunnels blasted through solid rock and over rickety-looking trestles spanning fast-rushing creeks.

In shorts and golf shirts, we hustled down to the depot.

"It's cooling off," I said, always alert for unexpected blizzards.

We were seated on a bench behind the depot, waiting for the train to pull in. Passengers were gathering. The wind off the cold ocean and off the cold glaciers was whipping through the train station. The late afternoon sun fell below a distant mountain peak, immediately dropping the temperature ten degrees.

Peter checked the depot clock. "We don't have time before we board to return to Sergeant Preston's to get our sweaters," he said.

"They got sweaters in the shop inside," I said.

At this point we were shivering just a little. The train ride was three hours long. In three hours the temperature could be below freezing, and I'd left my mittens back in the Yukon.

"Let's go shopping," Peter said.

It took us maybe two seconds to shoulder our way inside the shop. Peter and I got separated in the throng of tourists who were feverishly buying overpriced cribbage boards shaped like train engines, li'l engineer kits for kids, and White Pass and Yukon Route Authentic Spike Bottle Openers, your choice—red or green—for only $18.95. The shop also had racks of jackets, sweaters, and coats, all of them price-tagged at $100.00 or more.

Outside, the shrill sound of a train whistle announced the engine was pulling into the station. Time was running out.

I spotted some navy blue hoodie-type sweaters for a mere $25.00, ripped one from the rack, and shoved my way to the cashier. The place was jammed with people. I looked around but didn't see Peter. I paid and exited. I put my sweater on. Ah, nice and warm. It boasted in bold letters across the chest, "WP&YR." Okay, so it looked a little touristy, but it would do the job.

Then Peter emerged from the crowd, wearing exactly the same sweater.

We looked at each other.

"This is nice," Peter said.

"Maybe we should be holding hands," I said, grinning.

"We look like a middle-aged gay couple," he laughed.

Which was very complimentary, I thought. No, not the gay part, the age part. Peter might be middle aged, but for me, middle age had been so long in the past I couldn't even remember it.

We lacked the courage to ask anyone nearby to take a picture of us in our matching his 'n' hers outfits.

About five minutes after boarding (we'd barely chugged past the maintenance yard and the gold rush cemetery), I noticed I was sweating. I looked at Peter in the seat beside me. Perspiration glistened on his forehead.

"Warm," he said, "when we're away from that north wind."

"Very," I agreed.

Without further comment, we stripped off the brand new sweaters and left them off. The temperature that year in the north was such that I never wore mine again. Based on a per-minute usage formula, that hooded navy blue sweater is absolutely the most expensive garment in my wardrobe.

The year before the railway was completed through the pass, three thousand pack animals died at the hands of the prospectors. Overloaded, underfed, and whipped till they dropped, the horses and mules staggered up the pass, burdened with miners' supplies, during the winter and spring of 1898–99; they were literally worked to death.

Burdened only with cameras and hastily purchased sweaters, Peter and I survived the canyon trip. Back in town we hustled to the motel, replaced the sweaters, and reconvened at Moe's Frontier Bar.

There was a grand old jukebox belting out tunes from the '80 s (1980s—not 1880s), a pool table with red felt, a bar with mismatched stools, and a scattering of tables. We ordered drinks and were considering plans for dinner.

"Can you recommend a good place for chow?" Peter asked the chubby waitress.

She gave Peter a quizzical look.

"You want a good place to shower?" she repeated, surprised.

We erupted with laughter.

And got things straightened out.

"Must be your Canadian accent," I said to Peter.

"Well, the way she was smiling, I thought for a second there she was going to invite me back to her place and offer to scrub my back," Peter said when the waitress was safely behind the bar.

The shower thing became a highlight, and we wore it out repeating the story to anyone who would listen.

Think about it. Two guys go into a shabby bar and the first question they ask is, where can they take a shower? Oh, well. Maybe you had to be there. But we laughed about it a thousand times, and even today, remembering it makes me smile.

Tuesday afternoon we drove back to the log cabin home on the lake. It was time to phone the Admiral and tell her the gory details about Lori and Peter going their separate ways. I screwed up my courage (worried she'd blame me, somehow, for the breakup), borrowed the phone, and walked with it to the beach.

"Don't tell me you're spending money," Pat said when she picked up the line back home.

"Lori and Peter have broken up and already Lori has a new guy and Peter's on the hunt for a female with a big smile and pleasing tits who owns a pub and it's not my fault," I wailed.

"What's this about Peter having big tits?" she asked. "Have you been drinking?"

"Other than Scotch, gin, and beer, no. Oh, and some red wine," I added. Full confession always worked best with the Admiral, or so I thought. "Plus, a woman tried to pick me up in a parking lot in front of Extra Foods, which I'll tell you about when I get home, and in Skagway for about thirteen seconds I had lustful thoughts concerning a chubby waitress and a shower, but other than that I've been steadfast and true, I swear."

"Okay," said the Admiral. "I'll forgive you all the other stuff, but I want to know everything about the pick-up in the parking lot."

"She had red hair and she sweet-talked me about golf and…"

"Not now, when you get home. What I want to know right now is all about Peter and Lori and this new guy, whoever he is. And the thing about the big tits, tell me about that, too."

So I did.

And she forgave me for screwing up Lori and Peter's relationship, probably because her Coast Guard Auxiliary pager went off right then, distracting her.

"Stand by!" she yelled at me in her best unit leader voice. "Stand by" was official Coast Guard talk. What it officially means is, *don't move, don't think, and don't even breathe until I get back to you.*

While holding my breath, I could hear her on the other line, speaking to whoever had paged her, "Don't bother me right now just because someone's drowning. My daughter is getting a divorce and lecherous women in Yukon parking lots are accosting my husband! Call me later!"

Then she came back on the line.

"Wish Lori and Peter good luck and happiness," she said. "And tell them I love them both."

"What about me?" I asked.

"You want love, go see the bimbo who tried to pick you up in the parking lot," the Admiral said, hanging up.

Uh-oh.

We drove to Dawson City on Friday. All three of us. Just like the old days when everybody was happily married. I remembered being happily married myself, not so very long ago—like yesterday. But now, with the Admiral aware of the parking lot pickup hussy, I knew those happy days were likely long gone.

The drive took almost six hours. I got to sit in the front with Peter while Lori took a rear seat and caught up on some reading. Lori has driven the route maybe three hundred times, plus she has a low boredom threshold. Trees are trees are trees, and there's not much else to peer at. Except, now and then, there's a sweeping view of a blue lake, or distant mountains and empty green valleys, or the broad Yukon River twisting its way north.

Along the side of the highway, blackened scars of recent forest fires were evidence of how bad the fire season had been. We'd heard about how thick the smoke was in Dawson, but when we got there the skies were clear, the air was pure, and the annual Dawson City Music Festival was about to begin.

Of course, through the windshield we couldn't tell if the skies were clear. We couldn't see the sky, or anything else, through the glass. The Yukon had a very healthy bug population. Perhaps now it is not as healthy as it once was, but anyway there was a whack of bugs up there. Many of them hung around the highway, joyfully turning themselves into bug goo on the windshield as we thundered along. Some of the bugs were so big the *SPLAT* they made against the glass made me duck and cringe. But the windshield held strong, and although we couldn't see out of it very well, at least we weren't picking the bugs out of our teeth. So the lesson was, windshields were good things, especially in the Yukon.

Dawson City probably has a year-round population of five hundred hardy souls. The music festival draws young people from Whitehorse and from small communities throughout the Yukon. Plus there're tourists crowding the boardwalks, and the streets are made dusty by visiting pickup trucks, house-sized fifth-wheel trailers, and assorted RVs from the United States of America. Tour buses with their white-haired passengers from places like Kansas and Iowa and Idaho also add to the traffic. In the summer, Dawson City bustles with visitors from all over North America, and there were lots of Germans and other Euros there as well.

The music festival was held under a big striped circus-style tent, and beside it there was a grass field with picnic tables, a beer garden, and a long row of Porta-Johns. I hate it that bathrooms share my name, but what's a John to do?

While Peter went in search of his large-breasted-smiling-bar-owner dream spouse, Lori and I checked out the music. We were listening to some musicians jamming (or is that jamming musicians?) when several women approached Lori, the Yukon's preeminent hairdresser.

The first woman came up and curtsied and said, "I've heard so much about you, your majesty. You absolutely *must* do my hair."

Her hair looked like it had been trimmed with a bread knife and styled with an electric toothbrush.

"Phone my receptionist," Lori commanded. "I think I've got an opening in, like, February," and she turned away.

The second woman had hair that looked like it had been caught, possibly by accident, in a blender, with the dial on *puree*.

"I need you, O Goddess, I *need* you," she sobbed.

"I've been trying to cut back to maybe eight days a week," Lori said. "Try my apprentice. She's pretty good what with all that practice she's been getting at Bart's Sled Dog Training and Grooming School." Then she made a quick squiggle in her notebook: something about increasing her referral fee.

The third woman to approach the Yukon's preeminent hair surgeon had hair that looked pretty good. She strode right up, gave her bangs a flip and said, "Thanks, Lori. My hair looks great. Ever since you cut it I've been getting laid regularly. I owe you *so* much." And the woman flounced away.

Lori made another notebook squiggle: something about doubling her price for those customers with an improved sex life.

Another great thing about Dawson City was the breakfasts. On three successive mornings I had sausages with eggs, then eggs with sausages, and on the final morning, just to vary my diet, sausages, eggs, *and* bacon. When you get to Dawson—and you should go, you really should—stay at the Westmark, where the rooms are comfortable and clean and the breakfasts are great. The other place I liked for breakfast was Klondike Kate's. That's where the staff all lined up at the bar in midmorning and downed a quick round of shooters. Maybe it's a ritual, maybe it's a major drinking problem, or perhaps they'd just had a bunch of hard-to-please tourists from Germany. I don't know. Anyway, shooters it was at ten in the morning.

My time in the Yukon was running out, like sand from an hourglass.

On Monday, after the music festival was over, we drove back to Whitehorse. At a roadside pullout there was a stunning view of a distant mountain range, the Tombstone Range, barely visible on the horizon, and in between a vast green landscape so empty and beautiful it made my heart ache. (Either that, or it was Klondike Kate's coffee backing up on me.)

The Yukon *does* cast a spell, and it's hard to describe. So I'll borrow some words from Robert Service to help me out. They're from his poem, "Spell of the Yukon."

> *It's a great, big, broad land 'way up yonder,*
> *It's the forests where silence has lease;*
> *It's the beauty that thrills me with wonder,*
> *It's the stillness that fills me with peace.*

Epilogue

The next morning I was on Zip Airlines again, flying home, leaving the big, broad land behind. I had said good-bye to Lori and Peter, and I was hoping the new direction in their lives would work out fine for both of them.

But I had my own troubles. Waiting at the airport in Vancouver would be the Admiral. And she'd be expecting the story about the pickup—make that *attempted* pickup—in the parking lot.

And no, I didn't forget to write about it. If it were written down it would haunt me for the rest of my married life. This way, by *not* writing it down, I'm hopeful the Admiral will soon forget about it because, really, nothing sinful happened. Really. Honestly.

So if you want to know about the pickup story, you'll have to ask me in person. And if the Admiral's not around, and you ply me with a scotch or two, I just might be able to recall some of the scandalous details....

* * *

Not Tonight, Dear, the Spinnaker Hit Me in the Head and I Have a Headache

I now know everything I ever needed to know about spinnakers but was afraid to ask, thanks to a certain Skipper, who shall remain anonymous.

The Skipper will remain anonymous because she made me promise never to tell the story of our first attempt at spinnaker flying. So, for my own protection I'll simply refer to her as the Skipper, capital first letter and all, just like God.

The scene of the crime was English Bay. The Skipper had decided it was time to hoist the spinnaker. She'd read about it and discussed it at great length at her group therapy session, the one on Thursday nights at Stamp's pub. Now she had dragged me out on the water and was about to enlighten me on the fine art of spinnaker flying.

"Listen up," said the Skipper.

"Yessir," I said.

"This is the guy," she explained. "This is the sheet, and this is the uphaul, and this is the downhaul."

"The what?"

"Pay attention. When I give the signal, you have to pull this line, that line, or the other lines, depending on the signal. Got it?"

"I think so," I said. "What was the part about the guy again?"

"Just don't screw up," said the Skipper.

I nodded.

"Plus," she added, "you'll be on the tiller."

"Okay," I agreed. I always agree with the Skipper. "But while I'm doing nine or ten things all at once, what will you be doing?"

"I'll be on the foredeck yelling at you, dummy," she said, and went forward to the spinnaker bag way up there in the pulpit, the stainless steel railing at the front of the boat.

The Skipper began yelling and making wild motions in my direction. Instantly alerted, I yanked a little on some ropes, then I yanked even harder on some other ropes. The yelling, motioning, and yanking combination resulted in the blue spinnaker rising upward like a giant blossoming flower.

For exactly nine seconds everything was perfect. Then the flower died.

The spinnaker began wrinkling, creasing, and twisting.

The spinnaker started flapping.

The spinnaker tangled itself around the forestay, spreaders, and shrouds.

Distracted by all the up-and-down hauling, I'd forgotten about the tiller part of my instructions. The boat had turned and was now pointing into the wind.

Not good.

The Skipper was trying to communicate with me from the far end of the boat. Something about me being an idiot, but it was old news. I already knew I was an idiot from previous sailing expeditions with her.

Later, when the spinnaker was back in the bag where it belonged, and when it appeared we had safely avoided cardiac arrest, the Skipper said, "I sure hope there were no club members watching,"

She peered furtively around until she was convinced there were no club members in the vicinity, then the Skipper fixed me with a deadly gaze and made me swear never, ever to tell anybody, ever, about our first time with the spinnaker.

"Don't worry," I said. "Nobody would believe me anyway."

So, if you happen to ask me: No, I wasn't there. No, it didn't happen. And no, the Skipper's name is not Pat. Definitely not.

* * *

Of Course It's Raining, We're On Vacation

In Vancouver that year, rain poured down in March, April, and May. More rain fell in early June. Any moment the weather had to change, right? Sooner or later the sun would appear, the temperature would rise, and summer would begin. Or so we hoped. Our vacation was scheduled for late June. Surely it couldn't rain forever. Could it?

Hunched against the rain, Pat and I stood on the Heather Marina dock, staring gloomily westward. We were on vacation. Somewhere out there, beyond the curtain of mist, was English Bay. And beyond English Bay was Georgia Strait. And miles and miles to the northwest lay Desolation Sound, our vacation destination.

"We could change our minds and fly to Hawaii instead," I said, wiping rain from my chin.

"But our clothes are packed, groceries are aboard, we're ready to go," Pat said, brushing rain from her jacket.

Wimps would stay home, or go to Hawaii. We were not wimps. Well, at least Pat wasn't. And I would never admit to it.

So we went.

To Gibson's.

In the rain.

Pat donned her red Wetskins, and I struggled into my butter-yellow cruiser suit. My cruiser suit seemed to have shrunk since the last time I'd worn it four years ago. It had shrunk especially around the middle and felt tight against my tummy. Either it had shrunk or…my belly couldn't possibly have expanded *that* much. During the five-hour jaunt to Gibson's, rain swept against the mainsail and cascaded off the end of the boom in silvery streams. The gray-green sea was calm. Rain beat the wind into submission. We motored.

At Gibson's we plugged into dockside power, and the two portable heaters battled the creeping dampness.

Monday dawned with a broken sky. There were periods of actual sunlight. I suggested we get some exercise.

"Let's walk to Mom's," I said.

Pat gave me one of those looks. "Walk?" she said. "I'm on holidays. Plus it's uphill."

But I persisted, and she relented.

She packed my knapsack with frozen chicken.

"We'll cook it all at your mom's. That way, we won't have to worry about it going bad."

Sounded like a good idea.

Until I slung the knapsack on my back.

There was about two hundred pounds of frozen chicken in the knapsack. And we had a long, hot walk ahead of us. All of it uphill, as Pat had pointed out.

Pat had stuffed her pockets with Jujubes. For energy. Every time we came to an incline in the road, she ate Jujubes. For energy. We were always coming to inclines in the road, and Pat was always wolfing down Jujubes.

Fueled by Pat's Jujubes, we made the one-hour jaunt to Mom's in only two hours.

Away from the blocks of ice in the ice-box, the chicken began to melt. By the time we limped down Mom's driveway, the chicken weighed a lot less than two hundred pounds. Now it weighed only one hundred pounds. The one hundred pounds that was missing had melted. A dripping river of chicken blood and ice melt had soaked me from the hips down. My shoes were filled with chicken runoff. My boat shoes made mushy, squelching sounds as I trudged along. I left miles of wet footprints in my wake.

Pat cooked the chicken in Mom's frying pan. We ate some. Even Mom ate some, and she's a vegetarian. I think she ate some just so I wouldn't wrench my spine lugging it back to *Temptation*.

At dusk, we left Mom's and set off for the marina.

"Take the short cut through the woods at the end of Chaster Street," Mom said.

Pat liked the idea of a shortcut mainly because she was running low on Jujubes. Into the woods we went, my knapsack radiating the delicious smell of fried chicken.

"Uh, there aren't any bears around here, are there?" I asked Pat when we were deep within the woods.

"Naw, no bears," she replied. "Cougars, though. I've heard there's cougars on the Sunshine Coast." I looked behind me. I imagined cougars stalking us, lurking in the underbrush, licking their chops, the smell of fried chicken making them ravenous. Big cougars. Big as…bears.

I arrived back at the safety of the marina well ahead of Pat.

Tuesday we left Gibson's bound for Lesqueti. We hoisted the sails, the wind was brisk, and we sailed.

It was June 22. Our wedding anniversary. The sky was overcast. It got more overcast as the hours went by. A few scattered drops of rain fell. It was sort of like being spit upon by the gods of vacations and anniversaries.

Positive thinking. That's what had gotten us through three hundred years of married life. Okay, it only seemed like we'd been married for three hundred years when we were on holidays and it was raining.

In a fruitless effort to enhance a mood of positive thinking Pat inserted a CD in the CD player, on the surface of which raindrops collected. Majestic music flowed through the speakers. We felt like we were players in a movie with the soundtrack blaring.

"This is so romantic," Pat said.

"More like *Mutiny on the Bounty*," I said.

"What?"

"Nothing, dear," I mumbled.

Low on the horizon, Lesqueti was dark edged, with the gray belly of a rain cloud hanging pregnant and slow moving in the sky above it. There were skirts of rain on either side of *Temptation*, but they avoided us. We feasted on cold chicken for lunch. It was very tasty. The cougars had no idea what they'd missed.

To the west, gray boulders of clouds tumbled over the dark shape of Vancouver Island. To the east, swirls of cloud were draped over Texada Island, allowing mere glimpses of the terrain, as though it was a forbidden, secret place.

Squitty Bay was a narrow, rock-sided hideaway on the southeast shore of Lesqueti. It was a marine park, but the dock there was jammed with small, moldering local boats. Because the locals, who, we were advised, hated tourists with passion, had clogged up the dock with their own boats, *Temptation* had to raft to another sailboat, this one belonging to a New Zealander. The kiwi and we were the only tourist boaters there, the other tourists likely having had their throats cut by the local, crazed Lesquesti-ites who, no doubt, then dropped the corpses into the sea.

Lesqueti lacks the ridges and mountains of other Georgia Strait islands and is relatively flat. It is rife with hippies, sheep, and mosquitoes. We walked nervously along a dirt road over which tall trees formed a thick canopy. We were nervous about the throat-slitting locals, but on this day we managed to steer clear of them. The roadside which we strode along was fringed with foxgloves, spiky and bright with jolts of pink blossoms. Gigantic, green ferns prospered, like in a Disney cartoon, and the lack of electrical power and the isolated, makeshift houses gave the place a touch of whimsy. We climbed over black slabs of rock to a point overlooking the strait and bulky Texada Island, where scraps of cloud lingered. Woolly sheep hustled to make room for us on the rocks. Mammoth red-barked arbutus trees sprang from cracks in rough, black rock, and juniper trees looked like dead sticks stuck in the thin soil, fringed in green. For decades, strong south easterlies had tortured tree trunks, limbs, and branches, resulting in twisted, nightmarish shapes.

Overnight, the wind accelerated and swells marched aggressively into the narrow bay. *Temptation* rocked and shuddered throughout the night, and sleep was an elusive thing.

At nine the next morning, Wednesday, we were below listening to the marine radio over the rustle of falling rain. The forecast wasn't good. On this holiday, no forecast was good. The day would bring high winds and rain. We formed a committee (Pat was chairperson) and called a meeting and resolved to spend another day rafted to our neighbors while the storm blew itself out.

The New Zealander, whose first name was Grey, invited us over for tea. When I could put the visit off no longer, we clambered aboard their boat for weak green tea and stale Fig Newtons. From Grey, Pat picked up a new word: *mawzy*, short for mosquito.

For the rest of the trip, at night, I would hear Pat's startled cries from the V berth (I slept below in the salon; ships' captains rarely sleep with the crew). "Mawzy, mawzy!" Pat would holler.

Then would come the thump-crash-bang as she splattered the dreaded mawzy's against the bulkhead with her fist. She was exuberant in her mawzy slaughter, and I feared one of these times she'd pierce the hull with her knuckles. But, either her fist wasn't as hard as it used to be, or the hull was well built, for there was never a puncture despite the hundreds of noisy slayings.

One night, while trying to murder an irritating, droning mawzy, I struck myself in the nose hard enough to bring tears to my eyes. I never realized that skeeter killing was a contact sport!

Thursday dawned without rain or wind. I was determined to leave. I wanted desperately to avoid any more stale Fig Newtons. By eight thirty we had set off from Squitty Bay into a flat, calm sea. With clouds draped low over the world, we motored up Bull Passage. We were heading north in search of sun and heat (ha ha ha), and we wanted to check out Jebediah Island, a marine park off the eastern shore of Lesqueti.

But first, a rescue.

Sort of.

Just then off the starboard bow, a couple of hundred yards away, a bald eagle was floundering in the water. Seagulls dive-bombed the big bird, swerving away at the last moment. And other eagles spiraled nearby, keeping a wary eye on their comrade.

The eagle's hindquarters were submerged, his white head was up, and his broad brown wings were beating slowly, methodically. We thought he might be tangled in something, a net maybe.

Pat grabbed the tiller.

"I'm going in," she shouted, and *Temptation* veered eagle ward.

I bounced around the cockpit due to the sudden direction change, and coffee and cushions went flying.

As we closed in, Pat clenched our small fishing net in a white-knuckled fist.

"You take the tiller," ordered the Admiral. "This is your first rescue so don't be nervous. But if you screw up, I'll kill you! This is the kind of thing for which I've trained extensively with the Coast Guard." She took a deep breath. "I might get a citation, a plaque, or even a medal for this," she added.

Pat had never personally had the opportunity to rescue a real live human being in civilian life, though she'd assisted in about a thousand rescue missions with the Canadian Coast Guard, so this hapless eagle was the next best thing.

As the boat drew nearer to the struggling bird, the eagle seemed to grow in size. It was huge. And as the distance separating us dissolved from twenty feet to ten, I judged the eagle's wingspan to be about six feet across.

I was looking forward to watching a skilled Coast Guard member get a wild six-foot eagle in a two-foot fish net. I was also curious about what we would do with this giant, feathered predator with its hooked beak and powerful talons once it was safely aboard.

Somehow, *Temptation* didn't seem big enough for all three of us.

But Pat was in the middle of life saving and it was no time to pose questions.

Pat leaned over the lifelines, extending the net in a firm grip. The net was only a yard from the eagle when it turned its head, gave us an over-the-shoulder glare (do eagles have shoulders?), and lifted gracefully out of the water, foiling Pat's rescue attempt.

It had had a dead seagull hooked in its talons. Pat scooped up the feathered corpse, realized it was beyond resuscitation, and plopped it back into the drink. When *Temptation* turned back on course, the eagle returned, slanted in, dove, and nimbly made off with breakfast.

Ah, well. Poor Pat. All that rescue training and no one to practice it on. Maybe another day. But the good news was, I had handled myself in true Coast Guard fashion. I hadn't panicked, nor had I done anything stupid while in command of the tiller. If I kept up this high standard of seamanship, Pat would likely soon try to recruit me. (Weeks later, I'm still waiting for her to try to recruit me. Something tells me it's going to be a long wait!)

Jebediah's Long Bay wasn't very long, and it was shallow. Not wanting to take any chance of running aground, we motored on, and halfway up Texada's long shoreline, with Lesqueti growing small behind us, the clouds cracked apart, revealing a wide seam of blue sky. The sun popped free and we peeled off coats and sweaters and applied sun screen. Summer, at last, had arrived.

Enjoying the first (and only) sunny day of our vacation, and taking advantage of the flood tide, we decided to chug all the way to Rebecca Spit on Quadra Island, a journey of more than fifty miles.

The diesel engine labored away, giving us six knots of speed, the mechanical racket spoiling an otherwise perfect day. On either side of us the clouds were piled up like snow at the sides of a plowed road, but directly overhead the blue sky was brilliant with sunshine. The sea was so glass smooth it looked polished, and, where *Temptation's* bow carved into it, blue turned to frothy white.

By three in the afternoon Quadra Island was on the horizon, shrouded in clouds the color of campfire ashes. The heat we had enjoyed for hours began to seep out of the afternoon, and cloud cover crept across the western quadrant of sky. Summer, after a brief debut, was already in retreat.

The next four hours ever-so-slowly unwound. The closer we got to Rebecca Spit, the slower our progress seemed, like one of those dreams where you're trying to run away from something in slow motion.

It was an afternoon to gaze at the clouds and visualize the shapes of cartoon characters, birds, planes, and, yes, even naked women. But that last part was probably due more to my overactive imagination than to actual cloud shapes.

A rainstorm, like an expanding ink stain, swept towards us from Campbell River. When its advancing edge darkened the sun, the air quickly cooled and we reached for our jackets.

Raindrops began to leak from the sky at six o'clock. We cleared books, charts, and cushions from the cockpit into the shelter of the cabin below. But the dark bruise in the sky was merely a threat, and we were wetly kissed only occasionally by raindrops.

Finally, at seven fifteen, we dropped the hook at Rebecca Spit after almost eleven hours of nonstop motoring. Silence rang in my ears as I sat, fidgety, in the cockpit, watching for drift and drag of anchor. The first hour or so after anchoring, I'm always nervous, until I'm confident *Temptation* is firmly tethered.

There were four or five neighboring boats anchored, like us, near the beach; a couple of trawlers, a trimaran, and a sailboat or two. On shore, the rusty caw of a crow broke the hushed quiet of evening, and towards the opposite shore, a small motorboat purred by, curling a small wake behind it.

Pat's neck was stiff from a day on the water, and her face, neck, and arms were glowing with sunburn. My forehead felt hot and the skin on my face was tight, as though the sun had shrunk it against my skull.

Around us, the water was dark green. A breeze stirred out of the northwest, gently flapping the Canadian flag on the backstay. Wavelets flopped against the dinghy. A tiny fish—a mere flash of silver—jumped, and slow gray clouds clotted the sky.

Pots and pans rattled below as Pat prepared dinner. The gas stove hissed. *Temptation* lazily turned on her anchor line. Dusk rolled out from under trees, darkened a far ridge, and smudged a mountain with shadow. Pat hovered over the wok, and the smell of hot garlic lifted out into the cockpit where I was feverishly scribbling in my journal. Beef, baby bok choy, mushrooms, and sticky rice were on the menu. I was almost salivating at the thought of dinner.

The rain that had stalked us for hours now closed in for the kill. We were driven from the cockpit, where we were eating, and we ducked below clutching plates and chopsticks.

Rain pattered against the deck. We stared out of the narrow window as the world closed in. The cabin was soon gloomy with night. Cabin lights were clicked on, and books replaced plates in our hands.

The night was a restless one for me. I got up at least fifty times to check on the anchorage. A northeasterly blew in hard, fitful gusts, shaking the dodger, rattling the rigging, and making *Temptation* shudder on her rode.

We slept late on Friday morning. I was up first for a change and over boiled the coffee. Which is a good reason why I should never be allowed in the galley.

The sky was—surprise—overcast, and a stiff wind thrummed through the rigging. Drops of rain ticked against the windows while Pat lay snugly submerged in her thick comforter, radio headphones on, listening to a Vancouver radio station. The radio station advised that Vancouver was suffering under a deluge of rain. We weren't surprised. Outside, a sailboat glided by, no doubt seeking sunnier places. But where to find sunnier places? Not around here, that was for sure. The morning was lazy and quiet, accompanied by the creak of the boat and the rich, warm scent of fresh coffee, which fizzed and bubbled in small puddles on the stove, thanks to me.

Breakfast was typical of those we had on the trip. A pear each (sometimes an apple), a bowl of cereal, and a mug of black coffee, sometimes, for me, with a teaspoon of honey added.

Then we had a thorough wash-up and shampoo, as thorough as is possible when the hot water is tightly rationed. We had to get rid of body odor and grime and look sharp, for later that morning we were going to visit the thriving metropolis of Heriot Bay.

We shrugged into clean shirts and Pat hooked the electric motor to the dinghy. I assisted mainly by watching, but also by lifting the forty-pound battery which accompanied the five-pound motor.

We pushed off. The electric motor gave a gurgle like a baby with a bottle and we glided into the waves.

Heriot Bay was a mile or so across Drew Harbor. The sky was a dismal gray, and periodically a few raindrops splattered down on us during the half-hour commute.

There was a ferry slip at Heriot Bay, home to one of the British Columbia ferry fleet's tinier craft. It churns between Heriot Bay and Whaletown on Cortez Island, ten miles away. There was a marina—the Heriot Bay Inn Marina—and a government dock, the latter home to a wild assortment of fishing boats, open speedboats, and sailboats, none of which looked in prime condition.

Downtown Heriot Bay, about a mile's walk from the Government Dock, boasted a four-way intersection. Also located there were a grocery store, a Legion Hall that cried out for fresh paint, and a combo business that sold everything from ice cream and fishing licenses to used books and fishing gear.

In the well-supplied grocery market—one of the best ever in an out-of-the-way place—we stocked up on beer, bread, and broccoli. We lugged our supplies back to the dinghy and returned to *Temptation* with a mere whisper of engine noise. The little electric motor wasn't fast, but it sure was quiet.

Part way back to our sailboat, a floatplane—Nootka Air—roared into flight behind us. Can't they soundproof those things, I wondered angrily, as the plane lifted off, the ear-pounding noise splintering the stillness of the bay, and sending a rolling thunder of racket across the peaceful sea.

Lunch was turkey sandwiches with Russian mustard on thick slabs of fresh bread. Then around five o'clock, after reading and napping away the afternoon, we clambered once again into the dinghy and cruised smoothly to the beach fifty yards away. The tide was high and the sea was glass smooth and dark green.

The beach that ringed the lengthy finger of Rebecca Spit was clogged with weathered logs. I had never seen more logs on a beach anywhere. Sure, okay, logging built this province, but it was a messy, sloppy industry and it left behind shamefully scalped mountains and beaches plugged with driftwood.

Rebecca Spit Park had picnic tables, fire pits, and benches for viewing either Drew Harbor to the west or Desolation Sound to the east. Ancient fir trees towered skyward, and there was a swath of grass, freshly mowed, and pit toilets and fabulous views. The spit itself is maybe a mile long and forty yards wide, its stony beaches piled high with driftwood, logs, and stumps. A wide trail led through the forested parts, and the smells of grass and forest and ferns and earth were thick and strong in the nostrils.

As we passed a light on the beach—it was ten feet tall, a warning for boats to avoid the spit—Pat explained that the light was solar powered and battery operated.

"Do they ever have to change the light bulb?" I asked.

"Not very often," she replied seriously. With Pat, all Coast Guard business is serious. "But," she added, "sometimes they have to replace the battery."

Pat gathered a few dry sticks—and that's not easy after weeks of rain—and lit a fire in a fire pit near one of those famous British Columbia cedar picnic tables. The flames had to be encouraged to ignite the damp wood, and after much blowing, smoke curled upward and flames crackled and grew, sending out waves of heat.

With a grin, Pat said, "It's a Stan fire."

I watched smoke billowing out of the rusty grate straight into our faces, and agreed.

A Stan fire. My father would contentedly sit all day tending a smoky fire.

By the time we returned to *Temptation*, rain began to fall earnestly. Fresh green beans, butternut squash, and new potatoes were on the dinner menu. Pat added beef ribs to her plate, dripping hot fat and barbecue sauce. They smelled delicious, but I abstained. The little galley seemed swamped with dirty plates and pots and pans. Every dish, every kitchen utensil we owned was piled overflowing in the sink. I washed. Pat dried. It was probably a good thing that darkness fell as we cleaned up. We were low on water and the cleanliness of the dishes as they were returned to their various cupboards was suspect.

On the far shore of Drew Harbor, a rock 'n' roll band started pumping out raw, thumping noise. It drifted unimpeded across the water. But as late night descended, we fell quickly asleep, oblivious to the intrusion of someone else's music.

Saturday was another—wait for it—overcast day. We were going to Gorge Harbor Marina on Cortez Island, about ten or twelve miles away. The plan was to plug into power (cushions and bedding were growing damp, damper, dampest) and we were lusting for the hot showers that were available there. There was no wind in evidence. It looked like the iron sail would have to once again propel us over the water.

But before I risked my back hauling up the anchor, the bilge had to be emptied and melted ice water from the cooler had to be drained off.

Hey! Hold it! Overhead, the sky seemed to be getting brighter. Maybe the sun would peek out!

But no. Not yet. It was only toying with us. The sun was still imprisoned by cloud. Over by Vancouver Island's serrated profile, a small patch of blue showed through in a wide field of charcoal gray cloud. Come on, sun, I implored. Come on out and play.

And it did, briefly, as we crossed Sutil Channel. Bits of blue sky appeared among broken cloud, but a northerly wind gusted up and blew the heat out of the day and the sun out of the sky. Whitecaps appeared, choppy and irritated, and we sipped from steaming mugs of black coffee, glad for the warmth.

As we approached Whaletown, the wind died and sunshine poured over *Temptation* like hot syrup. It sparkled off the waves and warmed our necks and hands. As if in celebration of the brief sunshine, two bald eagles spiraled above Whaletown's small harbor. On our right was a red marker, warning of a rock shelf that lurked just below the surface. Whaletown boasted a dock, a ferry slip, a few scattered homes, thick evergreen forest, a collection of boats, and a big rock in the middle of the harbor. The ferry slip was built with tar-blackened pilings and sat across the harbor from the government dock. As usual with government docks in this area, the fishing boats, prawn boats, and crab boats looked like candidates for the scrap yard. Some locals watched us from high up on shore, one man with a shaved head. We were just looking, and after looking we putt-putted in a tight circle and headed out. Not that we had anything against guys with shaved heads, but the lure of hot showers at Gorge Harbor tempted us to keep moving.

Sunshine became thin and tentative. Dark clouds with skirts of rain blew in from the west.

Lunch consisted of tuna fish sandwiches on poppy seed bread, a can of beer, okay, two, and a handful of peanuts.

We enjoyed the scenic trip through Uganda Passage, past Shark Spit, using green and red markers to guide us safely through the narrow and shallow channel. A sandy beach, some big, fancy homes built on rocks with awesome west-facing views, and a splash of sun. Then, for the twenty-seventh time that week, clouds sealed off the sun, and raindrops, fine and soft, swept in.

By midafternoon we were attached by spring and breast lines to Gorge Harbor Marina's dock and plugged into power. The twin heaters blasted warmth into the cabin in an all-out war with dampness.

Later in the afternoon, we hiked one and a half miles to Whaletown, ignoring the leaky sky. For this hike I was not lugging a knapsack full of frozen chicken, or any kind of chicken at all, and I was much more relaxed than at Gibson's. Bears and cougars were not preying on my mind. And, unlike Lesqueti and its tourist-hating hippies, Cortez seemed a friendly, civilized island. They had electricity, paved roads, and stores. Stores with beer and ice cream for sale and videos for rent. Very, very civilized.

The road, sure, was paved, but it was narrow. Every fifteen minutes or so a car would pass us. Often the occupants of the car would wave at us. There were colorful growths of foxgloves, and huckleberries and salmonberries that weren't quite ripe, and tall white daisies along the roadside. And there were grazing deer that barely took note of the two overweight hikers trudging past them.

Immense Douglas fir and cedar trees loomed on either side of the road, and deserted orchards ran wild. Where did the orchardists go? And why? There were no answers. Maybe they moved to Lesqueti and became hippies.

On the outskirts of Whaletown was a tiny, ancient Anglican church. I opened its unlocked door to peek inside. A waft of moldy, stale air assaulted us.

"What are you trying to do, kill me?" Pat, who is allergic to mold, said in a non-friendly tone.

Now there's an idea, I thought.

But I kept the thought to myself. Without the Admiral in my life, who would yell at me? So I quickly closed the door and we continued on to Whaletown's most prosperous and—by coincidence—Whaletown's only grocery store, where ice cream was purchased and consumed. Pat won't walk, bike, or go anywhere without ice cream waiting for her at the end of the road.

Returning, we detoured to investigate a replanted section of forest. Infant fir trees were incased in sheaths of hard plastic. There were thousands of these things spread over many acres. They looked like something invading aliens might have planted. In the middle of a darkening and silent forest, hundreds of rows of upright plastic shapes. Eerie.

But not as spooky as being tracked by hungry cougars seeking fried chicken.

Once again, we arrived safely back at the boat.

The marina owner told us that business was dreadful due to the lousy spring weather. He had a completely vacant lot of RV campsite pads nearby, each with electrical hookups, and there were only half a dozen paying customers at his spongy docks. I was glad I didn't have his cash flow problems. I had cash flow problems of my own. You'd be surprised by how much the consumption of books (by me) and ice cream (by Pat) can deplete one's bank account!

Sunday, we set off motoring, heading for Surge Narrows and beyond, to the Octopus Islands. The Octopus Islands are a marine park, and we'd read that anchorage was good there and the scenery beautiful. We were now into our final week of vacation. The plan was to anchor for a night or two up there and then head back home, making short day voyages as we returned. But we misread the tide/current book, and passage through Surge Narrows was impossible at the time.

Oops.

So we U-turned and chugged up Cortez's shore, heading for Von Donop Inlet, a three-mile narrow inlet where anchorage was easy and oysters prospered. Under thickening skies, prawn boats plied their trade in Sutil Channel.

We entered the narrow mouth of Von Donop and within one hundred yards Pat had two, yes, two strikes on her trolling pink hoochie. But, despite my reckless dive below for the fish net—risking broken bones, contusions, and other injuries with the eagerness of my dive (if Pat asks you to get the net and get it in a hurry, well, you hurry)—when Pat reeled in her line there was no fish hooked there. Either time.

We ghosted into the head of the inlet, where the black skin of the water perfectly reflected the forested shore. We dropped anchor in about fifteen feet of water. We had neighbors. We had a large sloop on one side. We had a forty-foot Canoe Cove in front of us. We had rocks behind us.

Pat glanced around and came to a decision.

"We better tie a stern line so we won't swing around and bash any of those other boats," Pat said.

"Great idea," I agreed.

And, now, with a full week of boating under my belt, I was ready to do something bold and daring and helpful. I would volunteer to do the stern line thing.

"I'm your man," I said boldly and with daring. "I will do whatever it was that you said."

"Tie the stern line," Pat said, somewhat doubtfully.

"I've always wanted to do that," I said.

"Do you know how?" Pat asked, very doubtfully.

"Of course not," I replied. "But just tell me what needs doing and I'll do it."

"Well, okay," Pat said, extremely doubtfully. Now not only was she doubtful, but she was skeptical, too.

I listened carefully to her instructions.

Then I floundered into the dinghy, which is sort of like a floating trampoline. I splashed the oars into their sockets and got a little damp. I tied one end of the four thousand feet of stern line around my paunch. It was one of my special knots. Even in a hurricane the knot would hold. On this critical mission I would not fail. From the bouncy depths of the dinghy I got the feeling other boaters were watching gleefully. Pat still looked doubtful.

I set out for shore.

It was about twenty feet away.

I rowed furiously, and in a short period of time, the dinghy, the oars, the four thousand feet of line, and I all arrived on shore at approximately the same time. Well, not exactly on shore. The edge of the dinghy was nudged up against the shore. The rest of us were still in the dinghy. Floating.

Back on *Temptation*, Pat had picked up a bullhorn.

"Step out of the dinghy and wade ashore," she bellowed, her voice echoing from one end of Von Donop to the other. Other boaters, attracted by her voice, were lining up to watch.

"Step out of the dinghy?" I said.

"Yes, you idiot," came the reply. "Step into the water."

"But the water is cold and wet." I looked over the side of the dinghy into the icy ocean depths. The water was at least ten inches deep. I could see all the way to the bottom.

"There's *starfish* in there," I shouted.

"It's okay," boomed Pat. "Starfish don't bite."

Fearlessly, I teetered over the side and sank my feet into the cruel sea. My feet immediately went blue with cold. My right foot struck a starfish and skidded off, almost tripping me. By the time I caught my balance I was mostly, but not completely, soaked. And let me tell you, catching your balance with numb feet while treading on starfish is no easy task. Not with hundreds of people watching it's not.

I dragged the dinghy all the way up on the rocks, where it was safe from waves, tides, and currents. By this time I was getting sweaty, and just a little exhausted.

"Put the line around that spruce tree," Pat's voice crackled with the electronic aid of the bullhorn.

I looked towards the tree. The tree was up a mud bank. A steep mud bank. There were barnacle-infested rocks between the mud bank and me. And the rocks were slimy with seaweed.

"Oh boy," I said.

Taking a deep breath, I charged forward.

And became entangled in the four thousand feet of stern line.

When I finally reached the spruce tree, I was muddy and bleeding. And out of breath. And really exhausted.

Then I couldn't undo the knot in the line that was tied around my waist. I wrestled with it, becoming increasingly muddier and bloodier, while Pat screamed encouragement through the bullhorn. Some of the gawking boaters were smirking. Others were just shaking their heads.

Finally, I undid the knot, looped the line around the tree, and fought my way back to the beach. I lugged the dinghy back to the water and hurled it in. Then I stomped into the water, to hell with the starfish, and collapsed, totally exhausted, into the dinghy.

Eventually, I scraped up enough energy to man the oars.

The stern line, attached to the spruce tree and reattached to my middle, caused me to row in circles. Tight little circles, like doughnuts. *Temptation* was only a few meters away but it might as well have been parked in Japan. The harder I rowed, the tighter the circles became.

I got dizzy.

I also got nowhere fast.

Where was the damned Coast Guard when you needed it?

Sitting in *Temptation*'s cockpit, laughing uproariously, that's where!

Epilogue

In Vancouver, rain poured down in March, April, and May. More rain fell in early June. Any moment the weather had to change, right? Sooner or later the sun would appear, the temperature would rise, and summer would begin. Surely it couldn't rain forever. Could it?

Well, no, it couldn't rain forever.

Our vacation expired. We arrived back home on July 4.

We went back to work the very next day. And the clouds vanished, the sun came out, and the first heat wave of the summer began.

* * *

The Admiral
Takes a Vacation

The provisions were packed and ready. Our sailboat, *Temptation*, was packed and ready. I was packed and ready.

My wife, Patricia, a.k.a. the Admiral, was packed, but she wasn't ready.

"I'm not leaving until I've got a huge Coast Guard Auxiliary burgee flying from the starboard spreader," she said.

She was wearing her ball cap with the official Coast Guard patch on the front when she said it. She was a proud member of the Coast Guard and wanted every boater in the vicinity to know it.

So, for twenty-four hours I sat and waited while Patricia went out and searched for a CGA burgee. Which she finally found and flew from the starboard spreader.

She hoisted the battleship-size burgee proudly.

"If someone sees my burgee," Patricia said, "they might ask me to rescue them."

The Admiral's lifelong dream is to rescue somebody—anybody—out on the water. Later in the trip she would realize her dream when she rescued a sailboat called *Temptation* with us on board.

In English Bay the strong westerly was blowing whitecaps off the swells. We reefed the main and put up the small jib and set off on our vacation, listing slightly to the right due to the weight of the CGA burgee.

Waves exploded over *Temptation*'s nose like foam out of champagne bottles.

"You better put your cruiser suit on," the Admiral warned.

"Later." I wasn't in the CGA, but I was no wimp.

Near Point Atkinson, a big, frothy wave slapped the hull and, rising, crashed aft, drenching me from head to foot. God, that water was cold!

My head ached from the shock of it. My sunglasses were awash. My face smarted. My jeans felt like they'd been dipped in ice. Beneath the jeans I suffered major shrinkage.

The Admiral looked at me.

"You should have ducked," she said.

Ducked where? The whole boat was dripping seawater, except for the Admiral, who was sitting under the protection of the dodger. If my teeth hadn't been chattering uncontrollably, I might have said something in return, but all I could manage was a dirty look, which probably didn't get past the film of salt on my sunglasses.

I stumbled below. The floor was filled with junk fallen from the shelves and drawers as the sailboat bounced and lurched through the heavy swells. Pretty soon I was sharing the floor with cushions, clothing, and charts, struggling into my cruiser suit, shivering with cold, being flung around the cabin like a pinball.

"This is a vacation?" I screamed. "This is what I've worked hard all year for?"

Out in the cockpit, the Admiral smirked but had no comment, which was highly unusual. Not the smirking part, but the not-saying-anything part. We were about two hours into our trip and off to a flying start.

Earlier, the Admiral had taken me aside and pointed out on the charts where she was taking me on her—I mean *our*—vacation. Desolation Sound was her goal. And mine too. "Yessir," I agreed.

For a moment I thought she was going to charge me a chartering fee, but in the end she agreed to take me along for free, exhibiting her charitable side.

We ended up in Centre Bay on Gambier Island that first night with a couple of other CGA-ers.

A guy called Larry, who owns a sailboat, and Tony, who owns a power yacht, were moored to a dock. Their boats were moored, I mean, not themselves personally. Neither the sailboat nor the power yacht had a CGA burgee, so we were one up on them.

The next day we went to Gibson's. The Admiral fished. She didn't catch anything, but she didn't lose any fishing tackle either, so it didn't cost us anything. The Admiral has been known to spend whole pay-checks on bright, flashy, colorful fishing gear only to have it fall off the line and sink to the bottom. She is very sensitive about this topic, so if you want to avoid a fistfight, never mention fishing tackle to the Admiral, especially when she's having a bad day.

The next day after the next day, we arrived in Pender Harbor, mar-riage still basically sound. I hurt my shoulder, ripping my rotator cuff while winching during a squall. Blood spattered everywhere and raw muscle and naked tendon were hanging out all over the place. (I may be slightly exag-gerating here. Check with the Admiral for the true facts!) I was also struck down by pneumonia and had to have one lung removed. (Good thing Pender Harbor Marina has a decent lung surgeon on staff!) Because of my weakened condition, the Admiral was forced to do all the tough work, and all the easy work, too. On doctor's orders all I could do was sit around and watch while drinking cold beer for medicinal purposes. This turn of events put tremendous pressure on the Admiral who, with her crew (me) indis-posed, had no one to boss around but herself. She kept herself very busy.

We sailed through Malaspina Strait in a gale. We made it to Beach Garden Marina alive. We both agreed to avoid gales in the future if at all possible. Gales are bad things, and if the Coast Guard were smart they'd outlaw them.

So far, the burgee had done an excellent job of being a burgee, but still we had failed to attract any boats in distress, and the Admiral was considering taking the thing back for a big refund.

That's when our engine blew up.

Parts exploded into the air for hundreds of feet, and thick black smoke poured out like Mount Saint Helens. We were zillions of miles from help, adrift in the middle of the upper part of lower Georgia Strait, off to the left just a little. Hot flames roared from the cabin.

We were eating lunch.

The Admiral looked up from her bucket of raw oysters, wiping her mouth on the back of her arm.

"Shit," she said.

The Admiral hates when lunch is interrupted.

"Maybe we should call the Coast Guard," I suggested, hopefully.

"Fuck the Coast Guard," said the Admiral, who is independent by nature. "Wait a minute. I *am* the Coast Guard." She took another look at the billowing smoke. "I'll rescue us right after we finish lunch."

The first thing any auxiliary Coast Guarder does when it comes to a bona fide rescue is brag about it. The Admiral was so excited about the rescue she bragged first and rescued later.

Grabbing her cell phone after ordering me below into the storm of exploding gas and flaming fiberglass to wash the lunch dishes, the Admiral phoned a guy called Dennis, who happened to be at work back in Vancouver. Dennis is a CGA-er, and as he had loads more experience than the Admiral, his assistance was vital if we were to survive.

"Don't bug me right now, I'm on my coffee break," is what Dennis told the Admiral. "Phone the Powell River Auxiliary."

"That Dennis," the Admiral said, nodding. "He sure knows his stuff."

"But Powell River is about a hundred and nine miles away," I objected.

The Admiral was already phoning Powell River's crack team of Coast Guard auxiliarists.

"Goddamnit, you woke me from my nap," roared the guy in Powell River.

"But my sailboat's on fire!" the Admiral replied calmly.

"Oh. In that case I can recommend Powell River's best marine mechanic," offered the helpful and highly trained unit leader. "In fact, he's the only marine mechanic Powell River's got." He went on to give the Admiral directions on how to find him just in case we made it to shore alive and with enough sailboat left to fix.

"I love being part of a smooth working team," the Admiral said. Then, duct tape in hand, she proceeded to tape everything back together so we could sputter over to Powell River.

Parts had to be ordered from Vancouver. When they arrived, the mechanic with the five-star rating from the Coast Guard Auxiliary put them in backwards, or sideways, or something. And only charged what it would cost to buy, say, a brand new Toyota Camry, fully loaded. We went on our merry way right after the bank approved our loan.

For about half an hour we were merry and on our way.

BLOOIE! went the brand new marine parts.

We limped into a nearby marina. This time when the Admiral grabbed her cell phone, she was not in a happy mood.

"You sonofabitch!" she yelled at the five-star mechanic. "You've let down the entire Canadian Coast Guard, not to mention the armed forces and all decent people in the Western Hemisphere! Now, get you skinny butt down here and fix this thing immediately!"

Which he did, learning belatedly what thousands of people already know: Don't piss off the Admiral. Ever.

Shortly afterward the vacation was over and we were once again safely home.

My shoulder has not yet properly healed and I'm considering a transplant. I'd like something muscular, possibly with a tattoo.

The shrinkage I suffered due to the cold wave is still very much with me. My doctor, after she stopped laughing, suggested I get a transplant there, too. I'm currently thinking about it. The Admiral has kindly offered to help pay for the operation. She says I should get a black one. I'm not sure why.

The Admiral has graciously invited me back for another sailing vacation with her next year.

"I'll think about it," I said.

She gave me one of those Admiral looks.

"Yes, of course I'll go," I said quickly. "I can hardly wait."

Maybe next year we'll get to rescue somebody else!

* * *

Sears Chronicles, One and Two

For a few years Pat had two jobs, three if you count looking after me, but she got paid for only two of them. This was after retiring from her career as sales manager in a department store. When most people retire, they retire. When Pat retired, she went to work.

Last fall, after several months of working twelve-hour night shifts at the Coast Guard and eight-hour day shifts at her other job, she said, "I'm tired of rush-hour traffic. I think I'll retire again."

The real reason she quit her day job was because during rush hour, she had to slow her sports car to under one hundred in order to avoid collisions with trucks, buses, and cyclists. She hates cyclists and isn't all that fond of buses and trucks either. The two-seater sports car is so small that even if she decided to run over a cyclist or two, the sports car would likely come out second best.

So now that she has retired a second time, she has only one job, the Coast Guard. Seven days on, seven days off. Sometimes it's day shifts, sometimes night shifts. She gets to wear a snappy blue uniform, sit around drinking coffee while getting paid for sitting around drinking coffee, and every few months she gets to rescue somebody.

The irony of it all is she commutes to work riding her—yes, it's unbelievable but true—bicycle! After hating cyclists all those years, she has become one. Luckily for her, the Coast Guard base is only a six-minute pedal along the seawall, and the route is safe from sports car drivers with bad attitudes.

When Pat's on her off weeks, she's been plotting changes to our home. She hired a contractor, who is about to start smashing apart the two bathrooms. Hopefully, once they're smashed apart, he'll put them back together eventually. Joe the contractor wasn't contracted because his estimate was the best, or because he has a dependable reputation. Joe was hired by Pat six seconds after they met, and never mind the cost, because Joe is a good-looking Italian guy. A *very* good-looking Italian guy. So, while Pat spends our meager retirement fund before it's even a retirement fund on tile, tubs, and taps, not to mention lighting, mirrors, and other stuff, the only consolation might be that we're helping Joe the contractor with *his* retirement fund!

. . . .

"We need to lose some weight," Pat said a while ago.

"We?" I said.

"Go look in the mirror," she said.

At my age and in my condition, I hate looking in the mirror. The reflection seems to get worse every day. So I took her word for it, as I always do. I always take her word for everything, mainly because there is no alternative.

"We're going on the Fit for Life Diet," she announced.

I'll explain the Fit for Life Diet as best I can. It goes something like: eat fruit, then more fruit, then have some vegetables.

Breakfast is one strawberry, three red grapes, and half a banana. At coffee break there is no coffee, but you can have an apple. Lunch is two kilos of alfalfa sprouts. Dinner is broccoli with maybe a dab of cauliflower for dessert.

The diet started a month ago. This morning I looked in the mirror to see if I was thinner. The only part of me that seemed thinner was my hair. Progress, I guess.

There's lots of exercise involved in this diet. Mostly the exercise is walking back and forth to the market for fruits and vegetables. It's a good thing alfalfa sprouts don't weigh very much, or I'd be exhausted.

Golf. . .

For several years I worked for BC Tree Fruits. Aside from selling Okanagan apples, what I did there mostly was play golf. And when I was actually in the office and not playing real golf, I practiced my putting on the office carpet. My putting didn't improve, but it sure beat working for a living.

BC Tree Fruits closed their Calgary office, and Vancouver was next. My office closed in April of that year, thus terminating my golf career, among other things. Back in January, BC Tree Fruits said to me, "We'd like you to move to the head office in Kelowna, where you'll be on our head office golf team."

I said to BC Tree Fruits, "Will I be able to practice putting on the head office carpet?"

"Yes, but only when the CEO is out of town," replied BC Tree Fruits.

Patricia and I flew to Kelowna in February and looked at houses. Right away Pat noticed a few things about Kelowna. There was no ocean, no Coast Guard, and no seawall on which to pedal her bike. However, there was a nice lake, and golf courses by the dozen, and apple orchards. We looked at houses on golf courses, at houses near the lake, and at houses beside apple orchards. We looked at new houses in old subdivisions, at old houses in new subdivisions, and at lots where houses weren't even built yet. Then we returned home.

The next day I phoned BC Tree Fruits in Kelowna and refused the transfer. The main reason being the CEO was hardly ever out of town and my putting practice would be severely curtailed.

In the years since the death of my paid-for golf career, I've maintained my relationship with that sport. I play it, and it beats me, and I play some more. I guess I love the punishment. But the halcyon golf days at BC Tree Fruits are gone, and I miss them.

* * *

The Sears Chronicles, Two

Most of the following story is true, and all of the characters and events are real. Unfortunately, however, a few teensy, tiny facts have been slightly twisted. But only slightly.

Happy Birthday to You

To properly celebrate my wife, Pat's, birthday on November 21, I flung myself out of bed early. So early, in fact, it's likely I forgot it was a birthday day. Other things were on my mind. I had a plane to catch. I had a business trip to take care of, and golf to play. My hot shower was a quick one, and while shaving I managed to avoid opening any veins. So far my morning was going extremely well. I arrived at the airport on time, had no problem slipping through U.S. customs, and I was probably thirty thousand feet above Seattle heading south by the time Pat stumbled into the shower. In just a few short hours I'd be on a Palm Springs golf course in eighty-degree sunshine, cursing and swearing at a little white ball to my heart's content. Life was grand.

Probably the flight attendant was pouring me coffee when Pat turned the shower on. My coffee was hot. Pat's shower was cold.

It started cold. And stayed that way. Happy Birthday, Patricia. The hot water tank had gone bust. I was out of town in the nick of time.

Over Palm Springs, the plane tilted and started down. Out the window I was looking at about eight thousand golf courses. The sun was bright, the golf courses were verdant green. Heaven awaited.

Back in Vancouver, cold rain pelted down. After boiling water on the stove and pouring the hot water into the tub, Pat bathed in about an inch and a half of water.

She then celebrated her birthday by phoning around, trying to locate a new hot water tank. Then she went to work at Sears and remembered, hey, that's what she did for a living! Selling hot water tanks. So she bought one. Credit cards are wonderful things, and we have several. So the buying part was easy. Next, though, came the installing part. And plumbers were never around when you wanted one.

Fresh off the airplane, I strode up to the first tee and, pulling out my driver, whacked the ball. It arced high up against the wonderful blue sky. It went forever down the fairway. Well, it seemed like forever. This was thin desert air and golf balls cut through it like bullets. In the desert air, golf balls are like peas. In the thick, dense, humid, cold, wet November air of Vancouver, golf balls are like basketballs.

While I was smearing sunscreen on my arms and legs, Pat was doing a slow burn trying to track down somebody to install the hot water tank. Eventually, she found a guy, and after she grabbed him around the throat and threatened to rip off his limbs if he didn't get on it right away, he promised he'd install the tank the very next day, at a cheap price. When the Admiral wants something, not even plumbers have enough nerve to refuse her. It's that Coast Guard training, you know.

After golf, I luxuriated in a steamy, hot shower. That night my friends and I dined out on the patio of a Mexican restaurant. Overhead, in the black desert sky, there were a zillion fat stars. The breeze was pleasantly cool and rich with the scent of yucca and mesquite.

At home, Pat worked a sixteen-hour day, and in all that time the rain failed to stop even for a few seconds. When she finally staggered in the door of the condo, she treated herself to an invigorating wash in ice-cold water. Brrr.

The next day Palm Springs sweltered under a merciless sun. Out there on the golf course, it was almost *too* hot. Actual perspiration formed on my skin. I discovered that Palm Springs fairways were as plush as the felt on pool tables. Of course, this discovery was mostly by accident, because I was rarely on the fairways.

I slugged the ball off palm trees and into water that mirrored the perfect sky and spent many sweaty moments blasting my way out of sand traps. And shouting things like "OH NO!" and "UH-OH!" and "FORE!" just to prove I was having a great time.

But in Vancouver, if one happened to be outside, the only thing that would form on one's skin would be rainwater. Pat started her day with another cold shower, but it was no longer her birthday, so she wasn't as upset as she'd been the day before. And soon the new hot water tank would be installed. Things were looking up.

After thirty-six holes in twenty-four hours, it was time to head even further south than Palm Springs. This was the business part of the trip and not nearly as much fun. I flew to Tucson, rented a car, and drove down to Nogales, which is located in the beautiful Santa Cruz valley, right on the Mexican/American border in southern Arizona. Sure, I was on business, but there was good news. Palm Springs wasn't the only place with golf courses. Nogales had them, too. Also, my hotel had a swimming pool.

At Rio Rico Golf and Country Club, I wounded a couple of live oaks and bruised a mesquite and made some Arizona ducks run for cover. And, miracle of miracles, I scored under one hundred! Another perfect golf day.

By now the new hot water tank was alive and living happily in our condo, Pat was in a good mood, and it was safe to return home. So I did.

As often happens, life evens things up. By the time I lugged my suitcase through Canadian customs and immigration back in Vancouver, I was paying big time for having had so much fun playing golf. Somewhere down there, maybe on the sixth green at Rio Rico while three-putting, I'd caught a cold. Pat, who'd worked a solid week of sixteen-hour shifts, suffered through cold baths, and endured unending rain, was healthy as a horse.

This is where the story gets violent. Children should leave the room, adults should brace themselves, small house pets should seek their beds.

While Pat worked another late shift, I, travel weary, cold infected, and genuinely lazy, went to bed early. Only for a few minutes. A nap.

Catch a few zzzz's. That was the plan. Because daughter Lori was coming into town, flying back directly from London, England, where she'd attended a hairdresser's convention, and Pat was picking her up at the airport at ten o'clock that night, after the late shift at Sears. Pat would be tired from flogging overpriced hot water tanks all day, and Lori would be tired from partying for ten days solid and from a fifteen-hour flight. They'd come home. I'd greet them heartily at the door and usher them to bed. That was the plan. There wouldn't be much time for socializing. Lori was due to fly out on an early-morning flight to Whitehorse, and Pat had eagerly volunteered taxi service.

Ah, but the best laid plans…

So I went to bed thinking: I'll just lie down for a moment. Won't even take my clothes off. Ah, that pillow sure is soft. Maybe I'll just toss the quilt over me, get a little more comfortable. Mmm. Yes. Very nice. Then ZZZZZZZZZZZZZZ. Dreaming about dazzling white golf balls flying high into cloudless blue skies. Dreaming about that twelve-foot putt. Hearing that beautiful *thunk* sound as the ball pops into the hole. Dreaming about palm trees, and soft desert nights, and that shimmering swimming pool.

While I'm in never-never land, the upstairs neighbor flushes her toilet. She walks away. The toilet spills over. And continues to spill over. A flood of water washes across her floor, and gravity takes over and the water starts to sink. It sinks downhill. Apartment number nine, our apartment, receives this tidal wave through the kitchen ceiling and down the walls. All over the place. The flood keeps coming and coming and coming, until the ceiling turns to mush, and the bolts holding up the heavy oak kitchen cabinet slip free, and…

CRASH!

Huh? What was that?

Earthquake? Car accident? What?

I sat up, got up, looked out the bedroom window. (The bedroom is on the bottom of our three-level condo. The living room and kitchen are above.) I see nothing but blackness and rain. There are no sirens, no panicky activity outside. Everything is calm.

Geez, maybe I dreamed it.

Oh well. Silly me. I'll just lie down, continue the nap. If I'm lucky I've got thirty minutes' bunk time before Pat and Lori roll in. ZZZZZZZZZZ. Back to that sand trap on the tenth fairway at Rio Rico. One hundred fifty yards to the flag. Late afternoon sun slanting in, no breeze, green grass almost tropical-looking against the brown desert. Let's see. Yes, a six iron ought to do it. Smack. Holy cow, I'm on the green! *The green*!! ZZZZZZZZZZZ.

While I'm blissfully fantasizing, Pat and Lori are striding along the breezeway. Arriving at door number nine, Pat takes out her keys, opens the front door, snaps on the lights. Mother and daughter halt in the doorway, shocked at the sight before them.

It's an emergency and Pat knows exactly how to react. From her mammoth purse, which contains life preservers, flares, and other Coast Guard rescue stuff, Pat snatches her trusty cell phone and hurriedly punches 911.

Downstairs lies the horror, spread below them like the ruins of a hurricane. Chairs are tipped over. Broken glass is everywhere. The overhead (well, it used to be overhead) oak kitchen cabinet lies spilled open on the tile floor. Huge puddles of water cover the floor.

Into the cell phone Pat is saying, "My home has been burglarized! It looks like there's been a fight. I can't see my husband; he may be dead in the wreckage somewhere. Murdered! Should I proceed, or should Lori and I go shopping until the cops get here?"

The 911 operator responds in a calm, professional voice, "Don't panic, ma'am. You can't go shopping this late, the stores are all closed. Besides, the soonest a patrol car can get to you is tomorrow afternoon sometime."

"Okay," blurts the Admiral. "I'm going in."

She lacks a Colt .45, so she pushes Lori ahead of her, using her daughter as a screen, just in case.

"Gee," Lori is muttering as she's propelled down the stairs, "you guys sure are messy housekeepers."

Glass crunches underfoot. All the glassware that was in the cabinet is now smashed into teensy tiny pieces. The teensy tiny pieces glitter in the light. Broken glass litters the stairs, the living room carpet, and is lying in drifts on the tile. Also, water splashes underfoot. Little waves lap against the walls. Pat fails to find the dead body of her husband in the immediate vicinity and is disappointed. That lazy, good-for-nothing cur didn't die defending his home from drug-crazed burglars after all! So where is he?

There's water, water everywhere…the ceiling drips moisture. The walls are damp. The carpet is soaked. Little waterfalls splash down the stairs to the bedroom. Fish jump, a Canada goose swims past, and a beaver family starts building a home.

The noise of Pat complaining to Lori that I might still be alive awakens me from dreams of soft desert air, the whirr of golf carts, and the whizz of clubs whipping downward.

"Huh?" is what I say.

And the family comes together. United by crisis. And toilet water. Lori in from London. Me in from the desert. Pat in from the retail wars. We set to work sopping up water, vacuuming up glass, sweeping up debris. And collectively we curse the toilet-flushing overhead neighbor. There's nothing like cursing an outsider to bring a family closer together. It's the Canadian way. By two in the morning, the work is done and our home is mostly back to normal.

And Lori eventually crashes on the couch, and eventually Pat forgives me for not dying a martyr's death at the hands of drugged-out burglars, and we crash into bed. And the violence is over, and this story, at long last, is almost finished.

Except for the epilogue.

Which takes us into the new year. And Pat gives me the best gift a woman can possibly give a man.

Laryngitis.

Pat gets it. She can't speak. (Well, she can, but only in a whisper.) And if she can't speak, I don't have to listen.

I hope and pray Pat's laryngitis doesn't last beyond, say, July.

* * *

Visit to a Gentle Place

A visit to the folks' place is a journey to the quiet life. No sirens, no traffic rumble, no jet planes overhead, no medi-vac helicopters whacking overhead on the way to the hospital.

Instead, the drone of a bee, or the soft engine of a hummingbird as it zooms by the sundeck. Every half hour a car drives slowly by on Velvet Road. A large crow coasts from tree branch to telephone wire. There is no breeze this day. Everything is hushed, even the air, as if waiting for something to happen, and nothing does.

Alyssum and aubrietia cascade over the driveway's rock wall, dripping white and purple over gray rock.

In the vegetable garden there are green shoots of onions, pale green clumps of Swiss chard, wrinkled leaves of rhubarb, and the peas are mere sprouts. There are spokes of chives and strawberry blossoms.

Mom says she is getting ready to retire from gardening, her lifelong passion. With her failing eyesight, it's difficult for her to sort out which things to weed, which things to let grow. Facing a future without being able to see the rich and vibrant blossoms of spring and summer must weigh heavily on her heart.

A slug appears on the edge of a wooden planter, and Mom scurries to the garden shed for a pair of shears and cuts up the slug.

"I hate destroying things," she says, and after the destruction she trudges out back to return the shears to their place on the shelf.

Dad appears on the deck wearing black brogues, black pants, black shirt, and clerical collar sticking out of his breast pocket like a white band.

"I've got to see a family about a funeral," he says. "I'll be home for lunch around 12:30."

The regular minister is away this week, and Dad promised to handle the funeral.

I guess the binding clerical collar is the last and most uncomfortable part of the uniform to be cinched into place. He goes inside after leaning on the deck railing to speak with me and getting something on his pants leg off the railing—a damp cloth is required.

In a few moments he reappears, collar in place at his throat, wearing a gray jacket. His snow-white hair is striking in contrast with his dark clothing. He seems purposeful and focused and professional as he walks to his Cavalier, his back, as always, ramrod stiff, and gets in and drives off.

His appearance is a 180-degree turn from yesterday's ball cap perched on his head, dirt smeared, baggy trousers, and woolen work shirt with the sleeves rolled to the elbow. Which version is the real Stan Sears? Why, both, of course.

Sitting on the broad deck of their home is seductive, hypnotic, an easy slide into a lazy dreamlike state. Behind me and inside, I can hear Mom moving around in the kitchen. A footstep brings a creak from the linoleum floor. A cupboard door closes. A dish rattles against the countertop. Mom, as always, is busy: fixing lunch, preparing food, cleaning up, taking stuff out, putting it away, probably pausing occasionally in her chores to glance out the window at me sitting in the deck chair, madly scratching away in a spiral notebook. *What an oddball*, she must be thinking. *Why doesn't he do something constructive?*

Eventually I put aside the notebook, manage to shake off the smothering my-get-up-and-go-got-up-and-went cloak, and proceed to wash the Camry. The silver arc of hose water splatters on the driveway, rinsing soap suds downhill onto the grass like a flood tide of foam.

Dad's timing, or Mom's, is impeccable. Moments after he returns, parking his car on the street so I can back the Toyota out when it's ferry time, lunch is served.

Dad sprinkles brown sugar on his serving of mashed turnip, a child-hood habit deeply ingrained. Mom cheats on her vegetarian diet and has a minute portion of beef stew. At the table I'm given the seat of honor—the one with the view out the kitchen window overlooking Georgia Strait. The water is calm, the surface merely wrinkled by the stirring of breeze and current. Vancouver Island lurks behind a gauzy screen of haze and cloud the color of dishwater. The freshly baked rhubarb pie, still warm from the oven, is the perfect blend of sweet and tart.

Shortly after lunch, as I collect my notebook and bag, getting ready to leave, I'm struck by the differences between their lives and mine. Their world seems tranquil, while mine is filled with city racket.

Driving away, I wave goodbye, a touch of sadness nudging its way into the warm spring afternoon.

* * *

Mike and Me
Dedicated to
Michael James Sears
1952-1985

Don't Mess With Mike

Mike reached up, clamped sturdy fingers around my necktie, lifted his small feet off the floor, and swung like Tarzan of the Apes.

It's a good thing the fight was broken up several moments later or I might have actually punched him and got him *really* mad.

Like all brothers, we had our battles. This one had erupted in the kitchen while we were getting ready for Sunday school. Mike was six, I was ten. I don't recall what started the fight, but I certainly remember how it ended: with Mike determinedly dangling from my tie while my face went purple.

Shortly after the Tarzan episode, and perhaps bolstered by his success at licking his older brother, Mike shoved a lippy but wimpy doctor's kid into a urinal in the school washroom. Got the wimpy kid all wet. I don't know what precipitated action, but Mike always smiled when I would remind him of the dunking years later.

Mike's commando training began at a place called Thirty Islands in Ontario, where the family (Stan, Sybil, John, Mike, and Happy, the boxer dog) spent at least one summer vacation and maybe more at a lakeside rental cabin. We (Mike and I, not the whole family) would strap on those old-fashioned, pillowy life preservers and march into the nearby icehouse with its heaps of sawdust, where we would conduct boxing matches.

Being older, I had a longer reach than Mike, which was a darn good thing. Mike would just grit his teeth and keep coming. With protruding front teeth, short, thin legs, and brush cut topping off a round face, Mike looked quite harmless. I knew better. This little kid was tough.

The Wrestlers

In Victoria, where we lived in 1960 and '61, we did a lot of wrestling in the basement of our home on Fairfield Road. To project the proper wrestling image, we'd don long underwear left over from our sojourn in frozen Knob Lake, Quebec. The long underwear mimicked the tights some pro wrestlers wore. Sometimes we'd wrestle in our bathing suits, wearing woolen work socks pulled up over the calf to represent fighting boots. I think the socks were also leftovers from Knob Lake.

Mike's nom de guerre, so to speak, was Murderous Mike, and I was dubbed Wild Wayne. As we threw each other around, I usually did the play-by-play. It was a tough job, fending off the legendary Murderous Mike while at the same time doing the ring announcing work.

In two years we had about a thousand matches. We came out about even at the end. Murderous Mike had a pet full nelson he often used, but fell victim to Wild Wayne's wicked claw hold.

Some furniture was damaged, and one poor old couch was actually killed, but Murderous and Wild were left surprisingly undented, unlike their broken-nosed, cauliflower-eared TV heroes like Gene Kiniski, the Brunetti Brothers, and Bulldog Brower.

Providing Mom and Dad didn't hear anything shattering, smashing, or cracking, the wrestling went on almost nonstop on weekends and after school. But in the early '60s, other attractions came along, and soon Murderous Mike and Wild Wayne were lured away from the ring to raise tropical fish and to collect records.

Mike and the Church

Mike's early life was closely tied to activities around the church. For example, it seemed only natural to assume that if Dad could earn a living from the church (as minister), so could Mike, but in a different role than his father.

The collection plate scam. Drop in a dime, take out three nickels while pretending to make change. It's an old trick. Every Christian kid does it. Okay, maybe not *every* Christian kid. Maybe only a few *naughty* Christian kids, who probably weren't Christian in the first place. Anyway, I was proud to be the one appointed to show my little brother the ropes.

Mike learned fast.

Once we'd saved up enough of those nickels, we'd meet in front of Ray's Restaurant after Sunday school. This was in Sutton, Ontario, where we lived from 1956 to 1960. Mike was about five during the collection plate operation.

Everybody likes cute little kids; therefore, Mike was delegated to walk up to the counter in Ray's and tell the cashier his mother had sent him to fetch some Black Cat cork-tipped cigarettes. After the fistful of warm nickels had been exchanged for the smokes, we'd run home to our tree fort and light up. We had a great time sucking down those dizzying Black Cats and coughing and gasping.

After smoking, it was important to disguise the breath before meeting up with Mom and Dad. Tobacco breath meant a bawling out, grounding, and possibly the loss of allowance. (This was probably 1957. I had a three-figure allowance—$1.00 per week. Younger and in a different tax bracket, Mike's allowance was only two figures—$0.50 cents weekly.)

Mike (and I) hated being dragged off to Sunday school when, instead, he (and I) could be home wrestling or playing hockey. In Sutton we were too young to weasel our way out of attending Sunday services. By the time we got to Victoria, though, we were older, wiser and much improved at weaseling.

The family had only one car, and Dad, who had to get to church early, always took it, leaving the rest of us to manage on the bus.

Our strategy was to miss that darned bus, and therefore Sunday school and church, at any cost. Our plan went something like this: Take

Mike's shoes and hide them real good. Five minutes before bus time, we'd be charging all over the house hunting for Mike's shoes.

This tactic exerted tremendous pressure on Mom, who *had* to be at church no matter what. Yet she couldn't drag her youngest child on the bus without his shoes.

No matter how long or how diligently we searched, the shoes were hardly ever found in time to get the bus. So Mom was forced to leave behind her barefooted son, and her eldest son also, to look after the younger brother.

Many times we watched from Mike's bedroom window as Mom scampered for the approaching bus. When she was safely aboard and the bus had roared up the street out of sight, it was slam, smash, and crash to our hearts' content.

After a few years, pressure began to ease up about going to church, which was a good thing. We were running out of shoes, and excuses.

Sneaking and Peeking—That's the True Spirit of Christmas!

Mom and Dad were very strict about several things around the house. No smoking, no playing hockey in the living room—at least while we had company—no staying out late.

And no opening of Christmas presents until Christmas morning.

Waiting until Christmas morning to find out what goodies Santa brought you was cruel punishment. It could ruin your health, lying awake all night wondering if you'd got that new six-shooter cap pistol, or a new pair of hockey gloves. In order to assure ourselves of good health and lots of peaceful sleep, Mike and I learned to sneak and peek.

Mike had the hands of a surgeon when it came to opening presents. He could open any present, take out the toy, play with it, then rewrap it like new.

Christmas 1958, we knew every single thing we were getting well in advance of Christmas morning. As far as sneaking and peeking went, we reached the pinnacle that year.

Somehow we had persuaded the parents to let us have our own little tree upstairs in the TV room, with our presents under it. Foolishly, they granted our wish.

On Christmas morning 1958, our gifts were all a little worn because we'd used them already.

Dad had a serious, scowling attitude about this kind of cheating and had warned us many times of dire consequences if he caught us opening presents early. Sometimes he or Mom would come across a present all torn at the corners, crumpled, and with part of the present itself hanging out. When confronted, Mike would pass it off as a result of the dog playing with it. Dad and Mom didn't really buy this kind of weak explanation, but on the other hand they couldn't come right out and accuse their son(s) of deceit and trickery, especially not at Christmastime, when everybody is expected to be nice.

No sir, there was never anyone better at x-raying gifts than Mike. Of course, the reason *he* did it and not me was, he was better at it. Also, he was smaller and subject to less punishment if caught.

The Legendary Mike Lonergan

Mike Longeran lived a few doors away on Dalton Road in Sutton. He was a bit older than me, and six years older than Mike Sears. Two guys named Mike gets confusing, so let's call Mike Sears "Mike" and Mike Lonergan "Lonergan." Still with me? Anyway, among other things, Lonergan was a Catholic, a good athlete, and especially good at getting into trouble. At all times he wore a smirk and a cowlick. Of all the adventures my brother and I shared, the most memorable were those in which Lonergan played a starring role.

Mike always had a concern for animals. Cats, dogs, even bullfrogs. In particular one giant bullfrog, which had been imprisoned in a large mayonnaise jar in Mrs. Holbourne's classroom at Sutton Elementary.

Mike agreed with the idea of studying frogs, no problem; but what Mike didn't agree with was the way the poor frog was cramped into the jar of water. Drowning innocent frogs in a mayonnaise jar was not Mike's idea of a good time.

So on a Sunday evening towards dusk, a daring rescue plan was conceived. Remember, this was long before Greenpeace . In his own way, Mike became a pioneer conservationist with the rescue of the aforementioned bullfrog.

As break-ins go, this one was a piece of cake. The classroom was at ground level and a window had been conveniently left unlatched. The only real danger was being spotted from the police station, which was right next door to the school.

Each of us had a job to do. I was the lookout, this being before I needed glasses. Lonergan's role was lifting Mike through the window. Mike's job was to scoot into the classroom and snatch the jar.

Afterwards, the only evidence of the crime was a puddle left behind on the floor, slopped as Mike dashed back to the window, jar clasped to his chest.

If Mrs. Holbourne ever puzzled over the vanished frog, we'll never know.

In those days, the sound of breaking glass was music to our juvenile delinquent ears. Or maybe they made glass differently back then so it sounded more musical than it does now. Practicing our pitching techniques, we used to, on occasion, throw rocks at school windows and, on one memorable summer day, at a cottage's windows at Jackson's Point.

Cottages and summer homes along the shore of Lake Simcoe were often deserted except on weekends. One cottage in particular was screened by a big green hedge. It was so quiet we *thought* the place was deserted. Boy, were we wrong!

Lonergan and the Sears brothers lobbed some stones over the hedge like hand grenades and heard the *whack, whack* of them striking the roof. We lobbed a few more stones and were rewarded with the shattering sound of breaking glass.

Suddenly, a very angry caretaker appeared at the end of the hedge. He had only one arm, which was frightening to young delinquents, never mind getting caught breaking windows.

"I caught you, you lousy hoods," snarled the unshaven caretaker. "I'm going to have you arrested for vandalism!"

We were absolutely terrified.

"What's yer names?" growled the one-armed man, stepping closer.

"Don't tell him your real names," whispered Lonergan, revealing his experience in tight situations.

"Uh," I stammered. "I'm Billy Brown from Brown Hill."

It's true there was a community named Brown Hill not far from Sutton. I guess I figured if he thought I was from out of town he might leave me alone.

The caretaker turned his furious gaze to Mike.

"Yup," squeaked the little guy. "I'm Mike." Then he fell apart. "And this is my brother, Mike," he added, indicating Lonergan.

Two brothers, both named Mike? (For the rest of our years together, Mike and I would howl with laughter when remembering this.)

The caretaker gave us a strange look. Billy Brown from Brown Hill, and two brothers each named Mike! No wonder it was a strange look.

"You punks wait here while I get the car to drive you to the police station," he ordered. He turned for the garage.

We also turned. The other way. And ran like crazy, escaping the one-armed caretaker.

Mike Becomes a Hardened Criminal

Our biggest Lonergan caper also took place in the summertime, late in the afternoon, at Briar's Dairy. It involved vehicle theft, attempted escape, the brandishing of a firearm, and, later, the use of a blackjack.

Lonergan's dad worked at the dairy and sometimes Lonergan Jr. did, too, looking after the counter where they sold fresh dairy products to the public. On occasion, Lonergan would leave the back window unlocked when he closed the place down. Later, he'd recruit the Sears brothers for burglary. Lonergan would hoist Mike up into the window, just like the frog escapade. Mike would then crawl through the window and work his way around to the locked door, which he would then unbolt for us. Then we'd enjoy a free chocolate milk or two before retreating.

One evening after relocking up, Lonergan eyed the fleet of milk trucks parked in an adjacent field while he wiped chocolate milk from his upper lip. His blue eyes were twinkling wildly. Mike and I had come to recognize that special twinkle in Lonergan's eyes that occurred when he was contemplating something exciting.

"Come on, I'll give you guys a joy ride in a milk truck," he said, and led the way.

We got into a truck. Lonergan in the driver's seat, brother Mike in the back, and I in the passenger's. The motor started up and we went bouncing and charging across the field. We had a great time going round and round the field, circling the parked trucks like Indians around a wagon train. We were having such a great time we weren't even thinking about getting caught.

Briar's Dairy was situated right across Dalton Road from Lonergan's house. It was his dad who called the police, thinking some punk was joyriding in a dairy truck and not realizing it was his own son.

Meanwhile, we were laughing and enjoying the ride. Lonergan's driving skills—he was maybe fourteen—were rudimentary, but what he lacked in skill he made up for with unbridled enthusiasm. Mike, in the back with nothing to hold on to, was bouncing around like a rubber ball.

Suddenly, over the roar of the engine, we heard a loud noise.

Lonergan stomped the brakes. We skidded to a stop and looked out. We saw the police cruiser, the black one with the white side doors. It was parked at the edge of the field. Sixty feet away, Mr. Harris, the portly chief of police, was marching towards us, yelling and waving his arms.

We bolted from the truck and headed for the trees.

Lonergan, an excellent sprinter, took the lead. Puffing, I was following as fast as I could manage. But Mike, with his short little legs, although they were churning madly, couldn't keep up. Within seconds my kid brother was in the firm clutches of the law.

Lonergan and I pounded through the trees downhill to the edge of the Black River. The river was deep and dark, and to a non-swimmer like me, it looked about a mile wide. Lonergan was about to jump in and swim for it while I stood there dumbly contemplating drowning versus surrender when Chief Harris roared, "Stop or I'll shoot!"

We stopped and he didn't shoot. Later, Mike assured us the chief actually had his gun out. During post arrest discussion, Lonergan swore he heard a gunshot, but Mike and I knew what he'd heard was his imagination.

Harris, dragging Mike, herded us back up to the field and into the back seat of his squad car. The route to the police station led right by our house. Mike prayed Dad wouldn't see us riding by, criminals in a police car. Luckily for us, Dad was elsewhere when we cruised by the house.

At the police station, Chief Harris yelled at us some more. He showed us the cells with steel bars where bad boys could be incarcerated. He hammered a blackjack on his desk to reinforce what a mistake it was to joyride around in a milk truck. Mike bawled, and I'm glad he did. I think the tears caused the cop to ease up a little.

Eventually we were released after swearing to behave ourselves forever. And for a long time afterward we did just that—behave ourselves.

For at least a week.

Baseball and Mike

In the back yard in Sutton, there were three places where if you hit the ball it was BIG trouble: 1) Mom's garden; 2) the neighbor's garden; 3) the thick cedar hedge.

In Mom's garden, more radishes and tomatoes were killed by grounders, pop flies, and pursuing outfielders than by disease or drought or bugs.

Our neighbors were named Fox. They were a three-person family, all elderly. A blind guy, his wife, and his spinster sister. They were grouchy. Most of the thrill of backyard baseball came from hopping the old fence, retrieving the errant ball, and returning without getting caught trespassing and being yelled at.

In the thick cedar hedge, balls would disappear, sometimes for months, as though swallowed. (It was the same with hockey pucks in winter. The hedge would eat them in January and spit them out in May.)

Happy, the strong male boxer dog, was attached to the yard-length clothesline by chain. He joined our games as often as he could, and he did it with wild abandon and reckless enthusiasm. Getting tangled up in Hap's chain as he charged for the ball was a serious hazard. It certainly added excitement and sometimes injury to an otherwise mild game. Hap loved joining in the fun far more than we enjoyed his gung-ho participation.

Mike played his first serious ball in Sutton. He even made the local United Church team once, for an inning.

Mike was about seven at the time. Others on the team were twelve, and some were fifteen. I'd like to brag that Mike made the team on ability alone, but Dad was the coach. Facing accusations of favoritism for inserting his son into the lineup, Dad sidestepped the issue by implying it was all part of a certain clever strategy to throw the Anglicans off their game.

We were playing the archrival Anglicans, who were notorious for their semilegal recruiting practices. For example, Mike Lonergan, the Catholic, was their shortstop. Dad didn't protest that one too much, as in his mind Catholics and Anglicans were practically the same anyway.

Our team, resplendent in T-shirts with a just-hooked trout leaping across the front, was ahead late in the game when up to bat strode little Mike, the bat almost as tall as he was.

The Anglicans snickered and grinned. Barry McQue, their chucker, flipped a soft pitch to Mike.

Mike hammered it.

With everything he had, which was about sixty-five pounds.

Mike charged for first base.

The ball dribbled between a surprised shortstop (Lonergan) and an alarmed second baseman. When the dust settled, Mike was safe at first.

The Anglicans glared and spat into the dust. Except for Lonergan, who gave Mike a secret wink.

Then Mike stole second and the place went nuts.

For years Mike basked in the glory of playing with the big kids and stealing second. He always had nerve, my little brother did.

When we moved to Victoria in 1960, Mike played Little League and did well. But Little Leagues were the minor leagues. It was the Sears Brothers League where all the action was.

One notable incident occurred in pretty Beacon Hill Park. One sunny morning we were taking turns pitching to each other, Mike working on his curve ball, me just happy to get it close to the plate.

Mike was catching, and I was trying out my fastball, such as it was. A streetcar pulled by horses and called a Tally-Ho approached. It was filled with tourists taking a slow ride through the scenic park. The roadway led close to the backstop where Mike squatted behind the plate.

I reared back and fired one, figuring to give the tourists an up-close look at my best pitch. Mike didn't get his glove up in time.

Pow! Right in the nose.

Blood was everywhere. The crowd of tourists began to look concerned as Mike howled and staggered in pain, face and T-shirt blood splattered. Strangely, I got mad at Mike for crying and carrying on in front of the tourists, who by then had passed by but were staring back after us.

I ripped off my shirt pocket in lieu of Kleenex and offered it to Mike. Eventually the bleeding stopped, but Mike's nose, and my pocket, were never quite the same. Also, Mike never forgave me for getting mad at him for bleeding in front of the tourists.

Mike played ball, of one kind or another, everywhere. In Lynn Valley, in Surrey, in Saint John, and once at Paradise Valley using a fence post as a bat. Mike and his dad even played catch in the snow in Winnipeg on Christmas Day.

At a friend's cabin in the Cariboo, Mike dug out a pitcher's mound and a home plate in the uneven roadway and we played ball in the bush, watched by curious woodpeckers and grouse.

We played on grass, dirt, gravel, and pavement. In Jasper National Park we played in the campsite, but the ball kept nicking tree branches and deflecting away. We spent as much time searching for the lost ball in Jasper as we did playing with it.

Frequently we allowed others to play ball with us. In 1983, we played in Seal Cove on Grand Manan Island in the Bay of Fundy. Talk about road games! This one was three thousand miles from home.

When Patricia and I first started hanging around together, Mike and I let her join us for a few games. But the first time she hit the ball, a scorching line drive into the outfield, Mike gave me a hard-eyed look, and shortly afterward Patricia was dropped from the team. The Sears brothers refused to play with anyone who could outhit them, especially if that person was female.

Shortly after Mike met Patty, it was discovered that Patty could chuck the ball like a missile, numbing your hand to the elbow when catching it. So Mike and I retired.

No sense making fools of ourselves in front of our lady friends, we figured.

The Gridiron

Football was also popular with Mike. Touch, tackle, and a thousand variations in between. In Lynn Valley in the backyard at 1409 East

Twenty-ninth Street in 1970, Mike jolted one of my friends who out-weighed him by fifty pounds. Mike figured the guy was showing off a little and it was time to teach him a lesson. When it came to taking on bigger guys, Mike didn't hesitate. He was compact in size but strong and fearless when angered.

We played tackle on the sloping front lawn at Brand Street until Mom yelled at us to stop crashing into her flower bed, sending clumps of dirt, leaves, and petals flying. No matter how big the yard, we always seemed to end up in the flowers or vegetables, even when we were semi grown up and should have known better.

In the early '80s we formed a football league, naming it the Sears Brothers Football League, a rather clever name, we thought at the time. It was Mike and I, Mike pushing thirty or just over. We played three seasons running in the muck and rain of winter when we had the parks to ourselves. Of all the games we played, this one turned out to be the most fun. Maybe because we played together and not in competition with each other. And maybe because we realized we were no longer young and opportunities to be kids together were dwindling.

The football rules were simple. Three downs to make the field. If we made it, seven points for us. If we failed, seven points for the field.

At a well-groomed playing field at Bear Creek Park in Surrey, we carried our football past a large sign that boldly stated: NO PRACTICING ON THIS FIELD.

It was a great field—real goal posts, springy grass, and white yard-line markers. About halfway through our game, rain pelting down, two parks officials drove up in a pickup truck and parked and got out and strode out towards us.

"Can't you guys read?" stormed one of them. "There's no practicing on this field!"

Dripping wet, clothes filthy, I looked at Mike and shrugged.

Turning to the official, I said, "Practicing? What do you mean, practicing? We're playing for real."

And Mike and I turned and walked, grinning, back to my Datsun.

Mike chuckled all the way home.

Hockey Night in Canada

There were other sports. Soccer, lacrosse, croquet (is that a sport?), golf, basketball, tennis, Ping-Pong, Frisbee—just to name a few of the games we played together. In fact, Mike learned to play a very cagey game of Ping-Pong from our dad. A Ping-Pong table in the basement was a standard feature in many Sears households.

When Mike applied his savage backhand, the ball was a white blur. He always beat me, and in later years he even whipped the coach, the guy who had taught him the game.

Sometimes, Mike would put a spin on the ball by slicing at it with his paddle. No matter what I tried, the ball always bounced off my paddle in the opposite direction to where I wanted it to go. Mostly, my returns against the slice missed the table completely.

Mike enjoyed Ping-Pong immensely and approached each match with a confident grin and a bounce to his step.

But hockey was the greatest of all games, especially when we were kids. We played it everywhere—bedrooms, hallways, basements, tents, churches, carports, garages, streets, lawns, tennis courts, campsites, and parking lots. We even played hockey on ice surfaces.

We broke furniture and windows, ravaged walls, smashed lights, scarred floors, and every now and then we dented each other.

Using a garden hose, Dad made a square patch of ice in the backyard in Sutton. Mike and I took turns wearing thick goalie pads we'd bought from Eaton's catalogue. At first, Mike's slap shots were no big deal, especially with goalie pads protecting my skinny legs. I mean, how hard can a six-year-old shoot the puck? But as Mike grew older, his shot gained velocity. By strange coincidence, the harder his shot became, the less I played goal.

Mike's hockey career soared when we moved from Sutton to Victoria. He outskated, out-stickhandled, and outhit (yes, hitting was allowed way back then) all the Victoria kids his age. Mike was at his most dazzling one night in the Victoria Arena when Rocket Richard was in attendance.

It was Minor Hockey Night, and all the teams from Pups to Juvenile played brief games before all the parents. To little kids, the big arena seemed jammed to the rafters with noisy spectators. The year was 1961, and the legendary Rocket, freshly retired, was on hand to pick the star of each game and to present the star with a personally autographed stick. That night, Mike's play caught the Rocket's eye, and Mike was rewarded with applause and the highly prized, autographed stick.

For many years Mike kept the stick as a memento of his most famous hockey achievement, but eventually an emergency arose when we were playing garage hockey. Mike's regular stick broke, so he snatched the Rocket's stick into use. It served him well for a long time, but like all sticks it wore down, and finally splintered and broke. By then the famed autograph had been worn away.

Not only was Mike an enthusiastic hockey participant, but he also loved watching games on TV. Back in the '70s, Dad and I pulled for the Leafs while Mike supported Bobby Orr and the Big Bad Bruins. One night while watching the Bruins blow a game to the Leafs, and irritated by heckling from me, Mike grabbed a chair and hurled it at the wall. One of the chair legs punctured the paneling, and for a moment the chair hung there, suspended, an exclamation point to Mike's passion for the game. (Right after that I decided to quit heckling Mike during Leafs-Bruins games. No sense having a chair puncturing *me*!)

As a teenager, Mike picked up a few bucks working as a part time care-taker at St. Andrews church in North Van. Mostly he cleaned up after week-end weddings, which of course were conducted by our dad. On Saturdays, the two of them devised their own version of a hurry-up offense if *Hockey Night in Canada* was drawing near and the wedding was running late.

I was never a party to their schemes, but no matter how long the cer-emony or how large the wedding or how much sweeping up was required, dad and Mike always arrived home, sometimes puffing, just in time for the opening face-off. Between them they must have had the fastest pro-nouncements and the fastest broom in the west. Or the east, for that matter.

Mike taped the '82 playoffs, the year the lowly Canucks did the unbelievable by going all the way to the Stanley Cup finals. It wasn't unusual to come from work during the hot days of August, months after the Islanders had won the Cup—beating the Canucks four straight—to find Mike downstairs in front of the TV watching the Canucks whip Calgary, Los Angeles, or Chicago again and again.

When you're addicted to hockey, getting through those empty summer months can be super tough. At least during that particular summer, Mike had enough on tape to support his habit until the real thing started in September.

Camping—the number one pastime

If Mike had been allowed, he probably would've spent his entire life camping. This love started when Mike was a little kid, but he kept at it even after becoming an adult kid.

When he was small, every few months, Dad and Mom would get the urge to drive across the country. They'd pile us kids, along with Happy the boxer, into the back seat, load up the trunk, attach an overstuffed roof rack, and beat it for either the East or West Coast, depending on which was the longest drive.

Mom took everything but her piano on these marathon trips, including a special tarpaulin that covered three acres of campsite and took two hours to set up or take down. The huge tarp went up every single night, just in case it rained. It was the old-fashioned canvas- type tarp, which weighed tons. When it sat all folded up in the trunk, the front wheels barely touched the ground.

I don't know how this camping business got Mike so interested. All I can recall of those early trips was being jammed into a cramped back seat with a slobbering dog, the temperature eighty at least (no A/C), and driving twelve hours at a stretch. Good family fun.

In North Dakota, an event became notorious within the family. Over the years it took on legendary status, and for the remainder of our lives, we will never get together without repeating the story with much delight. Mike was especially fond of this one.

That particular holiday day, Dad chose a campsite that looked a lot like a gravel pit. Mind you, *all* of North Dakota looked like a gravel pit, but we were at the end of a long, hard day of traveling and were desperate for a break. Emerging from the car, we were a little nervous of rattlesnakes. Standing there in a tight group, we were surveying the gravel pit/campsite and watching for killer snakes while deciding to camp or not to camp when Dad felt his right foot suddenly getting wet.

Astonished, Dad looked down to discover Happy peeing on his foot. It wasn't really Hap's fault, although the dog did in fact do the actual peeing. In the whole wide area, there was only one small sprig of grass for Happy to aim at, and Dad had foolishly chosen to stand close beside it. Happy, after a long, broiling day in the car with a bulging bladder, had no choice but to let fly at the nearest target available. Both the blade of grass and Dad's right foot were thoroughly hosed down by Hap, who, when finished, smirked in a special doggy way and trotted off.

I can't remember if we spent the night.

On a camping trip to the Black Tusk in the summer of 1975, I tried to kill Mike, and failed. Along on the rugged hike were Mark Armenini and John Peacey.

We climbed the towering black rock, an ancient volcanic plug. The view from seven thousand feet was incredible, but it was spooky being up so high on the steep peak. The wind seemed to want to push us over the edge. The Tusk is all rock, and most of the way up to the summit you have to use your hands to climb it, as well as your feet. There's only one route up the last hundred perpendicular feet to the top—through a narrow chimney. The chimney is also the only way down. On the way back down that sunny August afternoon, I got lost.

"Which way?" Mike asked.

"Uh…over there."

Being polite, I allowed Mike to descend first. He peered over the edge. Nothing but sheer rock dropping away into thin air. And, far below, more rock.

"Are you sure?" Mike said.

"Well, sort of."

So Mike started down, very carefully. Slowly he worked his way over the edge until all I could see of him were his white knuckles where his fingers gripped the rough, black volcanic rock, and his rather pale face.

"Geez," Mike said. "I can't seem to find any more footholds."

"Keep going, you'll find some."

Just then another climber showed up from the other side of the Tusk. He looked a little startled at the way Mike was dangling over the edge.

"Is that a short cut?" asked the hiker.

"Short cut?" gasped Mike.

"Yeah. The trail is over here," said the hiker, gesturing off behind him.

"We knew that," I said.

"We did?" Mike asked.

The hiker shrugged and left. I helped Mike back up. He gave me a dark and dangerous look.

From that day onward Mike refused to listen to me when it came to directions. A wise decision on his part.

Around campfires, Mike was a fussbudget. Poke a stick here, rearrange a log there. His shoes and boots usually showed the charred results of messing with campfires. Sometimes he'd look at his boots and point out various burn marks, saying, "This is from that trip to Pemberton," or, "That black mark there happened in Banff, and this one at Alouette." Why keep a diary, was Mike's attitude, when all you needed was a glance at your boots to remind you of events past.

For years Mike wore a favorite pea coat. About the coat clung the smell of wood smoke from his many camping trips. When Mike entered a room, you didn't have to look up to know it was him. All you had to do was sniff a little, get the odor of smoke, and say, "Hi, Mike," without ever having to glance his way.

Finally, the coat wore out and was thrown away. When it went, a lot of fond memories of bygone campfires went with it.

Smoking, Cars, Bravery, and Dulse

Mike was a born smoker. The habit started in Sutton, when he lit up his first hollow stick. Inhaling hot, rough, hollow stick smoke prepared his young lungs for what was to become a lifelong addiction. Cigarettes by the thousand, cigars by the case, pipe tobacco by the bale. Mike never got enough.

First thing in the morning, no matter where he was—home, at a friend's, in a tent, in a camper, wherever—he'd reach for his smokes and fire up. Player's, mostly. He always saved one for the morning, 'cause without a smoke to start things off, the whole day was ruined.

The only time I saw him seriously try to cut down was during Patty's pregnancy, and afterwards when Leslie was born. Mike would stand outside on his front porch and puff away, trying to keep the home's interior as pristine as possible for the females in his life.

I'm sure he still owes every smoker of his generation in Lynn Valley at least two cigarettes each, he borrowed so many. Mind you, he was always the first to offer one of his, no matter how few he had. That was true of everything he owned, including money. Mike was generous and always shared everything he had.

Over the years, Mike owned several cars. The one I remember best was a huge old (1958) Chevy. Once, when my MGB was in for repair, Mike loaned me the Chevy for commuting from Lynn Valley to work at Park Royal. Not very many miles to commute, but then the Chevy didn't have many miles left in it.

Originally the Chevy had had a standard column shift, but somewhere in its distant past a stick shift was transplanted onto the floor. Which was fine, except I wasn't sure which gear was which. Try for second and you'd get fourth, try for fourth and you'd get third, or even first, or maybe even—with a horrible grinding sound—reverse.

Going east on Fifteenth where it crosses Lonsdale, I was returning home from work when the traffic light changed to red. The Chevy and I stopped. Here Fifteenth is on an incline. A couple of other cars came up behind me while the light was red. The light flicked to green and it was time to put the Chevy in gear and move forward.

Sounds simple enough.

Easier said, though, than done.

As soon as I released the brake, the heavy Chevy started rolling backwards. Frantically I ground the gears, trying to shove the stick shift into first. No gears seemed available. The car directly behind me honked in panic as the battleship-sized Chevy drifted towards his frail modern bumper. Finally, the stick shift thunked into gear. I think it was probably third. Flooring the gas pedal, I barely got the Chevy into forward motion before it steamrolled the car behind into junk. Thick blue smoke poured fog like from the Chevy's exhaust. At last, the Chevy crept through the intersection just as the light blinked amber. Other cars honked in frustration.

All the way home, I didn't take it out of third, figuring it might never go back into gear—any gear—again.

Later, Mike admitted the gearshift *was* a little sloppy, but, defending his mammoth Chevy, he accused me of not knowing how to drive. When it came to his Chevy with the crazy gearshift, he was probably right.

Mike was brave.

Not only was he brave enough to buy cigarettes with collection plate money when he was young, but he was also brave brave.

During the early '80s in Delta, we used the propane barbecue a lot. It sat on the wide back deck where we used to enjoy late afternoon sun. Patricia, Mike, and I would lounge around in lawn chairs while the steaks sizzled on the grill.

One afternoon the propane tank developed a leak. Flames blossomed and grew suddenly. We pictured the propane tank blowing up like a bomb.

While I ran into the kitchen for water, Mike calmly stuck his hand into the flames (all that campfire experience coming in handy) and turned off the connection. Almost immediately the flames died. The fire's heat melted the handle. It also melted some of Mike's wrist and hand. The resulting burn scar remained on Mike skin for years before fading.

If Mike hadn't acted so promptly and fearlessly, there was a good chance the fire could've burned down the house. I admired Mike for his quick, decisive action. Now I worry that I never thanked him enough for it.

Dulse was a favorite Mike snack. The world's best dulse grows on rocks near Grand Manan, New Brunswick. Each summer it's harvested, dried, and sold around North America. Dad got Mike hooked on it. Mom, and many other women folk, including Pat and Patty, thought it was yucky.

Pat even went so far as to allege there might be seagull guano mixed into it.

"Yup," Mike agreed, chewing heartily. Mike would nod and reach for more. "Adds flavor."

Dulse has a particular odor only true dulse gourmets enjoy. With Mom or Pat around, the stuff had to be squirreled away where their sensitive noses couldn't detect it. If they found it, and Mike or I wasn't around to stop it, likely the dulse would end up in the garbage. But Mike enjoyed eating dulse. And I did, too. But now that Mike and our dad are both gone from my life, dulse seems to have, somehow, lost much of its flavor. Perhaps the true flavor came from the sharing and not from the seaweed at all.

Leslie

A variety of interests and passions brought happiness to Mike during his brief life:

Music. He was always tinkering with a piano, a saxophone, a recorder, a flute. He collected a range of records, from old time rock 'n' roll to symphony.

Sports.

TV. His favorite all-time program was *M*A*S*H*. In Delta, where he lived with Pat and me for several years while attending college, he would hurry home so he could watch two shows played back to back on channel twelve.

Camping.

Friends. Mike had friends wherever he went. People liked him. He was quiet and sort of shy, and pleasant.

As he grew and matured, many things influenced and changed him. But some things flowed strongly through him and never changed. Far, far ahead of ambition and material things came friends and family and kindness and a love of freedom in the out-of-doors. He respected all living things, pulled for the underdog, always had time to do favors for others.

But nothing changed him, or brought him as much happiness, or changed his habits and thoughts as much as Patty did. He'd been alone a long time, and somehow a piece of him was missing. Until Patty.

And when daughter Leslie came into his life, Mike was filled with unsurpassed joy and love and pride. His world became full and complete. All pieces were in place.

He had his own family.

What more could there be?

The Final Chapter

Every year, in springtime, Mike visits me for a little while.

It's always on a warm day with sunshine and a clear blue sky. It's always in a park where there is a nearby backstop and infield. The air is perfumed with the fragrance of earth and growing things and fresh-cut grass, and the leaves are tender and new.

I stop and gaze across the park. Pretty soon I hear the crack of bat and ball, and when I look up I can see a white ball arcing higher and higher into the blue sky. The ball pauses for a millisecond before dropping swiftly down.

A figure trots out under the descending ball, makes an easy catch, and grins at the sheer joy of it.

It's Mike, of course. And for a few moments each spring we are kids again.

* * *

The Whiz Monster

Always, there were other cats.

There was the Big Siamese Male who used to lurk outside the bedroom door and call for Tasha to come out and play. His cries of endearment would wake us up in the wee hours of the morning. But at least he was a nice guy. He was friendly.

There were sneaky cats that used to steal inside at night and swipe Tasha's Cat Chow. They didn't wake us up, but they sent our cat food bill soaring.

There was the Black Cat With The Red Collar who continually beat Tasha up, ate her food, and marked out his territory on our furniture and walls. Which was bad, but at least it didn't *smell*, because the Black Cat With The Red Collar was neutered.

Through all this, the sliding door in the bedroom remained locked open. It was Tasha's doorway to the outside world, through which she came and went freely, day and night, in snowstorms and rain, and in balmy summer weather. So what if a few other cats sneaked in? It was a small price to pay for Tasha's freedom.

Well, maybe not that small.

Stormy easterlies howled through the three-inch crack of freedom from November to March, turning our bedroom into a deep freeze. To ward off hypothermia in the winter months, our bed was heaped high with thick blankets, quilts, and comforters. It was quite bracing to bound out of bed on a December morning and put your feet down on the carpet and feel…frost! And scraping ice off the mirror over the sink before each morning's shave, well, that was a lot of fun, too.

Anyway, until the arrival of the horrible Whiz Monster, no sacrifice was too great to preserve Tasha's freedom of movement.

The first clue the Whiz Monster had invaded us was the smell. Wrong. Stronger than smell. Stink.

"Whew!" said the Admiral. "What is that awful smell?"

"I think maybe a tiger or a lion has been in here," I said.

"Maybe a whole herd of them," said the Admiral. "Hurry up and clean up this mess. I'd help you but I'll be busy watching TV. Besides, I have an allergy to lion piss."

I got some rags and some cleanser and went to work. After four and a half hours of scrubbing and washing, the smell was gone, but the wall and furniture paint was blistered forever.

Two days later the odor was back. Our bedroom smelled like a stable. The Whiz Monster had returned.

This time after the cleanup, we closed and locked the bedroom door. Sleeping in a room that stinks like a zoo is not a good thing for humans. Or for Tasha, who wrinkled her nose at the smell and complained bitterly, as only cats can.

She also complained bitterly about the door. The closed door. Her gateway to freedom was no more. Now she had to make decisions. Should I stay in? Or should I stay out? And she didn't like it, and she howled and was miserable and glared at us and ripped apart the furniture with those razor claws she has.

So we, and our furniture, couldn't live with Tasha's dark moods, and we couldn't live with the Whiz Monster. What to do?

We formed a committee, the Admiral and I, and scheduled a meeting. The Admiral had the floor, as she always does, and I sat there and kind of nodded agreement at everything she suggested, as I always do.

Said the Admiral, "Well, what are you going to do about this feline home invader?"

I thought long and hard.

Said the Admiral, "John, wake up! I'm talking to you."

"I'm not sleeping, I'm thinking," I replied.

"Yeah, well, sometimes it's hard to tell the difference," the Admiral said.

"The Whiz Monster calls for drastic action," I said.

The Admiral agreed with me, which is very unusual.

"We could install a cat door," I suggested.

"And the Whizzer could come through it," argued the Admiral.

"We could get one of those electronic gizmos," I suggested further. "With a beeper thing attached to Tasha's collar. The cat door would then open only when it was her trying to enter."

"Too expensive," said the Admiral, shooting me down as usual.

I was getting a headache, brought on by way too much thinking.

"Maybe the Whiz Monster will just get tired of whizzing," I said. "Or, maybe he'll eventually run out of whiz."

The Admiral checked her watch. It was late evening. Time for her favorite TV police drama, *Due South*.

Said the Admiral, "This meeting is adjourned. Get back to me when you've solved the problem."

"Yessir!" I said.

There was only one solution to the problem, I realized. And it involved a gun.

I went downstairs. From deep in the closet I dug out the Air Pressured Super Soaker water rifle. I loaded it with tap water and set it handy to my side of the bed. I opened the sliding door, freedom's gate, and locked it open. I turned off the lights and waited for many hours in the darkened bedroom. The Whiz Monster must've been busy whizzing elsewhere, for he failed to appear.

Several nights went by in this manner, the door alluringly open, me waiting in the dark, the deadly Super Soaker within easy reach. But my prey avoided the trap.

Then one early morning, the Admiral kicked me awake. It was pre-dawn, and dark and quiet.

"Hey," she urgently whispered. "The Whiz Monster is under our bed!"

Tossing aside the thick covers, I leaped from the bed and snatched up the Super Soaker.

"Got you at last, you dirty rotten urine-spraying commie!" I screamed.

I dove to the floor and, lying prone, I madly opened fire, sweeping the cave like area under the bed with a burst of water.

"Uh, I don't see anything," I said. I sat up and looked at the Admiral, who was grinning at me. "There's no cat under the bed," I added.

"April Fool!" she blurted, snickering.

And it was, and I was suckered again.

Shortly thereafter, the Admiral was out at her Thursday night Auxiliary Coast Guard meeting, at which twenty or thirty mature adults sit around and complain about the appalling lack of suicidal bridge-jumpers, sinking boats, and drowning sailors to which the Auxiliary unit would be paged for rescue work. Another week had slipped by without any of them saving a single soul. Ah, frustration! While the Admiral and her cohorts were hatching a plan to secretly torpedo a British Columbia ferry so they'd get some action, I was left alone in an empty condo, Super Soaker at the ready, also waiting for some action.

My prayers were answered. The auxiliary unit's were not, mainly because they lacked access to torpedoes. Evidently, they're not readily available at local marine stores.

I heard a rustling sound, and in the murky blackness of the bedroom I glimpsed shadowy movement. At last the game was on!

Quickly, I opened fire. An arc of high powered water hurtled across the bedroom and splashed harmlessly against the carpet, the closet doors, the doorway, and, as I took up high-speed pursuit, the stairs, the railing, more stairs, the walls, some pictures, the TV set, the fridge, and, yes, even the chandelier over the dining room table received blasts from the Super Soaker. Lots of stuff got blasted, but not the Whiz Monster, who proved to be very agile for a forty-pound cat. More agile by far than the aging, overweight gunslinger who, gasping for breath, chased him wildly up two flights of stairs, through the living room and kitchen, and back down the stairs, where the Whiz Monster made good his escape through the dripping bedroom and out the door into the night.

Later that night, when the Admiral returned home from her Auxiliary Coast Guard meeting, she said, "I think we've had another flood."

I explained about the gun battle with the Whiz Monster. But she was distracted, her mind already plotting new strategies for rescue work, the latest of which involved bazookas and sailboats. If rescues weren't going to happen naturally, then, well, things would have to be helped along. In the rescue business, one has to be proactive.

The very next Saturday morning, we came face to face, the Whiz Monster and I. And the Super Soaker.

I heard him out on the patio, arguing with Tasha. Silently, I gripped my weapon and on tiptoes went to the sliding door. There he sat, big as a mountain lion, calmly watching me as I lifted the deadly gun to my shoulder. He was arrogant and unafraid. For a brief moment we looked at each other. He seemed to say, give it your best shot. So I did. My finger squeezed the trigger. A bolt of water shot from the plastic barrel. It struck him dead center in the heart. In a microsecond he was gone, a furry blur as he leaped into the bushes.

And the Whiz Monster has never returned.

And Tasha, her freedom regained, is happy. Once more the sliding door is locked open twenty-fours a day, every day. And I'm happy I no longer have to live in a place that smells like a zoo. But the Admiral? Is she happy? Perhaps. Recently, she's been paged to a few emergencies, none of which involved bazookas. I think she's holding off with the bazooka idea until things go quiet again on the rescue front.

The Whiz Monster? Who knows what this evil feline is up to, or where he is spraying his foul whiz? He is gone from our lives and that is all that matters.

And the Super Soaker is still stored close at hand, fully loaded, ready to help me defend home and hearth again, if required.

* * *

Cat Terrorism

Recently, a special meeting of the Alder Bay Place condo owners association was convened. Everybody attended and the room was jam-packed. The issue behind the massive turnout was something that affected all of our lives.

Motion: All cats must be leashed if outside. If caught running free they'd be given a quick trip to the pound.

The guy running the meeting was from Building Management. He wore an Italian suit, carried a leather briefcase, and owned a stern expression.

"Cats have been running wild," said one man.

"They've pissed in the hall," said another.

"I had to clean up cat shit in the corridor," stated someone else.

A lady with a German accent said, "A Siamese cat sneaked in our place and ripped up $10,000 worth of beautiful wallpaper."

Pat and I exchanged nervous glances.

"Yeah," agreed the German husband. For sure this guy had been on oven duty as a young Nazi. "And that same Siamese cat pissed on our $50,000 just-laid carpet."

Goodbye, Tasha, I thought.

The cacophony of catty cat complaints continued.

"Every time I come home with an armload of groceries, a little Siamese cat runs in the door," claimed a woman. "Then I have to run around trying to catch it."

"My cat is a well-trained cat," said a woman in a white sweater. "A little Siamese keeps walking through my patio, getting my perfect pussy all worked up."

"Cat fights outside my window keep me awake most nights," growled a bald-headed man.

"Cats are out of control," wailed a voice from the back of the room.

"Something must be done!"

"Cats should be illegal!"

"Hang 'em!"

"Any cat I see, I'm taking to the SPCA right away," said the guy in the dapper Italian suit. "And furthermore, we'll change the bylaws of this place so that this cat problem is fixed once and for all."

"Great!" said the former Nazi.

"Yes, yes!" said Mrs. Nazi.

"Now you're talkin'," said the bald man.

I glanced at Pat. She was giving off storm warnings. Suddenly she stepped forward.

"My cat doesn't get in the hallways and therefore doesn't use them as a toilet," she said, with that familiar bar of steel in her voice she uses to boss me around on *Temptation*.

Pat whirled on a pleasant woman from suite twenty-two. Pat stabbed her with a forefinger. "The piss and the shit came from this woman's cat!"

The woman began to sob. "I confess! It *was* my cat. I promise I won't let him into the hallway ever again."

Pat nodded. Now she aimed her high-beam glare at the Italian suit.

Pat said, "You lay one finger on my cat and I'll crack your skull like a walnut!"

The sharp Italian suit went all wrinkly.

Pat gazed at the Nazis and all the other cat owners. "Anybody messing with Tasha answers to me personally," she snarled. "Any questions?"

People squirmed in their seats. They were just learning what many had already known for years. Thou shalt not get Pat mad. Ever.

"Actually," said the Nazi, "the torn wallpaper gives our place kind of a rustic look."

"We like rustic," nodded his wife. "A lot."

"Any time your cat wants to take a leak, hey, our $50,000 carpet is very absorbent," added the Nazi.

"I think we can forget this silly meeting ever took place," said the guy from Building Management in the badly wrinkled Italian suit. Clutching his leather briefcase, he ran for the exit.

The meeting was six weeks ago. Haven't heard a cat complaint since.

Meanwhile, Tasha wanders in and out of patios, slips through open doors, participates in the occasional territorial dispute with trespassing outsider cats, and generally has a fulfilling cat career.

* * *

Banger Sisters

The Canadian sales director of BC Tree Fruits, the apple company, flew in from Kelowna.

"I'd like to promote you to BC sales manager," he said.

"I was happy just being a sales guy," I said.

"It means a raise."

"Oh," I said. I was thinking, *hey! I could maybe buy a new car.*

"Plus your bonus will be larger."

I was thinking, *BMW.*

"But not that much larger."

"Well," I said, thinking, *Okay*, a *Toyota. Slightly used.*

"As manager you can do just about anything you want," he said.

"So I could come in later and leave earlier," I said.

"Of course," he agreed.

"I could play more golf," I said. "With customers, of course."

He nodded.

"I'll take the job," I said.

"But there is one thing," he cautioned.

"Okay," I said.

"Debbie and Heather will report to you. You'll have to manage them."

"Uh-oh," I said.

The Canadian sales director left. I called Debbie and Heather into my office.

"I'm your new boss," I announced. "You'll be reporting to me."

They exchanged looks.

"But we still outnumber you," Debbie reminded me.

"And we have our girl union," Heather said.

I nodded. They had me.

"So don't get, like, *too* bossy," Debbie said.

"Or things will go bad for you," Heather warned.

"At least I shouldn't have to make the coffee anymore," I said.

"Hah!" said Debbie, and got up and left.

"Hah!" said Heather, and she too got up and left.

Leaving me alone with my plants.

"Looks like I'm still making the coffee," I said to my plants.

Unlike Debbie and Heather, my plants never argued back.

The next day I made a managerial decision, my first.

"I'm leaving early today," I announced.

"We're out of cream," Debbie said. "You'll have to get some before you leave for the day."

Heather said, "We're also out of chocolate."

So right after I ran those errands, I left early.

For several years after my promotion, the daily office routine remained virtually unchanged.

Each morning I'd grind the organic fair-trade coffee beans and fill the coffee maker with organically purified water and make the coffee. Then I'd zip out and buy some chocolate-covered almonds.

The only thing that changed was, I'd do these errands with a stern expression. I read somewhere that managers should be stern much of the time. It was supposed to send Debbie and Heather a strong message. The message was supposed to be, *I'm in control here!*

But as the months melted into years, and my face got more and more wrinkly from looking stern, I began to doubt the message was getting through.

After the coffee was made, mostly what I liked to do was lurk in my private office, where I could talk to my plants, or gaze out the window, or play computer solitaire. I did all these things in as managerial a fashion as I could muster.

Sometimes I'd try to flex my managerial muscle. I would stride boldly into the main office.

"Heather," I'd say. "Could you—"

"I've already done it," she'd reply, and she'd turn back to her main job, which was eating grapes, bananas, or oranges. When not eating organic fruit, she kept busy by offering opinions on the health system, politics, and just about everything else.

Once or twice a week I'd slip into Debbie's office, where she was almost always on the phone speaking with her husband, her son, her sister, or any one of about a thousand other family members.

"Uh, Debbie," I'd say after waiting several minutes for her to acknowledge my presence.

"Look," she'd finally say, cupping her hand over the receiver. "I'm pretty busy; you'll have to make an appointment."

"It's about your overdue performance appraisal."

"Oh, that," she'd say. "I did it last week, gave myself an excellent review, got a nice raise."

"Oh," I'd say. "Fine, then." And I'd creep back into my office and glare at my plants for an hour or so, until it was time to go home.

After several years of being outfoxed by the foxes, I had a great idea. Or so it seemed at the time.

I hired my old buddy Tom Yipp. Tom was mild mannered, hard-working, and male. I figured no longer would dominating females out-number me. Now, in the office things would be even. And when it came to casting his vote, Tom, who was, after all, my loyal friend, would stand with me.

Tom got off to a great start. Right away he assumed the organic-fair-trade-coffee-making duties.

A couple of days later, I called a meeting.

And a couple of days after that, everyone agreed to attend.

"I have some announcements to make," I addressed the group in my best speech-making voice.

"Why are you shouting?" Debbie asked.

"I'm not shouting, I'm making a speech," I said.

"Well, keep it down. I can't hear the talk show on the radio," Heather said.

I snapped off the radio. No more mister nice guy.

"From now on, things are going to be different around here," I said.

"Oh?" said Debbie.

"Oh?" said Heather.

"Yes," I said. "That's what it says right here in my notes."

"Maybe you better make new notes," Debbie said, smirking.

"No," I said firmly. "Things *are* going to be different around here, starting today. Right, Tom?"

Tom avoided my executive-style glare, which I'd been practicing in the bathroom mirror at home after my wife had gone to bed.

Tom was gazing at his shoes.

"Come on, Tom," Heather said. "Tell him."

"Er," Tom said.

"Um," Tom said.

"Oh, dear," Tom said.

"Tom joined our union," blurted Debbie. "He's one of us!"

And the three of them exchanged girl-power high fives.

"I'm sorry," Tom said. "But I've been a union man for years."

"Er," I said.

"Um," I said.

"Oh, dear," I said.

And I hastily returned to my plants, which were always happy to listen to my speeches and didn't know anything at all about betrayal.

Once again the Banger Sisters—three of them now—had won the day.

* * *

Conquest of the Rio Montezuma

It started in the dappled shade of a dusty parking lot a few meters from where Rio Montezuma flows into the blue Pacific.

"This could be dangerous," Pat said, just before we started up the nearby trail. "There's jungle, slippery rocks, and, at the top, a huge waterfall."

"I just hope we don't die," I said.

"I've had Kent Search and Rescue training, so I'll go first," Pat said.

I had noticed that all other hiking couples were led by the male. But when your wife is the Admiral, normal rules do not apply.

"This is Costa Rica, not the Fraser Valley," I said. "I'm not sure if your training is relevant."

Pat gave me one of her fearsome looks. It's the look that reminds me of heavy artillery fire.

"Try to keep up," she said.

She turned and started up the trail. I tried to keep up.

I was carrying my green backpack, into which Pat had carefully loaded nineteen bottles of drinking water, towels to be deployed after swimming in the waterfall pool, sunscreen, bug juice, a flashlight, compass, flares, camera, a first-aid kit, a misplaced topographical map of Kent-Agassiz, an entrenching tool, a machete, a CD titled *Survival in the Central American Jungle*, a booklet called "How to Construct a Shelter Out of Coconut Husks," and extra sunglasses.

Pat was carrying the Lypsol.

The trail led up some rocks pooled with clear river water and was canopied with branches. As far as I could tell, there were no man-eating snakes overhead in the trees. Nor did I glimpse any jaguars stalking us through the shadowy underbrush. We were off to a good start.

A breeze blew along the river, which was more like a creek, keeping us reasonably cool. That is if, when the temperature is thirty-five Celsius, you can use the term "reasonably cool."

But our pace was not fast. Or even quick.

Because every fifteen feet or so Pat would stop.

"Water," she'd say, thrusting out her hand.

And I would dutifully stagger out from under the bulging backpack, dig out the water, and hand it to her. Glug, glug, glug, and we'd move on. Occasionally the trail would lead off in several directions at once. Pat never wavered. We stayed on the main path exclusively. Pat's SAR training was paying off. That, and following the Tico guy ahead of us didn't hurt either.

This was the dry season, so there wasn't a lot of river in the riverbed. The path crossed the rock-filled river bottom and climbed the bank. Trees closed in. Tangled roots crisscrossed the trail, trying to trip us up. The bank fell sharply away.

"If you trip on a root and fall into the chasm and break a leg, don't worry," Pat said, during one of her water breaks. "I haven't forgotten my Coast Guard bone-setting course. Just make yourself comfortable and I'll be back for you after I've had my swim in the waterfall." Glug, glug, glug, and she continued on.

"Thank you, sir," I said, and followed, placing my feet very carefully.

Eventually we heard the distant thunder of water falling on rocks. The waterfall was close. We were almost there. But the trail went along the face of a mud cliff. Footholds were scanty and handholds were iffy.

"Damn!" Pat said. "I should have brought my SAR-issued mountain-climbing and avalanche gear."

"Not your fault, sir," I said. "They'd never allow those ice axes and carabiners and stuff through airport security."

Pat managed to cross the cliff face without losing the Lypsol. I followed, banging my knee on a rock so hard it made my eyes water, hooking my shoelace on a root stub, and, at the very end, submerging my right foot in a puddle of stagnant water. The stagnant, scummy water looked like it might contain malaria.

Before us, the narrow river gorge opened into a high-walled canyon. A waterfall glistened, plunging two hundred feet over a rock cliff into a deep, dark pool that may or may not have been the home of crocodiles.

The air was cool and hung with mist. Some people were already swimming in the pool, unmolested by crocodiles. A Rastafarian guy was setting up a display of primitive-looking jewelry. Other people were taking pictures of each other.

"I'm going in," Pat said.

And she did.

And then I did. The little fishes in the pool seemed startled to see me in there with them. The current produced by the force of the waterfall tried to suck me under the cool, dark surface. The curtain of mist that drifted across the water tried to get in my nasal passages and drown me. But then water always tries to do me in. I survived this latest onslaught and dog-paddled safely to shore.

Now, if I could make it back across the cliff face, through the snarled roots, and over the water-slick rocks to the parking lot, the Costa Rican adventure would continue full steam ahead.

* * *

Costa Rica

My wife and I were having dinner at home one evening in November in Vancouver. She was eating a single bean sprout with a glass of plain drinking water on the side. I was having Wendy's french fries, with a liter of red wine on the side.

"We're going to vacation in Costa Rica next year in May," she said. Patricia always makes the important decisions.

"Great, I said. "Land of safaris, lions, and elephants."

"Costa Rica isn't in Africa, you idiot," she said, using her knife and fork to cut the bean sprout into small portions.

"Ah, the South Pacific," I said, washing down a mouthful of fries with red wine. "Trade winds, coral reefs, and babes in grass skirts."

"Costa Rica is in Central America," she said. "Down by Nicaragua and Panama."

Instead of speaking, I chugged some more red wine. Half a bottle in, the $8 merlot tasted pretty good.

I asked, "Do they have babes with grass skirts?"

"No," she said, chewing. "But they have monkeys, cloud forest jungles, and beautiful beaches."

"Oh," I said, trying to hide my disappointment about the grass skirts.

She added, grinning, "What I'm looking forward to most of all are the zip lines."

"The zip what?"

"That's where you zip along cables from treetop to treetop."

"Like, way up in the air?" I said nervously.

"Way up," Pat said, sadistic grin still firmly in place.

"Er," I said. "I'm not good with heights." I was eyeing the last of the wine for fortification.

"It's completely safe," Pat assured me. "Hardly anyone is ever seriously injured, let alone killed."

I slugged back the remainder of the red.

"Bring on the zip lines," I said boldly.

"I'm on a new diet," she continued. "I'm going to lose so much weight I'll need a completely new wardrobe for the trip."

"If you buy a whole new wardrobe," I said, "we might not be able to afford the trip."

"What?" she said, giving me one of those frosty looks she specializes in.

"You'll look terrific," I said quickly. "No matter how much it costs."

"Gimme your Visa card," she ordered. "While you sober up, I'll book the tickets on the Internet."

And that's how it all started, our adventure in Costa Rica.

Almost Busted

The first adventure happened with Costa Rica Customs upon arrival at Juan Santamaria International Airport late on Saturday night, May 19.

Pat had packed nineteen bags, suitcases, and backpacks. Yes, nineteen. Many of them were heavy. All of them were full. And all but a couple were jammed with stuff for Corbie's friend Marlene.

Corbie was our son-in-law. Marlene was a transplanted Canadian living in Grecia, just outside of the capital city of San Jose.

"If there's anything we can bring you," Pat had e-mailed Marlene, "just let us know."

Four hundred e-mails from Marlene later, her shopping list was complete. And our luggage was luggaged out.

Ping-Pong balls, chocolate chips, and parsley flakes, among a whole bunch of other stuff, had been requested, purchased, packed, and shipped.

Anyway, in San Jose we got through the long lineup at immigration, had our passports stamped, collected our baggage, and lined up for Customs.

Pat was slender now after months of eating bean sprouts. And her new wardrobe looked terrific.

I was not slender, nor did I have a new wardrobe. What I had were sweaty palms about going through Customs in a foreign country. Maybe chocolate chips weren't allowed in Costa Rica. Or maybe foreign Ping-Pong balls were outlawed.

The bags, all nineteen of them, went on a conveyer belt and through a scanner. There were a bunch of uniformed Customs guys around, armed, scowling, serious-looking people.

When our bags went through the scanner, a young Customs agent fingered me over.

"Open that bag," he ordered, pointing at the bag bulging with the stuff for Marlene.

I zipped it open with my sweaty hands.

Frowning, the agent thrust his gloved hand inside and yanked out the bag of Save-On's finest green parsley flakes.

Brandishing the innocent baggie, the agent glared at me.

"Gulp," I said.

The agent shook his head. "You're crazy, man," he said. "We got good dope here. No need to import."

He shoved the oversize baggie back inside the suitcase and we were on our way.

"I Want to Live Here"

Daniel found us in the melee outside the airport terminal, got us in the hotel's Hyundai van, and we rocketed away into the humid night. Daniel worked for the Hotel Vista Golfo, our first destination.

The hotel was a couple of hours north of San Jose. The Pan-American Highway twisted and climbed, was narrow—no shoulders—and teemed with trucks and buses and cars and scooters, even at night. Daniel drove the van hard, riding the bumpers of slow vehicles, shifting gears up or down as required, tramping the gas pedal, flicking on the high beams, and passing across double yellow lines, in tight corners, and on blind hills.

In the back of the van I double-checked my seat belt.

Pat whispered, "We've got accident insurance, right?" and I nodded yes, which is when we veered off Highway One onto a steep secondary road and the van lurched and bounced over a series of potholes as big as bomb craters.

Daniel and the potholes failed to kill us, and we arrived at Vista Golfo after eleven o'clock. The night was pitch black and the hotel was also pitch black. The power was out. Temporarily, we hoped.

We stumbled to our room, our baggage was heaped on the floor, and we were abandoned, our only companion a weak battery-driven night light.

Pat, trained for emergencies by the Canadian Coast Guard, had a flashlight in her backpack. With its aid, we found the bathroom and the bed. In the darkness as I crawled under the single sheet (who needs blankets when it's twenty-five degrees Celsius at midnight?), I hoped there were no snakes, lizards, or spiders crawling in with me.

There weren't.

About four thirty, with just a hint of early gray light around the window curtains, Costa Rica's entire bird population began to celebrate the birth of a new day.

The power was back on, and it was impossible to sleep with eighteen million birds whistling, screaming, and singing at each other. I got up and showered in the tiny *bano* and made coffee in the tiny kitchen.

Pat, lying in bed and sipping her first cup of rich and fragrant Costa Rican coffee on the first morning of our first day in the country, and ignoring the power failure, the insane ride on the highway, the vicious potholes, and the racket of the early morning birds, said, "I've decided I'd like to live in Costa Rica."

I didn't respond. There were things crawling on the floor under the bed that made me hesitant about the whole thing.

It's a Bird. It's a Plane. No. It's Me on a Zip Line.

Below our room was the spring-fed swimming pool with rippled blue surface, the restaurant and office, and a fringe of green trees I didn't know the names of, and beyond was a valley flat as a billiard table, verdant green. A few soft white clouds were lower than we were on the mountainside.

We went downhill to the restaurant, which had an open view of the breathtaking canyons and ravines, and, way, way out there, the Gulf of Nicoya and, on the hazy blue horizon, the Nicoya Peninsula.

"We can do the zip lines today or tomorrow," Pat said.

Pat was grumpy. The only cereal available was Froot Loops. No granola and yogurt here.

Manana—tomorrow—or, heck, even next week had my vote for doing the zip lines. My reasoning was simple. Why splatter yourself against trees today if you can put it off 'til tomorrow?

But, as usual, my vote didn't count.

After eating a bowl of Froot Loops and cranked on the resulting sugar overdose, Pat signed us up for the zip lines tour.

Hotel Vista Golfo is located at an elevation between rain forest and cloud forest. Within minutes of signing up to commit suicide, a grayish mist descended over the area, which made it a cloud forest day.

Daniel, the mad driver of the night before, was partnered with a colleague named Jesus. Jesus was very good looking, with a jet-black mustache and piercing dark eyes. While Pat gazed at Jesus, I was gazing at the cables that were slung high above the jungle, from one side of the ravine to the other. Zip lines.

"Because it's the slow, green season, you're our only customers," Daniel explained. "We cannot give you the full-day tour with the twenty-five cables. Only the twelve-cable, half-day tour is available."

"Great," I said at the same time Pat said, "That's too bad."

When it came to cables, twelve were better than twenty-five, in my opinion. With luck we'd—er—zip through the zip lines just in time for lunch, providing there were no accidents, injuries, or deaths.

There was heavy gear to be strapped into: helmets, thick leather gloves, harness, carabiners, clips. Pat and Jesus and Daniel were grinning and having fun as they got harnessed up. While they were enjoying themselves, I was trying to remember any prayers that might save my soul, if not my body. I couldn't remember any, but then I can never remember anything when I'm convinced the Grim Reaper is waiting just around the next corner, or zip line.

Through the mist we tramped, jingling and clanking with gear, to cable number one. We clambered up on the wood platform. The cable was maybe one hundred meters long and not very high. It was sort of like a bunny slope for zip liners.

"This carabiner clips on to the cable, you sit down and extend your legs, cross your ankles, placing a hand on the cable behind your head to control speed," Daniel explained. "Never place a hand in front of the wheels because you could lose some fingers. We'll start with a couple of easy ones, and then it gets exciting after that," Daniel said.

"I'm already excited enough," I said.

Daniel clipped me onto the cable. I sat down, felt the harness grip me below the buttocks and in the crotch. Great. They were going to neuter me before they killed me. I placed my hands as instructed, crossed my feet and…I was gone.

I avoided screaming. Also, I avoided having to sing soprano for the rest of my life.

The cable hummed and the ground was a blur and then I was on the other side.

Hm. Maybe this was okay after all.

After a few cables, somehow I ended up on a platform high in the treetops. I looked down. I shouldn't have looked down. The ground was almost out of sight. It was spotted with shadow, and among the trees the light had a green cast to it so that even the shade appeared green. Probably matched my complexion. In the next tree, monkeys were resting and watching us and maybe snickering a little.

Pat and Jesus took turns stepping off the platform into the void below. They called it rappelling to the ground. I called it crazy. I stayed on the platform. I may have *clung* to the platform. Rappelling is where you attach yourself to a line and descend vertically. Pat and Jesus seemed to enjoy rappelling.

The monkeys and Daniel and I stayed in the treetops. We were halfway through the zip line tour. I had yet to wet my pants, so things were looking up.

On the second to last cable Daniel warned, "This one's fast and steep and you need to watch your speed at the end."

The cable trembled, treetops flashed by underneath, and the platform came at me in a rush. But I landed safely, if somewhat clumsily.

When we were all across, Daniel said, "Now for the last one, and the longest. It's 750 meters."

We had to drive there, uphill, in the van.

The cable was wrapped around a huge, spreading tree and anchored to a concrete pillar. It disappeared into a ravine filled with swirling mist.

Seven hundred and fifty meters.

Going as fast as you can ride a bike downhill.

Jesus first, me next, then Pat, and Daniel last. Green jungle below, white mist all around, the song of the cable, and suddenly the platform emerged from the cloud and it was over.

The only notable incident on that last zip line was Daniel's cell phone ringing. He calmly answered it a hundred feet in the air, speeding through the clouds, and had a conversation during his hell-bent-for-leather trip. From the platform I could hear his voice long before I made out his shape flashing out of the curtains of mist.

The warm air was thick with humidity, our clothing was sodden from perspiration, sweat trickled out from under our helmets, and we gasped for breath in the thin atmosphere of the mountainside.

Worth every nickel. Worth every semi-heart attack. Next year, I plan on doing it all over again. Maybe even the full-day, twenty-five-cable package.

Quads

Above the hotel was a corral. In the corral were some horses. They looked pleasant enough, but they also looked tall.

Pat said, "Next, I'd like to go horseback riding."

"Next, I'd like to laze around the pool drinking Imperial beer," I said.

I was nervous about horses. Likely these were Spanish-speaking horses and I didn't know what Spanish for "Whoa, horsey!" was. And one other thing—I hadn't been on a horse in many years, and I still remembered the aches and pains of that long-ago ride.

"I'm sorry, *senora*," Daniel said. "We cannot do horses today, but I could rent you some ATVs."

"ATVs wreck the environment, are too noisy, and I don't like them," Pat said.

"I'll go," I said.

"Oh dear," Pat sighed. "I better go along to make sure you don't kill yourself."

But it wasn't me who almost got killed. It was Patricia.

The ATVs were quads, bright red, and loaded with power. The route was up the mountain and along several ridges, the roads rocky and potholed and steep and twisting and narrow: typical Costa Rican roads, in other words. The views were spectacular on the three-hour drive.

We roared past Brahma cattle and pastureland, through jungle, and past small houses. We also passed some horses. I gave them the finger as I thundered by.

There were four of us: Daniel leading the way, Pat and I, and bringing up the rear was Jose-Luis, a hotel guide.

The dirt road descended steeply into a hairpin turn at one point, and there was a creek and some trees in the tight corner.

Pat blasted downhill, her fat tires spitting pebbles and dust. Suddenly she was almost into the trees and creek. Jamming on the brakes, she came to a dust-swirling halt fourteen centimeters from the creek and half a centimeter from a tree.

"This wouldn't have happened with a horse," she said later, when she was able to talk.

We climbed above the clouds into sunlight, and we were instantly sweat drenched. At this high elevation, the tropical sun stung the flesh. Daniel found a small cantina at the summit of our trip and we off-loaded for beers and Cokes. My hands felt numb from gripping the handlebars, but I wasn't complaining. The views were of distant green ridges and steep-sided canyons and soft clouds. The area seemed deserted, and it was nice to have the tour with just Pat and me instead of sharing it with a dozen other tourists.

Despite the fact the ATV was alive with power under me, bucking powerfully over rocks, skidding through turns like a mechanical beast with an angry iron heart, my only bad moment came when I forgot to lift the visor before spitting out a mouthful of saliva thick with dust.

Pat had one other almost-bad moment when a tethered goat near the cantina wandered into the road in front of her. For a brief moment I had carnivore dreams of goat stew for dinner, but Pat wheeled sharply around the animal, thereby crushing my dreams of goat meat and leaving the goat crush-free.

After the cantina break it was downhill at great speed, and we splashed and surged through a creek on our return to Vista Golfo.

Later, we sampled the hotel's spring-fed pool. The pool, being fed from a mountain spring, was colder than the Imperial beer from the bar, so we didn't linger long in it.

It was off-season and the hotel was about half full. One night during dinner at the almost-deserted restaurant, we were treated to a lightning show—sheets of it flickering and pulsing, lighting the whole quadrant of sky below us all the way to the Pacific Ocean. Spectacular.

What was even more spectacular was the discussion Pat and I had about buses.

"Tomorrow we catch the public transit bus to Quepos," she said. No longer restricted to bean sprouts or Froot Loops, Pat was cutting a steak into large chunks with a very sharp knife. I paid careful attention the knife.

"I hate buses," I said.

"The public bus is cheap and it takes the scenic route," Pat said. "Plus, it'll give us a feel for the country."

"I don't need a feel," I said. "I need transportation with air conditioning and comfortable seats. We could get a cab or one of those executive buses."

"You'll get a feel and like it," Pat said firmly.

She may have brandished the steak knife just a little.

The argument, I mean discussion, was over.

And I'd just lost for the ten thousandth consecutive time.

Our final morning at Vista Golfo was sunny and hot, and a German named Hans in a dilapidated blue truck drove us bumpily over a dirt road to view some nearby mountainside properties, the panoramic view of the best of them seeming to go into a wispy, blue eternity.

"I want to buy this place," Pat said, reaching for her checkbook, "and live here forever. It's got a pool and everything."

The driveway was steep, but no more so than a cliff. Plus, as far as I was aware, we had yet to win the lottery and therefore lacked the money to buy a Costa Rican home.

"We have a reservation at Hotel Verde Mar in Quepos," I said. "We paid already."

"Okay," Pat said. "I'll leave for now, but you haven't heard the last of this."

(Months later—I *still* haven't heard the last of this.)

Putting away her checkbook, Pat boarded the hotel bus along with our nineteen bags and me. Daniel drove us to the old port city of Puntarenas, about a forty-minute trip.

As clouds carrying a cargo of rain swept in from the sea, Pat dragged me aboard a crowded, noisy public bus bound for Quepos.

Quepos by Bus

The bus was jammed when it left Puntarenas and got more jammed as it meandered south. Students smartly dressed in blue shirts clambered aboard at every other stop. Vendors selling cold drinks and snacks also got on and off. Some windows were open, others weren't. The interior was sweltering. Pat had the window seat; I was stuck with the aisle.

The feel I got for the country was that of the stomach of an overweight woman who stood in the packed aisle beside my seat. Every time the bus sped up, slowed down, or hit a pothole, she lurched against me. And the bus was always speeding up, slowing down, or hitting potholes. This woman was marinated in perfume strong enough to make my eyes water. After an hour or so I probably knew her more intimately than did her husband.

Another feel I got was from a slender teenage girl who replaced perfume lady in the aisle about halfway through the trip. She had long, black hair, which she whipped across my face every fifteen seconds while talking on her cell phone. The whipping and the cell-phone talking went for about twenty kilometers. This wasn't all bad, though. The hair whipper had a very short skirt, a short blouse, and nice proportions.

"This feel thing isn't all bad," I said to Pat when a sudden braking of the bus caused the girl to rub a couple of her proportions against me.

"I knew you'd come around," Pat said.

We passed groves of gigantic mango trees and acres of palm-oil palms and a stand of teak, the teak twenty years from harvest.

Near Quepos, I looked out the window and said, "They've got to be kidding!"

Pat was busy studying the proliferation of *se vende* signs. Bulldozers and earthmoving equipment were at work ripping open the earth, spilling red soil. The world has discovered Costa Rica's cheap land prices, and development and condominiums and gated communities were sprouting.

"That bridge," I said. "It's too narrow for the bus." I was calm. The bus wasn't moving very fast and would be able to brake in time, no problem.

But the bus didn't brake

Pat didn't seem worried. Likely she was dreaming about real estate.

As the bridge drew closer, I realized narrowness wasn't the only challenge. It was dilapidated and sagged across a deep canyon.

The bus entered the bridge and I held my breath. It rattled over the planks of the one-lane structure, the side mirrors almost scraping the rusted-out iron girders.

Underneath, a mud-brown river flowed seaward. I imagined crocodiles and water snakes waiting patiently for the bus and passengers to free-fall into their domain like manna from heaven when the warped old planks burst.

But the "Oh my God bridge," as the locals called it, took our weight, and a few minutes later we were approaching Quepos.

The town was busy as an anthill. The streets were narrow, and across from the bus station, a block long line of red taxicabs waited in the heat for fares. It was a $5 ride to Verde Mar, our next hotel.

The road to Hotel Verde Mar went up over a steep hill and quickly down, with just enough narrow twists to keep your heart rate up.

Restaurants, large and small, and bars and hotels lined both sides of the road in a solid row.

I was happy to be in a taxi and not a bus. It was one of the few cab rides I would have during the entire vacation.

Our room at Hotel Verde Mar was small and square and was brightly decorated Mexican-style: big square floor tiles, yellow walls with pink highlights, a cast iron bed. There was a small kitchen, a blue bathroom, and, most important, a fridge. The room was comfortable, clean, and outside our door there was a swimming pool. Manuel Antonio Park was only a couple of kilometers away, and fifty meters through some palm trees lay Espadilla Beach, sparkling in the sun.

Catastrophe One and Two

Our first morning in Verde Mar, a Wednesday, started with a bang at 6 a.m..

Several of them, in fact.

I was sleeping, dreaming of babes in grass skirts doing the hula on a tropical beach. Possibly Playa Espadilla. Or it might have been Playa Kitsilano. Didn't matter. What mattered were the grass skirts.

Suddenly I was kicked awake. By my wife. The grass skirts and the maidens wearing them evaporated.

Patricia was whispering, "Something is on the roof! Go look! Hurry!"

The hotel had a tin roof. Somebody or something was jumping up and down on it. Or maybe the Air Force was dropping bombs on it.

"Boom," went the roof. "Boom, bang, boooom."

I got out from under the thin sheet. Blankets aren't necessary in Costa Rican beach country. Sheets aren't even necessary, but we had one anyway. I staggered into T-shirt and shorts while the roof continued to erupt. If it was workmen fixing something up there at the crack of dawn, I was going to raise hell. I practiced a few Spanish swear words as I donned my sandals.

The sun was barely up and the world was lit with weak greyish light. I went out by the pool and looked up at the roof.

A monkey ran along it and disappeared. Another monkey jumped from a tree branch and landed, boom, on the metal roof.

Monkeys. On the roof, playing, at dawn.

At Vista Golfo it had been birds. Now it was monkeys.

Didn't the wildlife ever sleep in?

More catastrophe a few minutes later. No coffee filters in room 207 for the coffee machine. Couldn't possibly start the day without freshly brewed coffee. Especially after the early monkey alarm clock. (Months later, still can't start the day without a cup of Costa Rica's finest.) Tried using toilet paper for the filter. Nope. Didn't work: coffee grounds and water all over the kitchen counter and floor.

Most of the remainder of Wednesday morning was spent cleaning soggy bits of toilet paper out of the coffee machine.

After successfully unclogging the coffee machine and acquiring proper filters from the lobby, we bused (I didn't dare mention the word "taxicab") into Quepos—105 *colones* fare, about twenty cents—where we extracted eighty thousand *colones*, a huge wad of paper money totaling roughly $160, from the Bank of Costa Rica. At the local *Supermas* across from the bus station we stuffed our backpacks with a bottle of Panama rum, tomatoes, cereal, milk, lettuce, some sweet sticky buns, and Salsa Lizano. Salsa Lizano is popular in Costa Rica. It's sort of like green Worcestershire sauce.

After a sweaty twenty-minute wait for the next bus, we returned "home."

We frolicked in the big, powerful breakers that crashed onto the beach, and then did some pool time. About four o'clock, rain clouds blotted out the sun and a few scattered raindrops fell.

Marlene showed up and we hand-delivered her load of chocolate chips, Ping-Pong balls, onion soup mix, and the troublesome parsley flakes.

After dark, Marlene drove us to the Barba Roja restaurant and dropped us off. She was on her way home to Grecia, and we would meet up with her there at the end of our trip.

The Barba Roja had a great menu, and we dined sumptuously on ahi tuna and *camarones*, the shrimp being anything but. They were huge. The food was good. Our server was better.

Our hostess/host/waiter/waitress had, among other things, a fantastic set of breasts. We were pretty certain, though, the fantastic set of boobs were attached to a male body. Difficult to tell, with the makeup and blonde hair and the Botoxed lips, but still…

The next morning Pat bought a watermelon, mangoes, and a papaya from the back of a pickup truck. The pickup truck was full of tropical fruit, and its driver was making door-to-door deliveries to restaurants, cafes, and tourists.

We ate some of the fruit each morning until it was gone. Most mornings I added a slice of toast and peanut butter to the fruit plate. Delicious.

We toured Manuel Antonio Park, where we viewed monkeys and sloths and sleeping bats. The two-hour tour was worth every nickel of the twenty bucks each it cost, but by early afternoon the humidity was so thick it felt like we were wading through it.

Old Man and the Sea

Sipping a Diet Pepsi at poolside, Pat said, "I'd like to catch a marlin or a sailfish. Something big."

I was drinking a poolside beer and conducting an important comparison test. Where did Imperial beer taste better—Vista Golfo or Verde Mar?

Discussion of any kind would distract me from the project, so I said, "Sure, whatever." And finally decided, after much research, the taste test was a tie.

Next thing I knew we'd spent a fortune booking a fishing trip.

Friday we shared in the chartering of the *Benidicio*—a small, older model sportfishing boat. Pat didn't catch a sailfish or a marlin. She had no more luck in Costa Rica then she had at home. Which was no luck at all.

Some dolphins followed the boat for several hundred meters, sliding through the water like grey missiles, and we saw a sea *tortuga* (turtle) and a sailfish. The only thing we caught was sunburn.

The day was beautiful, though; the water calm, the clouds like layers of milk in the blue sky, and on shore the big blue-green mountains ringed the coastline. The sparkling blue ocean lifted and fell; its wrinkled surface was stretched taut and bright to the curved Pacific horizon.

Rain clouds blew in at the end of the day, and warm raindrops fell as we returned to the dock.

Later that night we joined our new acquaintances from British Columbia—Lorne and Jennifer from Chilliwack, with whom we had shared the fishing charter, and their companions Cheryl and Sam from Abbotsford— for dinner at the El Avion restaurant.

El Avion was housed under some permanent tents with wooden floors and stairs and gave a panoramic view of jungle and ocean. It was named the *El Avion*, which means "the plane," because the bar was built inside the body and wing of a plane that was shot down in the 1980s by the Sandinista army, leading to a scandal that uncovered illegal CIA supply missions to the Contra rebels in Nicaragua. But on this night, there were no CIA types or rebels in sight.

El Avion featured steak and seafood. By now I was addicted to the big shrimp and ordered some. While I gorged on them a fireworks display started below us in Quepos, a wedding celebration, someone guessed, the reason for the show. And along with it lightning pulsed and throbbed, dwarfing the man-made light show as though Mother Nature had decided to humble the lesser effort.

The evening was fun and filled with good companionship. A few BC'ers connecting in a foreign land far from home.

The following morning Pat and I walked to the end of Espadilla Beach in bright sunshine. But beneath the palms that fringed the beach it was cool and dark, and in the damp sand, small orange crabs ducked into holes as we approached.

As we passed lounge chairs shaded with umbrellas, which the *playa* entrepreneurs would rent you for about six dollars, Pat spoke of Realtors and property and how, if we were living, say, in Miramar, we would weekend here at Manuel Antonio.

A vendor with a large cooler on his bony shoulders offered chilled fresh coconut milk, and other vendors with pushcarts sold flavored ice cones. Waves heaved onto the beach and rushed, foaming, at our feet before quickly receding. Above us, the layered clouds were many shades of white: vanilla, cream, silver.

"It's taken you a week," Pat said. "But you've finally slowed down."

On Sunday, the monkeys again were slamming against the metal roof at dawn. On this day we took an estuary tour where several varieties of mangrove crowded the riverbank and white-faced monkeys pounced onto the boat's roof from overhanging branches, looking for handouts. Our guide warned us not to feed them, not wanting them to become dependent on people for their food.

Sunday evening, our final night in Quepos, we were invited to Karen's home for dinner. Karen was the manager of Hotel Verde Mar and an expatriate Vancouverite. She had married a Tico—Albert—and they had a daughter, Makela. Karen served a delicious seafood soup, and when we return to this beautiful land, I plan to hold a gun to her head, if necessary, to be able to have it again.

Snit

We were up before the monkeys on Monday, packing for a 6:15 bus pickup for the ride to Samara.

Yes, a bus again. But not a public bus this time. This one was a Gray Line touring bus with air conditioning and comfortable seats, and there were only six tourists on board.

Of course, the bus was late; many schedules in Costa Rica run late. We'd been up too early for breakfast or even coffee and endured the three-and-a-half-hour ride to Limonal on empty stomachs before grabbing some *frutas* cups and banana cake iced with chocolate at the bus stop café. Limonal was a small town and a bus transfer depot.

And then it was on to Samara, Pat and I the only passengers in a Hyundai van as we traveled over the nationally famous Friendship Bridge, a joint project between Costa Rica and Taiwan. At least this bridge was wide and solid. The bridge spanned a muddy brown river and joined the Nicoya Peninsula to the mainland. We passed through cattle country, and acres of jungle and green hills, arriving in the Oceanside village of Samara about noon.

The day was scorching hot when we exited the air-conditioned comfort of the bus. The Hotel Giada, into which we were booked for five nights, looked old and worn. Our room was small and the toilet didn't flush and the pool wasn't much bigger than a bathtub.

"We'll leave right after lunch," I said, in a minor snit. "There must be a better class of hotel around this godforsaken town somewhere."

We were sitting on hard wooden chairs with slatted backs at an uneven table in Giada's restaurant. Although the restaurant had a roof, it lacked walls. Main Street was ten feet from our table. I expected maybe a truck or bus to jump the curb and join us in the dining area at any moment. There was a storm of flies around us, and dust and exhaust fumes. Plus the temperature was three hundred degrees.

"I can take the flies and the heat and the sagging bed in our room," I was complaining. "But what I can't take is a faulty toilet."

Faulty toilets seemed to follow me around. The year before, in Mexico, the toilet hadn't worked when we checked into our room and had leaked puddles onto the tile floor for our entire stay.

"As a beer drinker," I explained, "it's important that the toilets work."

"This was supposed to be an adventure," Pat reminded me.

Just then the friendly waitress brought me an ice-cold Imperial beer. Cold beads of moisture ran down the outside of the bottle. I tasted some. I tasted some more.

"Maybe this place isn't all bad," I said.

Managing to beat the flies away, we had a nice lunch. I had another Imperial.

The decision to stay and make the best of it was made easier when we discovered a bigger pool and a better room in a newer wing behind the older part of the hotel. In this room the toilet flushed perfectly. Let the adventure begin, I said to myself.

Ensconced in *habitacion* nineteen, where the shower's water pressure was equal to that of a fire hose back home and the hot water was scalding hot rather than tepid, we settled in. The staff was courteous and helpful, but in Costa Rica, everywhere we went people were friendly and helpful, and even when I couldn't figure out the security vault system—I locked it at least four times and four times had to have the young concierge guy come to the room to unlock it—he never called me an idiot. At least to my face.

The *Playa*

Only a couple of short blocks away along uneven sidewalks, *Playa* Samara itself was broad and gray and crescent shaped. We explored it the next day. Gently sloped towards the green ocean, the empty beach was ringed by coconut palms, which leaned into the steady ocean breeze, yellowed fronds stirring sleepily. Breakers creamed over the nearby black reef, and waves swelled and tipped and spilled up the sand in long strands of foam. The blazing sun was in a vast blue sky, with soft white clouds sailing past.

We swam in the shallow water near the beach, where waves surged and pulled sand from under my toes. I didn't worry about sharks. Somebody told me sharks couldn't get inside the reef. I didn't worry about the undertow, which on some beaches could suck you all the way to Australia, because the jagged reefs at Samara also protect from suction.

I didn't worry because I only stayed in the bathtub-temperature green water maybe ten minutes and was never over my head, nor far from dry land. Salt water always tries to drown me and I have to be cautious.

We visited a Century 21 real estate office and were toured through a condominium development across the street from Hotel Giada, the price tags way beyond our reach. But Pat had that dreamy let's-move-here-NOW look, and I did my best to get her out of there before she started, again, reaching for her checkbook.

That night, dining at open-air style La Brasas Restaurant, our table lit by soft candlelight, we shared a dish of Spanish paella while bats flickered above our heads seeking insects.

The weather during most of our Samara stay was like this: We'd awaken at six o'clock, or six forty-five if we slept in, to blue skies and blazing sun. Then, around two in the afternoon, a few clouds would roll in and maybe every other day rain would briefly fall, the raindrops warm after descending through tropical air.

Wednesday morning, after a breakfast of fried eggs and coffee, served with dust and flies, Pat dragged me to the local RE/MAX real estate office. We viewed a few pictures of houses and property on a laptop. Pat talked about cost per square foot, location, and swimming pools. I was in charge of nodding and agreeing with Pat. Mostly, I just sat there and enjoyed the frigid air conditioning. We were given a map and directions to a home with a pool that was in our price range providing we were able to successfully rob a bank, and off we went.

King Kong Lives!

Pat had the map clenched in her hand.

"We follow this street here," she said. "Then we turn up this road until we come to this other road, and then we turn left, and the house with the pool will be right there." She sounded confident.

I looked at the map. All I could see was a bunch of wiggly lines. There was an X marked on it like a treasure map. The X seemed to be a long way from anywhere.

"Okay," I said.

Soon the paved street turned into a dirt road. Houses were few and far between. The jungle closed in. Then it closed in some more until there was a dark canopy of branches over the road, which was by now a trail.

We walked, and walked some more.

At a fork in the road, Pat stopped and consulted her map. A dirt road went off to the left and disappeared into the maw of the jungle. Another dirt road went right and seemed to be swallowed by more jungle.

There was nothing but sinister jungle all around. No homes, hotels, or people.

"This way," Pat said. "I think."

She set off to the left.

That's when King Kong almost killed me.

High up in the jungle something ROARED.

The hairs on the back of my neck stood up.

It roared again. More than a roar—a prehistoric and evil and threatening kind of growl-roar-howl.

The racket reverberated through the jungle.

Among the overhead branches something stirred. Something dark. Something…alive.

"IT'S A FUCKING WILD KILLER VAMPIRE GORILLA!" I screamed.

I figured maybe I could outrun Pat, and while the beast was devouring her I would make my escape.

But cold terror rooted me to the spot.

When I tore my gaze from the dense jungle, Pat was looking at me.

The monster bellowed again and clouds rolled in and trees shook, and I'm pretty sure the actual ground under my sandals trembled. Or maybe it was my knees.

"WE'RE GONNA DIE!" I screamed.

"It's only a monkey," Pat said calmly. "A howler monkey."

"Oh," I said.

"I see," I said.

"Loud little devil, though, isn't he?" I said.

"Are you all right?" Pat asked. "You look pale and your eyes are all bugged out."

"I'm fine," I said. "I think."

"That monkey didn't scare you, did it?" she asked, grinning.

"Who, me?" I said. "We better turn back, though; I think I just felt a raindrop."

Monkey? Sure. You bet. A mammoth, flesh-eating gorilla is what it sounded like.

To this day I firmly believe King Kong is alive and living in Costa Rica, in a gorilla condominium just outside Samara. I also believe he eats tourists when given the opportunity, likely swallowing them whole.

First there was one raindrop, soft and warm on my cheek.

And then there was another one.

We were marching homeward along the dirt road, leaving the threat of King Kong behind. I felt confident that soon we would be back in civilization, and safety. We passed a farm and some cows in a pasture and could see the sky was thick with rain clouds.

We were seconds away from the greatest deluge I had ever experienced.

Raindrops Keep Fallin' on My Head

I kept looking over my shoulder. Good news. No sign of a pursuing gorilla. We passed a hotel, and down the road there were houses coming into view.

The raindrops were increasing, raising steam and dust from the hot dirt of the road and ticking on the nearby trees.

Then somebody threw a bucket of warm water on me. And another. And another. At least that's what it felt like.

Moments later the hot deluge was roaring on banana leaves and thrashing branches and crashing onto the ground and sluicing across the dirt road, turning dirt to streaming mud, filling potholes to the brim and running though ditches, puddles instantly swelling into chocolate-colored soup.

Water flowed off the brim of my Tilly hat, stuck my shirt to my skin, and ran down my sunglasses in sheets. I glanced over my shoulder, and through the downpour I could barely see Pat ten feet behind me, her hat spilling a gout of water, her blouse and shorts tight as skin to her bones, and brown waves—yes, waves—of water on the road, her sandaled feet splashing through them.

We were within a chip shot of our hotel when Niagara Falls paused and stopped and the water on streets and in ditches began to vanish like oil in a hot frying pan. The air was thick with moisture and humidity.

I strode to Giada's pool, stripped off my backpack and sandals and plunged in, shirt and all. Somehow, the pool seemed drier than the rainstorm.

The rain started again later, crashing against rooftops and tile, gushing along ditches, pouring off palapa roofs. We ate dinner in Giada's restaurant, the street outside flooded, the rain blasting parked vehicles, roofs, and pavement like machine gun fire. Main Street was a river and rain poured from the restaurant's roof like a waterfall, trapping us like war refugees. No way was anyone here going to venture into the storm, so the restaurant was full. We ordered pasta and marveled at the lightning that trembled in the flowing black sky, and we flinched as thunder exploded just above our heads.

The plan for the remaining three days of our dwindling vacation was to visit Marlene at her home in Grecia. She had graciously offered a free stay at her bed and breakfast.

"We'll go there tomorrow," Pat said between bouts of thunder. "The bus leaves at nine o'clock."

I was having some red wine. Red wine was mandatory with pasta. It's an international law fully recognized in Central America.

I had a second glass, girding myself for the long bus ride tomorrow to Marlene's, about a six-hour commute.

"We could take the plane," I said hopefully.

I'd read about the nearby airport and the quick flights available to San Jose.

Pat didn't reply. She was busy finishing her pasta, which was very rich and tender. While she demolished her dinner, I remembered something important.

Pat often became agreeable to just about anything when dessert was on the table, especially after six months of bean sprouts.

"Maybe we should have dessert," I said and ordered some.

"We'll take the plane," Pat said, scooping chocolate syrup.

I had a celebratory third glass of wine.

This is an Airport?

With morning came a slight red wine headache. But there was good news. The storm of the night before was long gone, the sun was bright and hot, and the humidity was back with a vengeance.

A red taxi took us out of Samara to Cordillo Beach, ten minutes down the road. On the right was the beach, fringed by palms. The green Pacific sparkled and surged against a reef. On the left was a field surrounded by jungle, and there was a hut with a tin roof beside the road.

The taxi stopped and the driver unloaded our pile of bags. The taxi drove away.

I looked around. Already the temperature was well into the thirties. The road was deserted. The beach on the other side of the road was deserted. The field was deserted except for a turkey vulture, which was gliding overhead.

I examined the field. In the long grass, twin tracks pointed towards a mountain.

"I think this is the airport," I said. "The hut is the terminal and the field is the runway."

Pat inspected the field balefully. "It's a dirt runway with potholes, but at least it's short," she said.

"Is it too late to catch the bus?" I said.

It was.

While we waited, a few more turkey vultures took off and landed on the runway.

Eventually a woman walked out of the jungle pulling a wire cart. She had a cell phone and a radio transmitter. In the cart were an orange traffic cone and a fire extinguisher. She looked at our tickets and looked at the sky and went silently back into the jungle.

The departure lounge was a square of shade thrown by the hut. Pat and I stood there and sweated and waited and glanced occasionally at the empty blue sky.

Three or four other passengers showed up. The woman came back out of the jungle, put on a bright red vest and carefully placed the traffic cone from her wire cart near our luggage. While she did those things, I wondered if the fire extinguisher in the cart was used often.

Suddenly Pat said, "Look out!"

And the plane roared in, barely missing the power lines by the road, thumped down in a swirl of dust and blue smoke, and taxied to the end of the track. It turned and came back and rocked to a halt, and the engines shut down and the propellers stopped. The plane seemed to wheeze in gratitude.

When the blue smoke cleared, we were able to see the plane was painted blue and white and wasn't new. It would hold maybe twelve people. And maybe three kilos of luggage.

The pilot and co-pilot were calm and smartly dressed. They looked at our heap of baggage. They shrugged and loaded it. They maintained their look of calm.

I regarded the little plane, the heavy cargo of baggage, and the mountain at the end of the short runway.

"I like the idea the co-pilot is a woman," Pat said.

"I like the idea of getting the bus," I said.

We boarded and buckled up. The interior was like a sauna. It was also narrow and crowded, and the windows were fogged with age. The pilots took their seats and the engines fired up.

The cabin was loud with engine noise and vibration.

The plane bounced and rattled as it taxied towards the mountain. It turned and faced the ocean.

I was relieved. We wouldn't crash into the mountain. Instead we'd crash into the sea, where sharks would feast on our body parts.

I thought I saw the co-pilot gripping a crucifix. Then the plane rumbled forward, gained speed, and lifted into the air, missing the power lines by maybe a meter.

Blue Death Machine

We flew over the Nicoya Peninsula and *Golfo* Nicoya. The green ocean was snowy white where it shattered against the rocky coastline, and the interior mountains rose like a green fortress against the sky. We flew over the town of Miramar and Hotel Vista Golfo, where our trip had begun. We avoided hitting the mountains or splashing into the Pacific.

Descending out of a vast white cloud, San Jose was suddenly below us. The little plane landed safely.

I strode up to the rental car counter and ordered a four-wheel drive in case we got involved with potholes. The four-wheel drive turned out to be a neon-blue Suzuki.

Pat had the map and I had the wheel. Somehow we wobbled our way out of the airport and onto the Transylvania Highway, or maybe it was the Trans-America Highway.

The blue Suzuki bounced and shook, and when it wasn't bouncing and shaking it shuddered. Pat's knuckles were white where she gripped the dash.

"Is it safe to be driving this fast?" she said.

"I'm only doing eighty kph," I replied. I was busy trying to control the steering wheel.

Buses, trucks, and cars were passing us in a blur of speed.

"Remind me never to rent another Costa Rican Suzuki," I said, careening through the turnoff to Grecia on two wheels at sixty kilometers an hour.

"Try to stay out of the ditch," Pat said helpfully.

"Yes, dear," I said.

Grecia was a sprawling town on a mountain slope, its center a red Roman Catholic cathedral with a wide plaza planted with grass and shade trees. The streets were narrow, many of them one way, and all of them lined with parked cars.

But I wasn't looking at the sights. I was fighting for control of the car. Marlene's home was high up, on the outskirts, in a residential area.

Marlene's home was more than a home. Marlene's home was an estate. Ten acres, a couple of houses not including the two bed-and-breakfast rooms, a coffee plantation, plus fruit and citrus orchards, a gate, and a high surrounding wall. Not to mention the flowing creek through dark jungle forming a series of waterfalls, two friendly dogs, a nervous cat, and two energetic kids, Daniela and David.

Not only did Marlene serve us breakfast, but she also made sure Pat got a real estate tour. Marlene had enough energy to power a small city.

We looked at every house for sale in Grecia and in Atenas: big ones, little ones, and medium-size ones. Pat wanted to buy several of them, but held off. For now. We visited San Jose. We sat around a crackling fire in Marlene's living room while rain crashed on the roof of her home.

Up, Up, and Away

On Monday we drove safely to the airport, turned in the blue death machine, and boarded an American Airlines jet for home.

As the green mountains fell away below the wing and the plane banked and turned north, Pat said, "They certainly have some good deals on real estate in Costa Rica."

"Especially the swampland," I said, knowing where she was going with this: pitch number 1,500 for a house in Costa Rica. But I was prepared. She could pitch all she wanted; I wasn't going to weaken. I was going to be strong, yes I was.

"What a wonderful country, and seeing it by bus was a real adventure."

"I hated the buses," I countered.

"And the zip lines were exhilarating," she said.

"The zip lines almost killed me."

"And the climate was perfect."

"I got heat rash," I said.

"And remember the monkey," Pat said, laughing.

"You mean the man-eating gorilla."

"You were very brave," she purred. "With the gorilla."

"I was?" I said, sitting a little straighter in my seat.

"My hero," Pat said, giving my arm a squeeze.

I nodded and squeezed her right back. We were smiling at each other. The way this was going, I figured we'd be joining the mile-high club in another five minutes.

"So," Pat said, very softly, "we should buy a place and move there, right?"

"Well," I said, thinking why spoil the mile-high possibility, "we could come back for vacation next year and talk about it."

"I already booked the tickets," she said, grinning.

And, once again, I knew I'd been had.

* * *

Pat's Diet

It's the New Year. Okay, it's March already, and the year isn't new; it's slightly used, but it's almost new.

Anyway, the New Year. On the eve of which I made my annual resolutions; at the top of the short list was: 1) Lose some weight.

After two months of accomplishing very little in the weight reduction department, Pat took over. She went to Save-On and bought $300 worth of groceries. Thankfully, she has a small car. Pat doesn't shop with a budget in mind. Pat shops until her sports car is full.

She trundled the load from the parking garage, up the elevator, to our kitchen, puffing only slightly from the exertion. She began to unpack some of the hundred or so plastic shopping bags.

"I don't see any potato chips," I said, watching from a safe distance. When Pat's in the kitchen it's best to stay clear.

"No potato chips," Pat agreed.

"I don't see any brownies, either," I said.

"Nope," Pat replied.

"What I see is a lot of yogurt, salad stuff, and Lean Cuisine frozen dinners," I said, growing just a little concerned.

"We're on a diet," Pat said. She said it exactly like she was condemning me to life in prison, no chance of parole.

This has been a problem in our marriage for years. No, not the prison thing. Although, sometimes…never mind. I better not go there.

Dieting. That's the problem.

When Pat goes on a diet, we both go on a diet. No, it's not fair. And no, there's nothing I can do about it.

Pat filled the freezer with stacks of Lean Cuisine.

"Here's the deal," she explained. "For breakfast, one-third of a cup of cereal. At coffee break, yogurt. Lunch is a salad. Dinner is Lean Cuisine."

"There's no such thing as one-third of a cup of cereal," I said. "Is there?"

"My friend Dennis lost fifty pounds in two weeks on this diet," Pat said.

"Is he still alive?" I asked, horrified.

"Barely," Pat admitted. "But at least he's *thin*!"

All that happened just a couple of days ago.

On the first day of Pat's diet, I fell off the wagon just after seven o'clock in the morning. I was seduced by a muffin, which I ate in the office lunchroom. I ate five pounds of lettuce for lunch to compensate. I was pretty sure that five pounds of lettuce would counter the ill effects of one muffin.

Pat was working late that first diet day—or so she claimed—and was not yet home at dinnertime. (If I smelled french fries on her breath when she got home, I would kill her. Or at least give her a nasty glance.) What I had for dinner, alone, was a Lean Cuisine. My first.

It came in a little black plastic tray. It was called, I think, Oriental Stir Fry. Five minutes in the microwave and it sort of came to a boil. Maybe I should've read the instructions, but, hey, I felt creative.

I placed the plastic dish on the table and peeled off the cellophane.

Steam rose in a cloud. The dinner consisted mainly of a scorched puddle of something that might've, in a former life, been gravy.

"Gee," I said to the cat. "This won't take long to eat."

The cat remained silent.

The dinner was gone in three spoonfuls. Yes, three.

"Great," I said. "I feel thinner already."

The cat went to her cat dish. What was in her cat dish was more appetizing than Lean Cuisine. And a bigger portion.

An hour went by.

I began to grow dizzy from hunger. I looked at the clock. Only seven.

"If I go to bed now," I said to the cat, "I may be able to avoid driving to Wendy's in a coma and ordering a triple burger with cheese and biggie fries."

But the coma was setting in fast. I was reaching for the car keys when Pat walked in.

"You don't look so good," she said.

"I might be slipping into a coma," I said. "But I feel way thinner. I think I may have lost some weight."

Pat gave me that up-and-down look. It's the look she gives boaters when their boat fails the Coast Guard safety check.

"I don't think I need to diet anymore," I said. "I'm happy with the new, thinner me. I'm going to Wendy's to celebrate."

Pat narrowed her eyes.

"Just kidding," I added, surreptitiously replacing my car keys on the counter.

Pat busied herself building a salad.

I went back to the computer and the keyboard, my empty stomach making odd noises.

Now it was seven thirty. I took comfort that I was allowed a snack later. The snack being approximately one spoonful of yogurt.

Maybe I'd use a smaller spoon, make it last longer...

* * *

Postcards from a Galaxy (Costa Rica) Far, Far Away (1)

The Beginning

I could tell you about the weather—eighty degrees (our thermometer refuses to speak Celsius) in the shade. Or I could tell you about the view from our deck out over the jungle to the infinite Pacific Ocean. Or about how the sparkling blue swimming pool is surrounded by banana trees, hibiscus plants, and the arched fronds of coconut palms. But no, I won't.

I could tell you about the tiny black hummingbird I discovered on our deck one morning, lying on its side on the tile floor. I thought it might be dead. When I squatted beside it for a closer look, it blinked at me and seemed to say, "Please don't touch me. I'll be OK in a minute." And in a moment the little bundle of feathers righted itself and flew away. And I thought it could be an omen of good things to come: that this trip would be a good one, maybe a great one. But no, I won't tell you about that, either.

The next morning there was another omen, which caused some reconsideration on the good trip/great trip idea and opened up the grim possibility of bad trip/terrible trip.

Bad and terrible are much more interesting than good and great. Right? So that's what I'll tell you about: the bad and terrible thing.

It happened in the kitchen, a place into which I should never be allowed to trespass.

I was preparing my breakfast. Into the blender went a few chunks of pineapple, some strawberries, a scoop of Vega the Whole Food Health Optimizer, and a glass of tap water. The tap water is OK to drink here, which is good even if it sometimes seems slightly bleach flavored.

Pat, always supervising, said, "It looks crooked."

Meaning the blender's various parts.

I looked, shrugged, said, "It's fine." And pressed the blend button.

But no, it wasn't fine.

It was crooked.

It blew up.

It barfed all over the counter, down the cupboard doors, onto the tile floor.

Green goo in a spreading puddle, with micro bits of pineapple and strawberry. Very sticky.

Yuck.

"I told you," Pat said, turning away.

I was pretty sure she was smirking, but I was too busy tearing off sheets of paper towel to notice.

So that was omen number two.

Which is it going to be then? Good trip/great trip, or bad trip/terrible trip?

Stay tuned.

* * *

Postcards from a Galaxy (Costa Tica) Far, Far Away (2)

I've Got a Scorpion in My Swimming Trunks

Okay, where was I? Oh yeah, Costa Rica. The beaches are great, the nearby howler monkeys howl a lot, the weather is perfect, and except for the flu I'm doing fine, thanks.

Yeah, the flu. If I was a dog, you'd shoot me I'm so sick.

Anyway, what else could go wrong? First, the blender blew up. Now the flu.

What next?

Ouch! Something just bit me. Really. Inside my bathing suit, on the thigh, right now while I'm writing this.

Oh my God!

I've been stung by a scorpion.

Gotta go. More later.

Maybe…

* * *

Postcards from a Galaxy (Costa Rica) Far, Far Away (3)

That Was Close

There I was, naked, facing a deadly enemy.

I gave my swimming trunks, which I'd just whipped off my body, a panicky shake, and out popped three inches of wriggling death.

It landed in my chest hair near my throat.

There may be nothing worse than being terrified while nude, when every precious body part is so pathetically exposed.

I knocked the scorpion to the floor, grabbed a broom and swept it out the door onto the outside deck, where Pat was in her hammock, enjoying the soft ocean breeze.

"That thing bit me and I'm dying," I said, brandishing the broom. I might have been screaming.

"Put some clothes on," Pat said. "You'll offend the neighbors."

So I did. I almost always obey my wife.

"Now kill it," she said.

I hammered it maybe twenty-seven times with the broom. I was red in the face, gasping with effort, trembling with adrenaline, and shaking with fear, which is not easy to do simultaneously.

But the scorpion just lay there wriggling.

"Okay, you bastard," I said. "I'm already a dead man but I'm taking you with me!" I might have been screaming again.

And I snatched up Pat's nearby sandal and turned the scorpion into a red Slurpee.

"Jeez," Pat said. "Not my sandal. Yuck. What a mess."

"Should we call an ambulance or is it too late for that?" I said.

"Too late for the bug, anyway," Pat said.

"Not the bug; the ambulance would be for me," I said. "And, hey, that thing was no bug. That thing was a poisonous scorpion monster killer thing."

"Oh, stop it," Pat said. "Scorpion bites are no big deal. You'll be fine." And she turned over to tan on her other side.

And that's the story about the scorpion sting.

Tomorrow, however, promised another disaster: the decline of the upper-downer.

Details to follow.

* * *

Postcards from a Galaxy (Costa Rica) Far, Far Away (4)

Decline of the Upper-Downer

When we booked the Costa Rica trip, Pat was looking forward to many happy moments.

One of her favorite moments would be regaling total strangers about Coast Guard rescues. Plus, she'd be able to jump all over my mistakes and blunders for three straight months. As her exclusive companion each and every day, and with no golf courses in which to hide, I could be trammeled at will. Her evil grin of anticipation sent chills up my spine.

But what she was most excited about, most looking forward to, and what she dreamed about for months was being aboard her upper-downer, reading her Kindle, sipping a cold drink while floating in the glimmering blue swimming pool.

Last visit to Costa Rica, when what Pat was floating on was an ordinary air mattress, a British lady called it an "upper-downer," never having seen one before. In a pool, with someone lying prone on it while reading a trashy novel and slurping a can of diet Cola, nope, doesn't happen in Britain, I guess.

Thus was born the upper-downer.

We shopped for just the right one. Found it at Costco. This thing was way better then a flat mattress. This new upper-downer had all the comforts of home. There was a comfortable headrest and back support, and a sort-of foot stool for the feet. Not to mention a drink holder.

Very posh.

And never mind the price. When it comes to Pat's comfort, no price is too high.

Into the suitcase it went, taking up more than its fair share of space.

Pat flung some of my stuff out of the suitcase and over her shoulder onto the floor to make room.

"You don't need all this stuff," she said. "One T-shirt and one pair of shorts is all you need."

Pat is always in charge of packing for these trips. Finally the upper-downer was crammed in, and off we went.

It passed its first test on day one at the pool. Pat rode the pool wave-lets proudly while drinking diet ginger ale and reading her Kindle with the special waterproof cover. The back rest gave critical support where it was needed, and the foot rest made everything wonderfully comfy.

Pat was the envy of the heavy drinking couple from Denver, the husband puffing on a cigar which smelled not unlike burning tires. The couple from Las Vegas were also impressed, the wife wearing a very skimpy black bikini. Not that I noticed.

On day two of the upper-downer's career, more success; the pool boy Oscar, was caught jealously glancing at Pat's apparatus.

But the next afternoon, disaster lurked.

I was at poolside fighting off the ever-present threat of tropical dehydration by drinking cold beer. Luckily there was lots of cold beer in case widespread dehydration broke out. I watched as Pat climbed aboard the upper-downer.

Getting on one of those things isn't always a graceful moment. With a small tsunami or two, Pat heaved herself onto the upper-downer. Dutifully I handed her the ginger ale and the protected Kindle and off she sailed, looking very elegant in her new designer shades.

"Gee," I said to myself. I almost always talk to myself when I'm drinking beer. "Either Pat is putting on weight, or…"

I was noticing the lack of freeboard between the wavelets and Pat's posterior.

"…the upper-downer is sinking."

It turned out it was.

Sinking.

Later, after the ginger ale, designer sunglasses, and Kindle had been rescued and Pat was safely ashore, she examined the deflated toy carefully.

Her first thought was, it was my fault. She always thinks it's my fault.

"Did you step on it, or drag it carelessly across the concrete?" she said, glaring at me.

"No," I said. "I've been busy with dehydration."

She looked around. We were alone. There was no one else available to blame.

"Maybe the raccoons got it," she said, scowling. There had been raccoon sightings the previous night. "Or maybe the local cotimundi chomped it." The cotimundi is like a raccoon but with a longer snout.

Pat wouldn't admit the damage might have been due to poor workmanship.

Anyway, the next day we hired a cab and drove to the local gas station for a patch repair kit. We drove through a swirl of dust, and the taxi driver, who looked a bit like the late comedian George Carlin, said, grinning, "We call this stuff hot snow." Meaning the dust. Which I thought was funny. But Pat was scowling and in no mood for humor and wouldn't be in any mood for anything until the upper-downer was fixed.

The glue was spread, the patch applied.

And now, as I type this, she is down in the pool either happily afloat or grumpily sinking.

Please excuse me while I go down to see which it is.

I'll let you know.

* * *

Postcards from a Galaxy (Costa Rica) Far, Far Away (5)

Attack of the Turkey Vultures, Sort Of

They dress like funeral directors.

They *are* funeral directors: avian funeral directors.

They hang out in tree branches, or on the beach. You see them in the sky, like black kites. They ride the thermal air currents, forever circling, searching for carrion. They're looking for a buzzard buffet of dead, rotting meat, road kill, jungle kill, anything that attracts flies.

Every time I go down to the swimming pool and lurch into the water, trying not to swallow chlorine through my nose, there they are.

Those black kites, mini Grim Reapers, sweeping in low overhead, like spy planes, checking me out with their beady little eyes.

I'm not ready for the meat wagon just yet, am I?

When I'm on the beach or walking along the road, they ignore me. But when I'm in the pool, even when it's the shallow end, there they are: waiting. Ebony harbingers of death.

Maybe they recognize my vulnerability.

Whatever kind of water I'm in, I don't swim, I wallow. My version of the dog paddle can actually make nearby fish laugh. I always manage to swallow some, usually through my sinuses. It's very painful, by the way, sucking water through your sinuses, especially salt water.

Water hates me. Every time I'm in it, it tries to kill me: lakes, rivers, oceans, swimming pools. The wet stuff is my enemy. Here in Costa Rica the vultures are playing the waiting game. It's only a matter of time.

Which is why, lately, I've spent most afternoons sweating it out in a lounge chair safely away from the refreshing temptation of the pool. The vultures will have to bide their time. I'm not ready yet.

I have beer to drink, Canucks' games to watch, pension checks to cash. I have a full life ahead of me, and a wife who would miss me terribly if she had no one to nag.

The attack of the turkey vultures will just have to wait.

* * *

Postcards from a Galaxy (Costa Rica) Far, Far Away (6)

My, What Big Teeth You Have!

There's a war going on down here and I am cannon fodder.

It's me versus the bugs.

I have been bitten, stung, poked, tweaked, and pricked. Yes, pricked. And gnawed upon.

I have the welts, swellings, bumps, and lumps to prove it.

I am a banquet for the insect world.

My inoffensive defensive arsenal includes a can of Deep Woods Off, with 25 percent DEET. I also have a stick of After Bite, the Itch Eraser. I have sprayed and sprayed. I have even considered drinking the stuff. I think Costa Rican bugs actually like Deep Woods Off. They use it as an appetizer.

Each morning I awake to new itches, new puffiness, new and mysterious nests of inflammation.

All this from just sitting outside on our balcony.

The real war, though, was about to begin.

"We should check out the real jungle," Pat said. "Hike among the mangroves, view the famous Guanacaste, and see the teeth of the crocodile."

"Crocodile teeth?" I said, nervously.

"The lagarto tree," she said. "It has big spikes shaped like crocodile teeth."

"Are there bugs?" I said.

"Maybe," she said.

We paid six bucks each and descended into the Reserva Biologica Nosara. The only positive thing about the whole affair was, at the end of the hike was a bar stocked with beer. The day suddenly turned dark. What made it dark was the overhead canopy of trees. That, and the massing clouds of bugs. Dinner was about to be served, and I was on the menu.

The jungle reminded me of Vietnam war movies. I was like the Americans, the bugs the Viet Cong.

I lost. They won.

Two hours later, when I staggered dizzily into the Sunset Bar of the Lagarto Lodge minus several liters of blood, I was grateful to be alive. I celebrated my survival with two quick Bavarian dark beers.

Pat was happy about all those crocodile teeth, and she was totally free of bug bites. She chose a table with a panoramic view of jungle, beach, and shimmering ocean.

"What a wonderful place!" she said.

And I said, sweaty and itchy and cranky from a platoon of fresh bites, "Pass the napalm, please."

I think she thought I was kidding.

* * *

Postcards from a Galaxy (Costa Rica) Far, Far Away (7)

Shake, Rattle, and Roll

The phone rang. It was Heidi, from Alamo car rental.

"It's not that your car delivery is late," she said. "It's just that it fell into a hole and the driver will be there as soon as he gets it out."

No surprise there. Costa Rica roads are mostly holes laced together with dust and rocks.

When the Suzuki Jimny arrived ten minutes later, the young Tico said, grinning, "It's an excellent four-wheel drive. It got me out of a really big hole."

"Excellent" is a word not often used in the same sentence as "Suzuki Jimny."

The Jimny reminded me of those bumper car rides at fairgrounds. Sort of like toys, built for kids, but made for adults. But it was cheap and the country was full of them. It was either that or a Daihatsu BeGo. We flipped a coin, chose the Jimny, and rented it for a month, hoping it would hold together that long.

"Let's drive to Samara for old times' sake," Pat said.

Samara was a small town only a few kilometers down the coast. We'd enjoyed several days stay there on our first tour of Costa Rica, several years ago. It has a palm-tree-lined beach, lovely, sparkling green water, and brilliant white breakers. It was twenty-seven klicks away. Twenty-seven klicks of unpaved road, a good initial test for our four-wheel drive.

So we packed up and left in a swirl of dust.

For the entire journey, I never took it out of second gear. Well, maybe I was in third a few times, but not for long. That's how bad, and slow, the road was.

It was narrow and twisting, with many blind corners and hills. There were bridges over creeks and rivers, but they were narrow and seemed temporary, as if the next monsoon would send them tumbling downstream. Trees and brush grew tight against the road. There were deep potholes, rugged washboard, and an assortment of rocks capable of busting axles and other important undercarriage stuff.

And always there was dust; choking, blinding, hot brown dust.

The Jimny rattled and banged and went clunk. But it kept going.

I kept looking around, checking that the doors hadn't fallen off.

Pat, hanging on tightly, and trying to be helpful, kept screaming things like, "WATCH OUT FOR THE CHICKEN!"

And, "WATCH OUT FOR THE DOG!"

And, "WATCH OUT FOR THE FARMER WALKING DOWN THE MIDDLE OF THE ROAD!"

When I passed a forty-foot container truck amid so much dust we couldn't see past the Jimny's engine hood, and it's a really short engine hood, Pat was suddenly quiet. I think, for the first time in years, she was praying.

Afterward, when Pat found her voice again, she continued with the, "WATCH OUT FOR THE STALLED CAR! WATCH OUT FOR THE GIRL ON A BICYCLE! WATCH OUT FOR THAT BIG HOLE!"

Only a couple of times did a bus, or a big truck, come barreling around a hairpin curve in our lane. We avoided those, and avoided falling into bottomless sink holes, and avoided also migrating dogs and chickens. We pulled safely into Samara an hour later, dusty, sweaty, and alive.

We had lunch at an outdoor soda (café) on the beach. We had to step around sleeping dogs to reach our table. Then we had to fight off buzzing flies while we ate. The lovely ocean breeze picked up pellets of sand and flung them into my fish filet.

"I think these are the very same mangy dogs and the very same disease-carrying flies that were here last time," I said.

"It's good to know some things never change," Pat said, sipping her Coke Light through a soggy straw.

On the return trip there was more dust and—get this—an actual, real-life cattle stampede. Yes, really, a cattle stampede, a Brahma cattle stampede—you know, those BIG ones—all over both sides of the road, a hundred of 'em, surrounding the little Jimny, running and shitting and having a great time while scaring the, well, shit out of us.

It was a memorable sight, sitting in the little Jimny, staring up, way up, at a defecating cow anus.

And there was Pat, winding down the window, thrusting out the camera, click, click, and click.

"Don't get shit on the camera," I said, alarmed. "And roll up the window before they shit in it."

But, miraculously we escaped, undented and unshitted upon.

There were wayward roosters, vagrant horses, and suicidal dogs. There were reckless ATVs and thundering trucks and swarms of other Suzuki's and Daihatsu's and Hyundai's.

In the end, I think the dust was a good thing. Within the thick clouds of it, we really couldn't appreciate the kind of danger that surrounded us.

So, with the first driving adventure successfully concluded, Pat, reading the guide book, said, "Let's drive to Arenal. It's an active volcano and it's only a four hour drive away."

"An *active* volcano?" I said.

"Yes, with flowing molten lava and everything."

"Uh…"

"And the roads are paved. You know, like real asphalt."

"I'm in," I said.

Real asphalt and a real, live, active volcano, with molten lava. Mount Arenal, here we come!

Life just couldn't get any better. Could it?

* * *

Postcards from a Galaxy (Costa Rica) Far, Far Away (8)

Washout!

The sign on the office door read "Massage, Taxidermy & Discount Psychology."

Being retired, I needed a discount, and being really depressed, I needed some shrink work done. It wasn't my idea. It was Pat's idea. I always do what Pat wants. So here I was, lying comfortably on the couch of Dr. Nogales Tijuana Juarez. He had thick glasses and a black hairbrush moustache.

"Call me TJ for short," said the doctor, creating an instant bond between patient and therapist.

"Since returning from the Arenal region yesterday I've been extremely depressed," I said.

"Si," he said. "Talk to me, Juan. Talk to me."

"We went there with great expectations," I said. "All it did was rain. We left early. I may have to kill myself."

"Well, if you really must, for an extra fifty bucks I can lend you a pistol. But first, give me some details."

I gave him some details.

I told him about the drive along the lake. About the potholed pavement, about how the deep holes were full of water made red by the red mud. I explained about how when the car hit them hard, my fillings fell right out of my molars.

I mentioned the wind whipping the lake into frothy whitecaps and how the low clouds scudded across the sky. I described how the rain came in bursts, like we were being machine gunned. The jungle grew tall, right to the edge of the road, and sometimes on tight corners trucks would have a wheel or two in my lane. I told the good doctor about how my hands ached from their tight grip on the steering wheel.

I whined about the dampness in our cabin, how the towels and bed sheets were damp and the air was damp and cool. No blue sky, no sun, for forty-eight hours, I said. The rain was torrential and of hurricane force and so loud it was deafening. But the jungle was green and lush, and the grounds of the Arenal Observatory Lodge, where we stayed, were thick with tropical plants and exotic bushes. Albeit dripping with moisture, all of it.

The power went out one night, I told him, and our cabin was as black as a bat cave for several hours. I could barely feel my way to the bathroom. And at night, lately, my bladder seems to want to visit the bathroom a lot, lights or no lights.

And at dinner in the restaurant, even with the power on, it was dark, with candlelit tables little islands of murkiness in what might as well have been a coal mine a mile below the earth's surface.

"If the candle on our table burns out," I remember saying to Pat, "we'll never find our way out of here."

However, the candle flame soldiered on until the meal was finished. Then we drove down the steep hill half a mile to our cabin in a fierce blast of rain and wind.

From the rain-soaked observation deck at the main lodge during the day, all we could see was cloud, I explained to the doctor: drifting cloud, curtains of cloud, gauzelike cloud, and plain ordinary cloud. If there was a volcano, 1,600 meters of one, it was just a rumor as far as we were concerned.

"Doc," I said, wrapping up, "if I'd wanted rain and cloud I would've stayed in Vancouver."

Dr. TJ for short steepled his fingers while he contemplated me through his Coke-bottle glasses.

"There is only one solution for you," he said. "There is only one thing that will allow you to throw off this cloak of depression and give you back your normal life."

He scribbled out a prescription and thrust it at me.

"Take six of these daily," he said, "And if you are not feeling better in a week, come back and I will lend you my pistol."

I got to my feet and looked at the prescription.

"*Gracias*, doctor," I said, grinning.

The prescription read,

"Imperial, *la cerveza de Costa Rica*." (Beer, in other words.)

I was feeling better already.

* * *

Postcards from a Galaxy (Costa Rica) Far, Far Away (9)

Road Trip, Part One

Bored with circumnavigating the pool in her upper-downer, Pat decided we needed a change of scenery.

"We'll go up to Playa Del Coco," Pat said, "take advantage of that stay-three-nights-for-free offer and maybe buy a condo."

"Buy a condo?" I said.

"Just kidding," Pat said. "But if it's nice maybe we'll rent there next year. Now go phone Edgar and set it up while I finish packing."

"Yessir," I said.

Edgar was a Realtor who'd been recommended to us by some friends back in British Columbia.

"I'm not selling real estate anymore," Edgar said from his cell phone, which sounded like it was being run over by a lawnmower.

I ended up talking to the new guy in the office, James.

"Great, super, wonderful," James said. "We're busy but come on up, we'll find a place for you to stay, no problem. I got a nice two-bedroom, right beside those friends of yours who bought that unit off Edgar last year. You'll love it."

So we saddled up the Jimny and headed out, looking forward to a pleasant three days.

I forgot about the roads. So the pleasant part didn't last very long.

The first thirty-five minutes of the trip were unpaved and therefore dusty, bumpy, and lumpy. Then there was pavement. There were no center lines, passing lanes, or shoulders, but by God it was pavement.

We drove for three hours. The Nicoya Peninsula is mostly cattle country, with big ranches spread over broad, flat valleys. Occasionally there were mango orchards or fields growing sugar cane, but mostly there were Brahma cattle, and sometimes cowboys on horseback tending them. The surrounding hills were still green from the rainy season. It's beautiful country, except for the driving part.

Fortunately on this day, no speeding trucks squashed us, no rusty bridges collapsed under us, and we ran over no dogs, horses, or wayward chickens. And the cattle stayed where cattle are supposed to stay. Except for the fact that my eyes were glazed from avoiding death every six minutes or so, my fingers were welded to the steering wheel, and my nerves were fluttering like butterflies, we arrived in good shape.

"Turn off the highway here," said the navigator.

Playa Del Coco was teeming with pedestrians, bicycles, trucks, cars, buses, and golf carts. Yes, golf carts, and not a fairway within miles. Main Street was clogged with T-shirt vendors, restaurants, and bars. The place had lots of energy, lots of crap to buy, and lots and lots of touristas. Of course, it also had a beach, but we couldn't see it just yet.

First, we'd settle into our pleasant, free condo, then we would deploy to the beach.

There were acres and acres of condos jammed together, with narrow, winding streets and now and then a patch of grass. We drove by Tropical Dreams, one of the nicer units and where we hoped to stay. Of course, as we've all learned by now, things don't always go as planned.

The girl, Ana, in the real estate office said, "James isn't here right now."

This should have been the first warning signal of uh-oh, now what. But I was too busy being overwhelmed to think about uh-oh, now what.

Ana was slender and pretty, with flashing brown eyes, plus she was wearing a very snug polo shirt.

"I'm here to buy a condo," I said, reaching for my wallet.

"No," Pat said. "You are not. And stop leering."

"Right," I said. I often get confused when confronted with attractive young women.

Ana checked her file. She was seated behind a desk. I got busy again, this time trying very hard not to peek down the polo shirt.

"There's been a mix up," Ana said, frowning.

"Oh, great," Pat fumed.

"The two-bedroom in Tropical Dreams James promised you is not available," Ana said. "But we have a nice one-bedroom in Forest Green, right across the street. Come, I will show it to you," she said, with a brilliant smile. She grabbed some keys and headed out.

I noticed, following her, that she had a spectacular, er, bottom, but I wasn't allowed to enjoy it for long.

"You get the car, I'll follow what's-her-name," Pat said.

I drove the car across the street and parked in Forest Green's gravel parking lot. I couldn't help but notice that the Forest Green building was, well, very green.

I had never before seen exactly that shade of bright green, man-made or natural. It hurt my eyes. I put on my sunglasses. It still hurt my eyes.

When I climbed the narrow stairs to room six, Pat and Ana were inside. The room was dim and small and smelled moldy in a hundred different ways. The bed was narrow and lumpy, and it looked like the kitchen had been cleaned fairly recently but maybe the cleaning staff had been visually impaired. Pat was standing there with her arms folded, looking grim. Ana looked sheepish.

I glanced quickly around the room. I sensed cockroaches lurking.

"We can't stay here," I said.

"Right choice," Pat said.

And we left.

The Jimny had heated up to approximately nine million degrees. Pat, after reminding me it would be better to park in the shade next time, pulled out her map.

"We'll go south to Tamarindo, the famous beach and high-end resort center, and find a hotel for the night" she said.

"OK," I said.

I was watching Ana return to her office. Man, those shorts were tight.

Pat caught me looking.

I put the Jimny in gear.

"Is it hot in here, or is it just me?" I said.

And I drove quickly away, knowing that on the journey's next leg Pat would find a way to punish me for my brief affair with Ana.

The punishment will be painfully unveiled shortly.

* * *

Postcards from a Galaxy (Costa Rica) Far, Far Away (10)

Road Trip, the Sequel

We left Playa Del Coco in a huff. Well, not really in a huff. We were in the Jimny. I was driving, Pat was navigating.

Sure, I had left Ana behind—whoops, maybe I better not mention Ana's behind again. I'm in enough trouble as it is.

Try again.

Sure, I had left the real estate office behind, and with it the opportunity to stay overnight for free, and, sure, it was early afternoon and the sun was blazing hot, but the good news was we were traveling on smooth pavement. I was happy. I love pavement.

My happiness came to an abrupt end a moment later.

We arrived at a fork in the road: to the left, nice, smooth asphalt; on the right, the road to hell was waiting, dirt and dust, ruts and rocks.

"Turn right," Pat said, with a small but evil grin. "We'll take the shortcut."

Thus my punishment for ogling Ana had begun.

"But it's kind of risky-looking," I said. "What if we get lost?"

"I have a map, we can't get lost," Pat said. Pat loved dirt roads and shortcuts and exploring the more hair-raising bits of Costa Rica.

"Besides," she added, "there's a golf course out there somewhere, and you might like to visit it."

"Okay," I said doubtfully. After all, what kind of golf course would be located a million miles away from anywhere pleasant?

On the other hand, maybe the golf course had hotel suites for rent, fancy ones, with air conditioning and mini bars in the rooms.

"Forward, ho!" I said.

But the golf course didn't have hotel suites for rent.

What the Papagayo Golf and Country Club did have was a tethered horse acting as the groundskeeper, grazing near the driving range. It also had a clubhouse, a restaurant, a bar, and an infinity swimming pool. It had everything but golfers, diners, drinkers, and swimmers. It was deserted, in other words.

Well, not quite deserted. There was a very enthusiastic young guy on duty. Other than the grazing horse, he was the only living thing I'd seen for miles, except for cattle and vultures. He was so lonely for a moment there I thought he might hug me. Fortunately for both of us, he didn't.

It was ninety-five bucks for a round, including golf cart. And it was hot enough to melt steel at two in the afternoon, and we had many kilometers of dirt road to explore. Or Pat did, and I was her driver, and Pat hated golf, so we broke the young guy's heart and abandoned him.

On the unpaved road to hell, I mean to Tamarindo, the Jimny bucked and heaved and sent clouds of dust heavenward. I bucked and heaved and sent a few curses heavenward. Pat bucked and heaved and smiled heavenward. She was in her element, enjoying the adventure, happily ignoring the damage to her kidneys and spleen caused by the rugged terrain. There were cows to see, and horses, and distant green hills lifting into puffy white clouds, blue sky, and flat pastureland all around.

Above us, ever hopeful and endlessly riding the thermal air currents, the vultures circled, just in case we had a flat tire or ran out of gas or something.

But the gas tank contained plenty of fuel, the tires remained firm, and the black vultures kept their distance. Things were starting to go our way, right up until we got lost.

The road just sort of petered out in the middle of San Blas, a village boasting two stop signs, a nice collection of chickens, and a few shade trees. The sun beat down. The air was still. San Blas probably hadn't seen a car drive through since last fall. There were no road signs, and the road forked. Now what?

In the nearby shade, which was black as night, three men with machetes lounged, giving us a predatory once-over.

I rolled down my window and hollered, "Filadephia, por favor?" Filadephia was the next town on the map. (And, yes, it's spelled funny.)

One of the hombres tipped his machete to the east.

"Gracias!" I shouted, and floored it. Gravel shot out from under the tires, dust exploded, and we were gone.

"Who says men never ask for directions?" I said to Patricia.

Eventually we found a paved road and arrived in Tamarindo hot, tired, and in desperate need of accommodations.

Tamarindo's main street was narrow, maybe a lane and a half wide, and crammed with cars, motorbikes, taxis, and wandering tourists. There was no ocean view. Instead the view was plugged with one- and two-story bars, restaurants, and dingy surfboard rental shops.

The first couple of hotels I tried were full. I bucked the congealed traffic, cut off a taxi or two, bullied an ATV aside—none of those things were easy to do in an underpowered Jimny—and finally found a place that would accept our stay. The room was small, with two single beds and, wow, air conditioning. The twin beds were probably a good thing, as I was still suffering Ana backlash from Patricia, who really knows how to hold a grudge.

OK, I thought. I'll take Pat out for a nice dinner, soften her mood, and then maybe later we could push those two hotel beds together.

After a long and treacherous walk over broken sidewalks, tilted driveways, and crumbling pavement, I chose a nice dark bar and restaurant. But every bar and restaurant in the country is dark. It must be an anti-light bulb conspiracy thing.

I was carrying, in the backpack, through mobs of sweaty people in ninety-degree heat, everything we owned. We didn't trust the thin lock on the flimsy hotel room door. The backpack weighed almost as much as I did.

I collapsed into a chair. Through the murk of the bar I could see a faint gleam of ocean and beach off in the distance.

"I'll have a Witch's Tit," Pat said to the waiter.

"The Witch's what?" I said.

"Tit," Pat said.

"Tit?" I said.

"You want a what, senor?" said the waiter.

"I better have a beer," I said. "Tits always get me in trouble."

"Only sometimes," Pat said, smirking.

The waiter went away. It turned out the tit thing was a drink made from fresh fruit juice and rum, which Pat enjoyed immensely.

Was my softening-her-up plan working?

For dinner, Pat had the tuna, a great whopping slab of it. Pat was happy.

Yes, my softening-her-up plan was working.

I had the fajita con pollo. It came with a dense swarm of houseflies on the side. Also, at the same time, my ankles came under siege. Little sharp things were gnawing on them. With one hand flailing away at kamikaze flies, and the other slapping futilely at my ankles, I didn't get much eating done. I did manage, however, to get through the beer okay.

Later, after we got back to the hotel room, I slipped into the shower thinking that when I got out, I'd slide the two beds together, taking advantage of my softening-her-up campaign.

When I exited the bathroom, towel draped roguishly about my waist, sure enough, Pat was really excited.

But the TV was on.

"We have satellite TV," Pat said.

"Oh, dear," I said.

"*Bones* is on," she said. "And right afterward, *House*. Isn't it great?"

My softening-her-up plan had sprung a leak.

"But it's in Spanish," I said.

"With English subtitles," Pat countered, grinning.

And my softening-her-up plan fizzled and died.

In the morning, after a continental breakfast of coffee, pineapple chunks, and baby wieners, we once again boarded the good ship Jimny and cast off.

Pat was poring over her now-much-wrinkled map.

"There's a shortcut to Santa Cruz," she announced.

"Of course there is," I sighed.

And there was. The shortcut consisted of several more miles of dusty, unpaved, bone-shaking road on which to pound ourselves half to death. But, after Santa Cruz, the end of the road trip was in sight. And although I was battered both emotionally and physically, I was confident that after a few beers with which to convalesce I'd be eager for the next adventure.

Within a week we would plunge into the dark, malaria-infested jungles of Panama's Caribbean coast.

God help me. Please.

* * *

Postcards from a Galaxy (Costa Rica) Far, Far Away (11)

In the Jungle, the Mighty Jungle...

Back in Costa Rica after a week in Bocas del Toro, Panama, I'm searching for a way to briefly summarize the experience of jungle living.

OK, I've got it.

Eight days, seven nights in the Caribbean jungle.

Are you ready?

Women and small children, please leave the room.

Here goes.

I hate the goddamned-blood-sucking-skin-probing-tiny-little-fucking-invisible-no-see-um-bugs-that-ravaged-me-all-over-my-sweating-overheated-humidity-devastated-fucking-body-causing-me-to-itch-and-scratch-all-day-and-all-fucking-night-the-dirty-little-nasty-fucking-fuckers!

That pretty much covers it.

And I didn't even mention the spiders.

I'll tell you about the spiders, including the black death spider, in the next postcard.

* * *

Postcards from a Galaxy (Panama) Far, Far Away (12)

Getting There

Patricia shut down her laptop and turned to me.

"We're going to Panama," she said.

"No," I said firmly. "We're not."

I was often firm about things while drinking beer. I popped open another can of Imperial. "I can't take any more potholed, river-fording, dangerous, dusty, crappy roads."

"No dirt roads, I promise," Patricia said. But there was a twinkle in her eye.

A twinkle in her eye was something I'd learned to fear.

"Really, no dirt roads?" I said.

"No roads, period," she said. "We'll fly all the way. From Nosara to San Jose, then on to Bocas del Toro on the Caribbean coast of Panama."

"Well…," I said, still wary of the twinkle.

"In Panama the beer is cheap," Pat said.

"I'm in," I said.

Ah, yes. Sucked in once again by the siren song of cold beer.

A friend drove us to the Nosara airport. That's wrong. It's not an airport. It's an air*strip*.

We watched the plane come in, land, and taxi up to the, er, terminal. The terminal was an open-air shed with a policeman, two Nature Airlines guys, and a baggage scale with a digital readout. Plus it had a stray dog or two. The airlines guys not only weighed our baggage, they weighed *us*. Pat didn't seem very pleased to have a bunch of people standing around reading how much she weighed.

"That's a very small plane," I said.

"It's Canadian built," Pat said confidently. "It's a De Havilland Twin Otter."

We flew at ten thousand feet to San Jose and landed forty-five minutes later without blowing a tire, catching fire, or otherwise dying a terrible screaming death.

Did I mention I'm a nervous flyer?

It's an even more intriguing flight for a nervous passenger between San Jose and Bocas del Toro. There are two mountain ranges to buzz over, some volcanoes, rivers, and lots of jungle that looks like broccoli from the air.

Fifty-five minutes out of San Jose, the plane wobbled out of a towering cloud that had swallowed us whole only a few minutes earlier. Below I could see banana plantations and fields of pineapple. Then the green/blue Caribbean and, coming up fast, the Bocas airstrip on Colon Island.

"The landing strip seems kind of short," I said. My knuckles may have been white as they clenched the seat in front of me.

"Yes, but the plane has good brakes," Pat said.

We bounced and lurched and arrived.

We disembarked on the tarmac and right away we were assaulted by the humidity. Our clothing was instantly sopping wet. The smells were of baking pavement, ocean, and that special moldy odor of jungle.

The immigration department consisted of a young guy wearing jeans and a polo shirt in a closet-sized office handwriting passport numbers onto a sheet of paper on a clipboard. Not a computer anywhere in sight. Our suitcases and backpacks were hand searched by a couple of guys who looked like they had just wandered in off the street. No computers, and no uniforms for anybody either.

Our passports were stamped. We were officially in Panama. We were greeted by our hostess.

Also, we were given a fast walking tour of Bocas, the town.

Hot and poor, the town was packed with hostels, hotels, open air bars and restaurants, and blocks of rundown houses. Most of the locals were of African/Caribbean descent. The waterfront and the brilliant green of the Caribbean Sea were blocked by houses and hotels sitting cheek by jowl at the waters' edge.

Our hosts rented a year-round mooring slip for their panga, a.k.a. a motor launch, but to reach it we had to walk through the dark ground-level basement of a stilt home. With a four-foot ceiling, we had to bend over to avoid banging our heads on the overhead beams. Luckily there were no rats, spiders, or muggers hanging around, and we emerged unscathed on the water side and piled into the panga.

Edgar drove. Edgar works for $11 a day take-home, looks like a young Eddie Murphy, and is somewhat taciturn, speaking maybe seven words to me in seven days. He drives the boat, humps luggage, runs errands, and is chief groundskeeper of the twenty-acre estate of Casa Selva del Mar.

We powered past waterfront bars and hotels, many of them ramshackle, and past anchored yachts, many of them big and sleek and expensive, and down the channel towards San Cristobal, the island we would soon be calling home. It was five o'clock and the sun was ruthless, but we were tearing a white, frothy wake through the calm sea, the wind of our passage keeping us cool. The many islands of the Bocas del Toro archipelago lay about us in lush green splendor.

Within thirty minutes we would be at the dock at Isla San Cristobal. Our first look at our rented villa would remind us of stilt homes in Tahiti, where the vegetation was thick and green, where flowers were always in vivid bloom, and where paradise awaited.

Yes, indeed.

Also waiting, little did we know, were more insects than you can imagine. Sitting there patiently, biding their time among the mangroves, hovering, hungry, and invisible, waiting for dusk, waiting to attack us, wave after wave of the little bastards.

In my backpack, I had half a can of Deep Woods OFF.
It would not be enough. Not nearly enough.
We were doomed.

* * *

Postcards from a Galaxy (Panama) Far, Far Away (13)

Never Turn on a Flashlight in the Dark in the Jungle and Shine it on the Floor. Or Anywhere Else.

We were in paradise.

Except for the bugs. My ankles and legs were raw from no-see-um bites, and my left shoulder and upper arm had so many bug bite bumps I couldn't count them all. Seriously. And my whole body seemed to be screaming about how itchy it was.

But enough about me.

Pat was the same.

Our stilt house had a screened wrap-around porch, wonderful water-front views, and—most important—a queen-size bed with netting that could be dropped and tied. The netting was shroud like, white, and no-see-um proof.

We spent a lot of time in that soft bed, day and night. Surrounded by the white shroud. Itching and scratching and wishing we'd brought more OFF.

The screened-in porch kept out mosquitoes, but the no-see-ums poured through unabated.

There were bi-fold louvered doors made from teak, and hardwood floors and walls, and when the lights were on after dark, the entire place, from kitchen cabinets to bathroom countertops to the rattan stools, glowed with that warm wood color.

"Warm" being a key word.

The humidity was murderous. So thick it felt like I was wading through it. The nights were cool, but as the sun rose along with the temperature, Pat's daily refrain was, "It's hot." Or, "I'm dripping." Or, going for the combo, "I'm dripping it's so hot!"

In the night, every time I snapped on the flashlight something different skittered across the floor. Usually small, usually with more than several legs, usually benign. But I started putting on my flip-flops. Just in case.

Imagine that. Putting on footwear to go to the bathroom. Gotta love the jungle.

Anyway, even with all this floor activity, I still had to get up and use the bathroom frequently during the night. I used the flashlight to find the bathroom because it was so very, very completely dark. I didn't want to bang my shins against unseen furniture or walk into a door or, even worse, wake up Pat by switching on overhead lights. Thus, the flashlight.

One dark night towards the end of our weeklong stay, I swept aside the gauzy film of the netting and reached for the flashlight. I was groggy with remnants of a dream about Ana the condo girl as I groped for the flashlight. I dropped my feet to the floor, got my toes into my rubber flip-flops, and snapped on the light.

HOLY MOTHER OF GOD!

The black death spider was trapped in the cone of flashlight light.

At least I think it was a spider.

It was close to my flip-flops. It was black, with three bright white dots on its back. It was thick and nasty. It had short and sturdy little legs, lots of them. It didn't have a spider shape. It had a square shape.

I was pretty sure it was going to kill me.

But it was confused by the light.

It went left, then it went right. Very quickly. Then it paused.

Pat, not realizing I was about to be massacred, snored peacefully on.

Even my scream didn't wake her.

I was on my feet. I lifted my right foot and slammed it down.

Right on the black death spider.

Take that, you creepy bastard!

Greenish gooey gloop squirted out from under my flip-flop.

I raised my foot.

OH NO! IT WAS STILL ALIVE.

I slammed down my foot again.

More squirting greenish gooey gloop.

This time, when I lifted the killer flip-flop, the monster was dead.

But, yuck, the sole of my flip-flop had a glob of greenish gooey gloop stuck to it.

It made sucking sounds as I walked to the bathroom.

Since then my nightlife hasn't been the same. Gone are the pleasant dreams of Ana and me frolicking naked in the surf.

Those dreams have been replaced by frolicking naked in the pitch dark with the black death spider's relatives that are lurking under my bed, seeking revenge.

* * *

Postcards from a Galaxy (Panama) Far, Far Away (14)

Paradise Lost, and Found

We were hiding in our Tarzan house one afternoon, avoiding bugs, when a gust of smoke blew past the screens.

A moment later the raw smell of smoke was permeating the house. "Are we on fire?" Pat said, looking up from her Kindle.

Pat was annoyed. She was reading the latest Kathy Reichs. How dare her house burn down while she was reading about Dr. Temperance Brennan, the famous forensic anthropologist character and Pat's all time favorite heroine.

"I'll check," I said.

More gray smoke was pouring past our view, thick, rolling clouds of it.

Under the stilt house, there was a barbecue on wheels, and in the barbecue were a bunch of blazing, smoking sticks. Adding more sticks to the smoldering fire was Edgar, the all-purpose helper guy.

"Keeps away the bugs," he explained.

So for several hours in the late afternoon, we breathed smoke while our eyes and lungs burned and the bugs came anyway. So we added coughing and hacking and wheezing to our retinue of misery.

* * *

Here's more bug stuff. But don't worry, all the bug stories are nearly finished.

Behind our jungle house, a wall of impenetrable jungle loomed. It was at least one hundred feet high and reminded me of a fortress. There were parrots and butterflies in there, and possibly boa constrictors. There were a couple of trails leading into it, trails that had been forged during the owners' eight year tenure.

My insect bites were in remission and I was feeling bold. I may have had a few cold Balboa's to ward off the humidity and to enhance my boldness.

"Let's explore the jungle," I said.

"Have you lost your mind?" Pat said.

"Probably," I said. "But it's there, and when will we have another chance to walk in a real live jungle?"

We started forward.

But our host stepped out of some bushes, blocking our path. He was wearing long pants, socks, shoes, a wide-brimmed jungle hat, and a long-sleeved shirt. He appraised us doubtfully.

I was wearing shorts, flip-flops, a T-shirt, and my Costa Rica baseball cap. Pat was wearing her deep tan, some OFF, shorts, a T-shirt, and her dainty but fashionable black flip-flops with the fancy toe-strap option.

"Take these," the host said, thrusting a pair of four-foot sticks at us. They were made from hardwood and were heavy.

"To sweep away the spiders," he added, when I looked perplexed.

Uh-oh.

"Spiders?" I said.

"Big ones," He nodded. "But they're fairly docile."

"Fairly," I said.

"They are harmless but there's lots of them," He said.

"Maybe we'll go kayaking instead," I said.

And we did.

But on another day, our host led the way past his garden of pineapple, papaya ,and banana plants. The trail ahead led into the jungle.

It was dark in there, like a subway tunnel. The undergrowth was very thick, and the higher-up growth was also thick, blocking out the sun.

He swept aside about a million spiders and their maze of spider webs, and into the maw of the jungle we tiptoed. We stayed very close to our guardian. We saw some sloths way up there in tall trees, moving slowly. We saw some toucans on tree branches.

"We used to have howler monkeys and an anteater," He said. "But the Indians ate them."

Mosquitoes started to close in, and we exited the jungle, never to return.

* * *

During the first few days in the Tarzan house, I couldn't see paradise for the bugs, humidity, and sweltering heat. It was so bad even the beer fresh out of the refrigerator seemed warm. Plus the gecko that lived near the coffee maker in the kitchen often startled me.

When we went for lunch to town, Bocas seemed cheap and broken down and smelled of stagnant water.

Then one morning, a miracle.

I was sitting out on the wood balcony, wondering where the hell was paradise anyway. The sun was just beginning its morning climb, there was a soft ocean breeze, and the no-see-ums were taking a day off. Sipping black coffee freshly brewed, I relaxed and looked around.

I could hear the palm fronds clicking in the breeze, the squabbles of parrots fussing in the jungle behind me, and wavelets slapping against the nearby dock pilings. There was the fragrance of blooming flowers, the tang of ocean salt, and the pure scent of thousands of acres of wilderness.

On the green, shelving mountains of the mainland, cloud shadows moved and, as the sun rose, the colors of the sea changed. Over the reefs the water was turquoise and clear, and in deeper places it gleamed dark blue, its surface shimmering in the sunlight.

Towing snowy-white wakes, motor launches and fish boats were busy far out in the channel. Every now and then a dugout canoe slipped past, often paddled by a single fisherman. A container ship steamed into sight, inching past the many reefs, heading to the Chiquita banana shipping terminal on the mainland.

We went kayaking—Pat looking like she was born for it, all that experience in the upper-downer finally paying off, and me wobbling and splashing and trying to keep up.

The sea was calm, and close to shore the tangled mangroves were reflected mirror like on the water. The silence of the day was almost overwhelming; the only sound was of dripping paddles. We drifted and paddled and drifted again. The coves were shallow and mangrove branches dipped into the sea. A nurse shark turned languidly below us, seeking lunch.

Overhead, the sky was cloudless and perfectly blue, and the unfettered sun hammered down, stinging bare flesh and bouncing like diamonds off the water.

The sea in front of Casa Selva del Mar was streaked with rock and coral. The shallow water was clear as gin, and we saw small fishes darting, like sparks of green, fleeing our slow shadows. Other fish were silver with black stripes, while others looked like butterflies. A brown spotted Ray shot beneath us. Its tail was probably ten feet long. The sandy ocean floor was marked with the dark shapes of fat sea cucumbers and spiked sea urchins. Here and there patches of underwater sea grass stirred and bent to unseen currents.

Maybe, just maybe, I had found paradise after all.

* * *

And on the eighth day we returned to Costa Rica, slamming through only one air pocket that tried to launch me out of my seat.

We overnighted in San Jose at the Isla Verde hotel, a Chinese-owned accommodation where we celebrated Chinese New Year by ordering platters of *fideos de arroz con curry, lechon y camarones, carne al estilo ze-chaun,* and *chop suey con pollo.* The food was excellent, we ate way too much, and, bursting at the seams, we staggered upstairs (no elevator) to our room.

In the morning we had the breakfast-included portion of our stay, gathered our luggage, and waited outside for the prebooked taxi to arrive.

"We better phone for another cab," I said. I was always nervous about getting to the airport on time.

"The cabbie who dropped us off yesterday said he'd be here at eight," Pat said. "Be patient for a change."

I was patient. For maybe five minutes. The arranged cab never showed. I hailed another cab.

There are two airports in San Jose. There's the big one, for international flights, and the little one, for domestic service. The taxi tried to take us to the wrong one, but made a correction in morning rush-hour traffic when I noticed the wrong signs pointing in the wrong direction. We got to the Nature Air desk at the right terminal in plenty of time to catch our nine thirty flight.

That was when I heard the four words passengers never want to hear. "We have a problem."

But it was a cute little Tica with fabulous brown eyes who said it. So how upset could I be?

"We are overbooked," she went on. "You and your wife will probably get on the plane but your luggage might have to go by earth."

"By earth?" I said.

"Si."

Hmm.

So we waited and waited and finally we boarded and learned, happily, that our luggage would not have to go by earth but would join us in the air.

I couldn't help but wonder if in fact the little plane was indeed overbooked weight wise and, overloaded, we might splatter into the side of a mountain.

We flew over Golfo Nicoya to Islita, where the landing strip has often been patched and by a colorful array of patching, but at least it was paved. The terminal was actually a hut with a palapa roof. Some people got off, some people got on. Everybody was sweating.

Fifteen minutes later we were back in Nosara. We were soon reunited with our luggage. We wheeled toward the crush of taxi drivers. I chose one.

When we were outside the terminal on the side of the street, Pat looked at the vehicle and said, "That's not a taxi."

Under a thick coating of dust I was pretty sure there was a car. Once upon a time it might have been a Toyota, or maybe a Hyundai, but now it was a dirtmobile.

I opened a rear door for her. Dust swirled. The rear seat was lumpy and had a few rips and tears in it. The exterior probably hadn't been washed since 1993, and the interior had never seen a vacuum cleaner, ever. But the radio worked. Spanish music wailed.

Giving me one of those crushing looks, Pat got in. The springs sagged. Or maybe it had no springs. Anyway, the swaybacked taxi sagged. I got in the front, and when the driver got in, the poor old cab could barely move. During the ten-minute ride to Casa Banda, which was mostly uphill, the transmission remained in first gear. The ten-minute ride turned into twenty minutes. Into the open windows powdery dust flowed. I heard Pat coughing. I didn't dare turn around to look at her. I couldn't take another of her crushing glares.

It got us home, though, and I survived Pat's seminar about choosing proper taxis, clean ones, with air conditioning.

I turned on the overhead fans, looked out the front windows at the wide, blue Pacific and at Playa Pelada where the surf crashed on the sand. Below our deck, banana trees stirred, the swimming pool shimmered, and in the kitchen, in the fridge, cold beer rested.

Ah, yes.

Paradise.

* * *

BREAKING NEWS ALERT

Canadian Upper-Downer Stolen, Taken for Joy Ride!

Dateline: Costa Rica

The proud floating vessel known fondly around the world as "the upper-downer" was recently stolen in broad daylight and taken for a joy ride by an unknown perpetrator.

The upper-downer's commander in chief, Patricia Sears, a.k.a. the Admiral, reported the crime to the Costa Rica Navy.

"But," claimed the Admiral at a hastily called news conference at poolside, "Costa Rica doesn't have a navy. Or an army either, for that matter."

"No wonder they didn't return her phone call," said Patricia's husband, John, a legend in the produce industry for his buy-high, sell-low philosophy of fruit flogging..

"I went down to the pool on Monday afternoon and the upper-downer was gone from its mooring slip. My heart was broken," said the Admiral, who has successfully skippered the upper-downer through ocean-breeze-tossed waters, high humidity, and once through the dangerous shadows of late evening.

"Plus, it really pissed me off," she added.

"Then, suddenly, it was mysteriously returned while my back was turned," claimed the woman who was once the champion arm wrestler at Stamp's Landing Pub.

"After a thorough examination I detected beer stains on the port-side cowling," said Patricia, whose training as a forensic technician comes from watching the TV show *Bones*.

"So it's likely the perpetrator was drinking beer, possibly Imperial brand," Patricia said.

"We're thinking of offering a reward," John advised. Taking a sip of beer from his can of Imperial, he added, "We want to nip this kind of flagrant nautical naughtiness in the bud."

Concluded the Admiral with a snarl, "If I catch whoever took my upper-downer on a joy ride, I'll strangle him or her with my bare hands!"

"But let's be perfectly clear," John said, "at this point we have no particular suspects in mind."

The Admiral will be accepting anonymous tips from the public in an effort to bring the culprit to justice.

If you have any information regarding this incident, please call 1-800-HOT-TIPS.

* * *

Postcards from a Galaxy (Costa Rica) Far, Far Away (15)

Lookin' for Adventure

Patricia kicked Ana the condo goddess, who was naked at the time, out of my bed.

Well, not quite.

What actually happened was, I was dreaming (again) about Ana the condo goddess early one morning when Pat kicked *me* out of bed.

"Get rolling," Pat said. "We're driving to Grecia."

So we rolled. In the Jimny. The backseat was stuffed with suitcases, backpacks, and extra stuff. The extra stuff, I guess, was in case we suddenly decided to spend the rest of our lives in Grecia. The front seat contained maps, water bottles, and snack food. When you travel with Patricia, you travel prepared.

I drove. Pat told me where.

Grecia is a medium-sized town located in the central valley of Costa Rica, not far from San Jose. There are lots of interesting places to explore in the area, and Pat was determined to explore them. Plus there were stores, coffee plantations, and furniture factories, and Pat planned to shop them rigorously.

It's maybe three hundred klicks from Nosara to Grecia. It shouldn't be a long trip, but it is. On the world's worst highways, it's an all-day, life-threatening adventure.

We drove to the town of Nicoya and turned right, past some cattle in a field. Next we drove over the Friendship Bridge, which cuts off the end of the Golfo Nicoya and connects the Nicoya peninsula to the mainland.

We turned right again at an intersection featuring a huge statue of a Brahma bull and eventually entered highway number one. The Inter-American Highway. If we had turned north we could have driven all the way to Canada. But we turned south and joined the stream of livestock trucks, tanker trucks, container trucks, buses, bicycles, and slow-moving scooters.

Sure, it's a major highway, but hey, it's Costa Rica. There were no painted lines, no passing lanes, and no shoulders. Even when it should have been flat and smooth, it was flat and bumpy. Sometimes the bridges, and there are millions of bridges, were wide and well engineered, sometimes they were dangerously narrow.

We slowed for school zones. We slowed while big trucks ground through their gears going uphill. We slowed when buses stopped. We slowed for just about everything.

Then we stopped. Stopped dead for thirty minutes on a ridge overlooking a steep canyon. Ahead we could see green mountains. We had made progress but there was still a long way to go. The reason we stopped, as did ten thousand other vehicles, was the bridge was out, or most of the bridge was out. It was down to one temporary lane. We eventually tottered over the bridge—it was a long, long way down to the canyon floor—and resumed our stop/start journey.

In Grecia, on a busy side street, we were greeted by our host, Denny. Big guy. Shaved head. A "sleeve" of tattoos on his thick right arm. Earring. Wife-beater T-shirt.

Denny looked like he was just freshly released from prison, but it turned out he was from Calgary. Fleeing a mangled marriage, he'd moved to Costa Rica three years previously and opened a B&B. Despite the biker persona, his grin was wide and friendly, and he was helpful, thoughtful, and kind.

Across the width of the house was a steel gate. And behind the gate, Denny kept his motorcycle and his white Jeep Cherokee. There were more bars on the windows. It was the same on every house, bars and gates and fences with razor wire. Petty theft is everywhere in Costa Rica. When it comes to protection, the police, on their little Yamaha motorcycles, aren't any help at all. Every resident is on his or her own. Every home—no matter the neighborhood—is a fortress.

"If I leave stuff on the patio, they'll use a stick with a nail in it to slip it out through the bars," Denny explained. "Out in the country, they'll even steal the tiles off your roof."

We had the penthouse suite. Which sounds much more grand than it really was. It was a humble Tico house, with thick walls, tile floors, and a cheap overnight price tag. Plus Denny and Rochelle were praised highly on Trip Advisor.

I left the Jimny on the street right in front of the B&B. Nobody would steal a Jimny, right? (It spent three lonely nights there, and no one touched it, although several dogs baptized the tires.)

Pat climbed the narrow, tiled stairs to our bedroom. I followed her up, lugging suitcases.

She looked in the bathroom.

"Oh my God!" she exclaimed.

* * *

Postcards from a Galaxy (Costa Rica) Far, Far Away (16)

Dead Man's Curve

"There's a big crack in the wall," Pat exclaimed, peering cautiously into the bathroom. "There's even a big crack on the bottom of the Jacuzzi bathtub."

Yes, there was.

But what was even more alarming to me was the size of the "queen" bed. If indeed it was queen size, the queen was a midget.

When you sleep with Pat, space is paramount. Pat is—how should I say this?—an aggressive sleeper. Her "half" of the bed is, often, three-quarters of the bed. Or more. (If she reads this, I'm in BIG trouble.)

And the bed was small, with a thin mattress.

But the good news was, we were staying only three nights. Clinging to the very edge of the bed, I could tough it out for three nights. Sleep is overrated anyway. And at least it was a low bed, so if I fell off the edge onto the floor, I could survive without serious damage.

Later, Denny explained about the cracks. We were out back in his postage-stamp-size back yard seated comfortably in rocking chairs. Denny was smoking Marlboros and drinking merlot that came in a box and costs about a buck and a half a liter.

"Earthquake of January oh-nine," he said. "Destroyed maybe six hundred homes, killed a bunch of people, and cracked up my bathroom." That night, street noises drifted up into our bedroom. Flatulent trucks and buses. The ripping sound of accelerating motorcycles. Horns, car alarms, and laughter from the bar on the corner. The smells were of pastry from the bakery directly across the street, hot asphalt, and exhaust fumes.

In the morning, Denny cooked bacon and eggs and Rochelle served coffee. Rochelle was a petite Filipina and every bit as friendly and nice as her partner. Plus, she taught Pat how to download just-published best-selling books for free from an Internet Web site. (If you want free best-sellers, talk to Pat.)

We drove to Sarchi, a town twenty minutes away, famous for souvenirs and furniture and home of the biggest ox cart in the world. The road went up over a couple of hills, snaked through steep-sided canyons, and twisted through crowded neighborhoods The neighborhoods—like almost all Costa Rica neighborhoods—were a jumble of residential homes interspersed with bars, restaurants, mechanic shops, convenience stores, and assorted small businesses.

To quote Denny the biker, "Sure, it's a country free of regulations and rules, which is a nice change. But there's nothing to stop your neighbor from opening a machine shop right next door."

Rochelle had told us about her experience living in San Jose before she met Denny. She said, "I had neighbors in the apartment next door who partied a lot and played loud music all night long. There were no bylaws, so there was no point in calling the police. I lived on sleeping pills and used ear plugs every night for two years."

So the neighborhoods are an eclectic mix of good, bad, and ugly. Sort of like Surrey, British Columbia. Only more so.

In Sarchi, we bought some stuff; then we bought more stuff. I ran out of Calones (the local currency) and switched to U.S. dollars, and when those were gone, I pulled out my Visa card. Pat kept stuffing shopping bags full of T-shirts, wooden bowls, and jewelry until the Jimny was full.

On the way back, we almost didn't make it past dead man's curve.

I was going downhill into a hairpin turn. I was in the outside lane, with a sheer drop-off beside us. The road, although paved, was narrow. Maybe I was going a little fast. Okay, maybe a lot fast. Below, coming out of the hairpin, slow and awkward and big as a *Tyrannosaurus rex*, was a flatbed truck carrying a bulldozer.

There was no pilot car, no red flags, no flashing lights.

The flatbed was taking up almost all of the road as it grunted through the curve. The big, wide blade of the bulldozer was sticking way over the side of the flatbed. And therefore way over the center line of the road, if there'd been a center line on the road. Which there wasn't.

The iron blade grew rapidly large, larger, huge as it closed in.

"Watch out!" Pat said.

I cranked the wheel hard right. I'm pretty sure the two passenger-side wheels were thrust momentarily into the thin air of the deep canyon.

The blade missed the Jimny by the thickness of a coat of paint.

I cranked the wheel hard left. The Jimny's four wheels screeched on the asphalt.

We had survived dead man's curve.

* * *

Postcards from a Galaxy (Costa Rica) Far, Far Away (17)

Hair

Our sojourn in Costa Rica was almost over. It was time to think about going home, about seeing old friends, about reentering Canadian society.

Pat looked in the bathroom mirror and said, "Uh-oh."

Then she added, "I can't go home looking like this."

"So maybe you put on a pound or two," I said helpfully. "Wear something flowing. No one will notice."

"No, you idiot, it's my hair," she said.

I looked. I shrugged.

"Looks OK to me."

"You're an idiot."

"Yes, I know," I said. "You already told me."

"I need color."

I nodded.

"But the question is, is Sandi up to the task?" Pat asked.

I ran a hand over my own hair.

"Sandi did a great job with me," I said encouragingly.

"You have a buzz cut."

"Good point."

Sandi was the local Tica hairdresser. She had a dusty little shop in downtown Nosara, tucked between a fly-infested outdoor cafe and a roach-crawling motel. Across the street was a laundry service in somebody's living room, and nearby was a pumpkin-colored Catholic church.

Great location. How could Pat go wrong?

"I don't think I'll go the highlight route," she said. "I don't think Sandi is good enough. Just a sort-of light blonde shade all over. Sandi should be able to handle that. If I go at all, that is."

Pat was under huge pressure. Her eldest daughter, Lori, is the Yukon's premier hair dresser, and her youngest daughter Teri has shoulder-length, honey blonde hair that's always perfect. A bad hair day can send Pat into depression for weeks.

"Okay," Pat said, decision made. "Drive me."

The Jimny rattled and bounced to Nosara, ten minutes away. I pulled up in front of the bright blue storefront. The *Abierto* sign was on the front door.

For a moment Pat was silent and unmoving in the front seat, screwing up her courage. At last she opened the car door and got out.

"Come and get me later," she said grimly, slamming the door.

Walking into the shop, Pat looked like she was on a mission to hell.

I drove away in a cloud of dust. Life is easy when all you have to worry about is a buzz cut.

I drove to the gas station, parked, got out, and locked up. I bought a cup of ceviche from the entrepreneur who sells it out of the back of his battered station wagon. Fish, lime juice, salsa, and cilantro. Very tasty.

Yes, I know. It's ninety degrees and he has no refrigeration. But so far no stomach pump had been required, and I'd eaten there several times.

I hoped Patricia was having as much fun as I was.

Hanging out at the *gasolinera*, I traffic-watched for a while. There was a guy on a brown horse. Yamaha and Honda motor bikes were blowing dust as Tica maids drove back and forth to work. A Bimbo delivery truck, Bimbo being the name of a bakery, lurched over the potholes. Several gringos driving ATVs wore masks against the dust. Cars and pickups passed each other . Pedestrians and cyclists paraded by, drenched with powdery road dust. Free-range dogs loafed. Guys were pumping gas and washing windshields—no self-serve here. A mother and infant child on an ATV, helmet free, roared over the single-lane bridge.

Meanwhile, back at the hair salon, Pat was in the middle of a hair nightmare.

I parked out front. When I opened the door there was an orange glow in the room. Pat was in the only chair with her back turned. I could feel the stress vibes crashing against the walls like waves on a beach. I looked at Sandi. She looked like she'd just been harpooned.

Something was wrong. Terribly wrong.

I looked at Pat. At the back of her head. From where the orange glow emanated.

Oh no!

Oh yes!

"It's gone orange," Pat growled. "Go away."

I went.

I thought maybe we'd have to emergency air-evac her to Whitehorse, where Lori would be tasked to save her mom's life.

But no.

When I went back a second time, everything was fixed. Pat's hair looked normal, and all the rest of Pat looked normal, too, if a little bit shell shocked.

"It looks, er, lovely," I said as Pat climbed into the Jimny.

"Shut up and drive," Pat said.

Which I did.

"You better not tell anyone about my orange hair," Pat said.

"Your secret is safe with me," I promised.

* * *

Postcards from a Galaxy (Costa Rica) Far, Far Away (18)

…In Conclusion

It's over. It's all over.

The fridge is empty. There are no more Imperials to drink. The bags are packed, all nineteen of them. Pat's beloved upper-downer has been pulled from the pool finally and for all time. It was left behind, too patched and scarred and worn to be taken home.

The murderous potholes that pit the roads, streets, and highways will no longer rattle my bones. My lungs have inhaled their final dust clouds. The little Jimny, trembling and exhausted, is resting gratefully.

There will be no more glorious sunsets to watch from our balcony, as the swollen orange disk of the sun glides into the ocean. No more barefoot walks along the beach while the waves batter the shore in rhythmic fury.

The grounds of Casa Banda will continue to be bright with hibiscus, ginger, amaryllis, and bougainvillea, but we won't be here to marvel at the vivid colors. The wall of green jungle that towers against the azure sky, branches and fronds and leaves ceaselessly stirring, will be seen by eyes other than our own.

Patricia's maps are tucked away. There will be no more dusty short-cuts for us, no unexplored territory in which to challenge my sanity.

The no-see-ums (called "little witches" locally), mosquitoes, and spiders will have to find other blood to drink. I'm taking what's left of mine home. Good luck to your next victims, you little bastards.

For the last time a waitress in an outdoor restaurant (*all* the restaurants are outdoor restaurants here) said to me, "Would you care for some bug repellent with your appetizer, sir?"

It's over. It's all over.

And I'm trying hard to be positive about going home.

I *love* cold temperatures. I *love* gray cloud cover. I *love* when it rains all week long.

See? I'm really, really trying.

BUT IT'S NOT WORKING, GODDAMNIT!

* * *

Made in the USA
Lexington, KY
27 January 2012